TALES OF THE DOGS
A CELEBRATION OF THE IRISH AND THEIR GREYHOUNDS

TALES OF
THE DOGS

A CELEBRATION OF THE IRISH AND THEIR GREYHOUNDS

John Martin

BLACKSTAFF PRESS

To the memory of James and Gertrude Martin

CONTENTS

FOREWORD   7

1   THE JOURNEY BEGINS   10

2   CELTIC ROOTS   18
     RACING COMES TO IRELAND

3   BORD NA GCON 1958–1968   26
     THE DEFINING DECADE

4   THE TOTALISATOR   34
     GREYHOUND RACING HITS THE JACKPOT

5   FLYING THE FLAG   42
     IRELAND'S 'SHIP' COMES IN

6   THE LIFE OF NED REILLY   50
     BORD NA GCON 1969–1994

7   'THE DOGS' UPDATED   56
     BORD NA GCON (1995 ONWARDS)

8   VICTORY AT WATERLOO   64
     MASTER M'GRATH

9   COURSING IN THEIR VEINS   72
     McGRATH–MATTHEWS–MULLAN

10   AN AFFAIR OF THE HEART   80
     MICK THE MILLER

11   THE GREENING OF THE WHITE CITY   88
     THE GRAND CANAL ... AND THE BANKS OF THE LIFFEY

12   THE MAESTRO FINDS THE RIGHT NOTE   96
     GER McKENNA'S ENGLISH DERBY DOUBLE

13   THE IRISH DERBY 1932–1952   104
HEADING FOR 'ROUGH WATERS'

14   TOM LYNCH   112
THE ARRIVAL OF THE 'SPANISH' ARMADA

15   SÉAMUS FARRELL   120
TRIUMPHS AND TRIBULATIONS OF A BOOKMAKER

16   CLASSIC CONNECTIONS   128
THE McKENNA CLAN

17   MATT O'DONNELL AND THE NEXT GENERATION   136
RAISING THE BAR

18   THE EASTER CUP   144
GATEWAY TO GREATNESS

19   OWNERSHIP   154
THE DREAM LIVES ON

20   BREEDING   162
WHEN MUTTON CUTLET WAS TOP DOG

21   GOING TO THE DOGS   170
THEN AND NOW

AUTHOR ACKNOWLEDGEMENTS   182

PICTURE ACKNOWLEDGEMENTS   182

BIBLIOGRAPHY   184

THE SPORTING GREYHOUND: A CHRONOLOGY   185

INDEX   186

FOREWORD

Dogs of one kind or another have been part of the Irish environment for as long as the stretch of either history, folklore or myth can accommodate. The Clan Taoisigh of centuries ago kept wolfhounds, partly for protection, but also out of respect for the loyal and noble animals. We learn from folklore that refuses to die that aeons before that, again, sporting dogs were ever present with the wandering warriors known as Na Fianna, the guardians of the ordinary people. We have all heard of Fionn Mac Cumhaill, one-time leader of Na Fianna, and of his many escapades and deeds of valour. I always had a great interest in his two star dogs, Bran and Sceolaing, and was convinced that if they had the gift of eternal youth like Oisín, the son of Fionn in Tír na nÓg, then the Derby and other Classics of modern times would be theirs for the taking.

In those far-off days the famous pair of hounds was kept for hunting purposes, as much as for the entertainment of witnessing the contest between dog and the fleet-footed deer, be it on the river plains or along steep and rugged mountain flanks. Numerous lays and lyrics detailing those thrilling chases survive in the folklore of both Ireland and Scotland; perhaps Laoi na Seilge (A Tale of the Chase) would be typical, though it led to a temporary metamorphosis of Fionn the all-powerful into a hapless and wizened *seanóir* by a lakeside. It began with Bran and Sceolaing giving chase to a leaping doe en route to a nearby mountain; there the flying young deer, having outwitted the chasing duo, was transformed into a weeping fair maiden apparently in distress; on arrival some time later the gallant Fionn offered assistance but his exertions in search of a lost ring of gold in the lake led to the temporary loss of his power and the wisdom for which he was noted.

It matters not whether the lay sprang from absolute fantasy or not but it does establish that dogs were part of the scene that existed in those bygone days. That aspect of rural Irish life has not changed much in the meantime and growing up on a farm in west Kerry I have memories of canines from a very early age.

The first I recall had the unusual name of Careless, a bilingual black and brown shepherd wise enough to know both cows and cattle by names like Bléinfhionn, Cluain Searrach, Bó Mhaol, Hereford and so on. And strangely a greyhound entered the memory chamber before I was two years of age. He must have been a special one, though, because he was housed in a tidy corner in what was then called the old home and I distinctly recall seeing a stream of people coming to see him. He belonged to my uncle Joe and had qualified to run in the Derby, a huge distinction then as now. Eventually he was unable to compete due to sickness but his litter brother owned by Dan Walsh of Moyvane, then known as Newtownsandes, actually won the Derby, making the name of Dainty Man famous forever more far beyond the bounds of the Kingdom of Kerry.

We learn from folklore that refuses to die that aeons before that, again, sporting dogs were ever present with the wandering warriors known as Na Fianna, the guardians of the ordinary people.

Greyhound racing
has meant a lot to me
ever since those early
days and I have worn
many a pair of shoes
going to tracks here,
there and just about
anywhere.

I believe I was well educated in the faculty of greyhound science before I ever set foot in a school at the age of six. My uncle, a teacher in north Kerry at the time, had more than his share and enjoyed a fair degree of success. One of his called Doonshean Banks won the Oriel Cup at the Dundalk track over seventy years ago and the trophy has rested in Kerry ever since.

I could not but have an interest in the sport with that as a background, and for good measure there was always a strong racing tradition in the area, with the usual mix of good, fair and middling practitioners being raced on track and field near and far. Greyhounds always acted as passports that encouraged people to stray from their usual surroundings now and then – always recommended for the soul's welfare.

Greyhound racing has meant a lot to me ever since those early days and I have worn many a pair of shoes going to tracks here, there and just about anywhere. I have great memories of both Shelbourne Park and Harold's Cross going back to the late 1940s when I first arrived in good old Baile Átha Cliath. Of course they were different then, with facilities fairly primitive, but nobody complained about the lack of either this or that; people simply went in droves to enjoy the racing and to have a flutter with the bookies, as the friendly tote had yet to make an appearance. Patrons were predominantly male and many got to the track on trusty bicycles; I remember the one-legged entrepreneur with his crutch who herded hundreds of them each night along the grey dull wall on the roadside of Shelbourne Park. He had

no fixed charge for the parking and understood why some people needed to let the account 'run' forward on certain occasions. And indeed I never heard of an incident when a bicycle was clamped!

It did not take long before I became directly involved myself and the first essay into the business was in partnership with a friend, Patrick Kavanagh. The dog was in training with a chemist in Dunlavin and won his first race in Newbridge. It was a bit far to cycle so we hitched our way to the heart of Kildare, enjoyed a good night at the track that circled the football pitch and must have managed to get back at some Christian hour as well. Since then I have been lucky enough to own dogs that won races at venues all over the country – from Dublin tracks to Cork, Limerick, Waterford and 'all stations in between', as the great pioneering railway men of the USA used to holler clearly and with feeling before the advent of the less entertaining public address or neon language.

I have always looked upon greyhound racing as a pastime, allowing also for the fact that it is a very successful business. Most tracks have been renovated to a degree that offers good racing surfaces and excellent facilities for those attending, with plenty of outlets for dining, wining and betting. The sport is governed by a state board set up in 1958 and known under the Act as Bord na gCon, its official name, not the Greyhound Board. The inspiration for all the developments in the industry over the past fifty years has sprung from that source, and under the immediate former chairman Paschal Taggart, facilities reached levels that attract huge crowds. The majority go for a night's enjoyment and it is noticeable that it has become popular with the young, both male and female; of course, it is pleasant to end up winning a few euro but that is not the yardstick by which the night's value is measured. Turning to the business end of this decidedly Irish pastime, it is a factor in the employment market; many hands are needed to run the country's eighteen tracks and as usual there are ancillary services that provide further employment also. I have seen the growth of big breeding and training establishments and there are many small farmers with a good knowledge of breeding who dabble in the business as a sideline. It is to those places that ambitious owners sometimes go in the hope of purchasing a future Derby winner or a champion in one of the many competitions run throughout the year. By the way, the monetary prize for winning the Irish Derby now stands somewhere close to €175,000.

Exporting greyhounds has been a feature of trade since the introduction of racing tracks in Britain over eighty years ago, though there is strong competition from home-based owners to buy the best in recent times. Indirectly that has led to greater successes by Irish-trained dogs in the big races across channel and it was nice to see popular Carlow trainer Séamus Graham claim the English Derby in midsummer 2008.

Yes, the show started by Fionn Mac Cumhaill almost two thousand years ago is still running and gaining in stamina. Its future can be equally long provided the fun element is maintained and the philosophy of hope fostered. There is nothing like hope and that reminds me to

persevere in the search for a Derby winner – and any Derby will do.

Micheál Ó Muircheartaigh

Coursing in Hatfield Park

1 THE JOURNEY BEGINS

The Earliest Days

The sands of time now cover the exact origins of the greyhound. What is known is that the breed, probably wrapped in a shape somewhat different and more hairy than that which we know in the twenty-first century, was recognised at least four thousand years ago.

Those who have chronicled the migration of the greyhound over four millenniums tend to agree that its trek began on the fringes of the Sahara Desert. The first pictorial evidence of this genesis was found in the tombs of the Pharaohs. The fact that hounds resembling our modern-day racing dogs were deemed worthy of overseeing and guiding the journeys of the ancient kings of Egypt into the next life speaks volumes for the high regard in which the breed was

held. Images of greyhounds have also been found on the earthenware of the nobility of what is now the Middle East – Persia (Iran), Abyssinia (Ethiopia) and Armenia – and it is believed that greyhounds were exchanged between the ambassadors of these kingdoms. They remained a valuable bartering tool until Norman times in Britain.

A hairy type of greyhound may have been known to the Egyptians as far back as 1500 BC, but the concept of two branches – Afghan, Borzoi and Saluki on one hand; a dog more like our modern greyhound on the other – arises between 50 and 200 AD. Early accounts of the greyhound ascribe the word 'feathered' to its coat. Later the greyhound altered in appearance from a long-haired hound to the sleeker version that we know today, with climate being a contributory factor to this change.

The fact that hounds resembling our modern-day racing dogs were deemed worthy of overseeing and guiding the journeys of the ancient kings of Egypt into the next life speaks volumes for the high regard in which the breed was held.

A pair of greyhounds from the Mastaba of Mereruka, vizier and royal administrator, who died in c. 2291 BC.

The one constant in the story has been the greyhound's connection with royalty and nobility. Whether etched on the panels of tombs in ancient times or as a prop to commissioned and romanticised paintings of later royalty in Britain, the association of the greyhound and aristocracy is evident throughout history. The greyhound of which King Solomon wrote has arguably changed slightly in its appearance but not in its attributes:

> *There be three things that go well,*
> *yea four that are comely in going;*
>
> *A lion which is strongest among beasts*
> *and turneth not away from any;*
>
> *A greyhound; an he goat also; and a*
> *king against whom there is no rising up.*

Proverbs 30:29–31

Now so accessible that everyone can own one – although few admittedly could ever afford the fastest and most prized of the species – the greyhound was once the preserve of the very highest in any land. Hunting with greyhounds was the original sport of kings and would remain so in Britain until the popularisation of horse racing less than a hundred years ago.

According to an old Welsh saying, 'You may know a gentleman by his horse, his hawk and his greyhound'. And, in around 1014, King Canute assembled his legislators in Winchester and introduced laws that ordained that only gentlemen and those of the bluest blood could own greyhounds. The Forest Laws stayed on the statute books right through the reign of King Edward III in 1377.

At the time of the enactment of the Forest Laws, the spelling of the name may have been 'gre-hound' or 'grieg-hound', prefixes that indicate that these hounds were premier or first in rank. In Middle English, 'gre' becomes 'gredus' signifying most important or first grade. The later 'grey' is thought now by some to have been a corruption of the 'grech', an old English word for dog. Other suggestions are that the title comes from 'Grais', meaning Grecian, as the dog undoubtedly was known in that centre of classical learning. It could be that the name

A sixteenth-century French painting of Diana the huntress

An A–Z of Greyhounds

A Age

All thoroughbred horses become a year older on 1 January each year, irrespective of their actual birthday. The age of a greyhound is given as the first day of the month in which it was born. So a greyhound born (whelped) on 31 December 2009 will be two years of age on 1 December 2011. Greyhounds tend to be at their racing peak between two-and-a-half and three-and-a-half years of age, although some pups mature more quickly than others. The evergreen Mick The Miller (born June 1926) ran in the English Derby in 1929, 1930 and 1931, and also won the 1931 English St Leger at Wimbledon. He died at the age of thirteen.

derives quite literally from the colour grey, as the hue of the dog's coat has also evolved over the centuries. However, the most popular interpretation is that the breed started out as gazehounds based on the fact that they hunted by sight rather than by smell.

The Roman poet Ovid, who lived at the time of Christ, has left behind descriptions of hare hunting, although historians believe that it was the Celts who introduced the idea of hare coursing – the pitting of one greyhound's skills against another – to Roman and Greek society. That event – the change from simple hunting to coursing – is dated around AD 150. By the end of that second century, the Roman writer Arrian had set down the first rules for competitive greyhound sport.

The hound traded by the Celts was the rugged forerunner of today's greyhound, named by the Romans as the 'Vertagi'; but the sport bore every resemblance to the coursing which was to be seen in Britain from the Middle Ages until 2005, and which still takes place in modern times in Ireland. The object of the exercise was to be the testing of one man's greyhound against another, rather than the killing of the quarry.

The greyhound still had some distance to journey yet. Even as it and the Celtic tribes moved through Gaul, or present-day France, it would seem that they had two types of greyhound in tow: the larger version was a working dog used in the practical field of hunting; the other was the forefather of our greyhound.

Greyhounds in Writing

Irrespective of the definitive type, greyhounds were cherished for two main characteristics: speed and an ability to hunt. Writing in the late 1300s, Geoffrey Chaucer told of a monk's prized possessions:

Greyhoundes he hadde as swifte as fowels in flight;
Of prikyng and of huntyng for the hare
Was al his lust, for no cost wolde he spare.

In 1486, Dame Juliana Berners, Abbess of Sopewell, set down what everyone should be looking for in terms of the physical conformation of the perfect greyhound:

A Grehound shold be heeded lyke a snake
And neckyd lyke a drake,
Backed lyke a beam,
Syded lyke a bream,
Footed lyke a catte,
Tayllyd lyke a ratte.

By 1576, during the reign of Queen Elizabeth I, essays on English canines were speaking of two separate varieties of greyhound. The smaller, smoother-coated type was that favoured by the monarch who, on witnessing the sport at first hand and being fascinated, instructed the Duke of Norfolk to set down the Laws of the Leash for the fair running of the sport of hare coursing.

An illustration from *Old English Sports and Pastimes: Coursing* by C.C.W. Aldin.

OPPOSITE
The Monk from Chaucer's *Canterbury Tales*, as shown in the Ellesmere manuscript.

egec
&

lualor

B Bitch

In horse racing, fillies and mares get weight allowances, which enable them to compete on 'level' terms with the colts. Greyhound racing is one of the few sports (human or animal) in which the female of the species competes directly with the male. While bitches need to be exceptional to beat the dogs over the Classic distances, there are many examples of them being triumphant.

Moreover, bitches come into their own over 700 yards and longer marathon trips, and generally possess more stamina. Muinessa – sprightly up the coursing field against her own sex – triumphed over the dogs in the 1937 Irish Derby. She was the second bitch in just six renewals to win this great race.

The First Coursing Club

Exactly two centuries later, the first coursing club in these islands came into being (coincidentally, in Norfolk) at Swaffham. The club was founded by Lord Orford who is famous for trying to achieve a hybrid hound by crossing the now established greyhound with the bulldog (or a strain of bull-terrier). He hoped to increase the courage and stamina of the breed by this cross-mating. His running of the first official coursing club was at least a success. By 1781, the organised sport could be found in Yorkshire where it would also prosper.

The impetus that would give coursing a national platform was the founding of the Altcar Club in the Waterloo Hotel

The Waterloo Cup coursing meeting, 1840

in Liverpool in 1825. Eleven years later, the Waterloo Cup was established and was to become not just the premier competition for greyhounds but an essential part of the British sporting calendar. It was to coursing what the Epsom Derby is to horse racing and, indeed, for a century it would dwarf even the premier Classic of the turf in social importance. The Waterloo Cup was to herald the sporting rivalry of the English and the Irish, and now reaches a high point at the Cheltenham Festival in March of every year.

The coursing season was, and still is, governed by laws relating to hare husbandry, and lasts just five months, from October to February. So greyhound racing – by contrast – was a sport not confined to the winter months and accessible to hundreds of thousands in the city. Just as in Rome, the greyhound was displaying its adaptability. From hunting for food in ancient times to providing sport for the landed gentry in the Middle Ages and beyond, the greyhound was now to thrill millions in yet another role and in the era of electricity.

The Waterloo Cup was to herald the sporting rivalry of the English and the Irish, and now reaches a high point at the Cheltenham Festival in March of every year.

Celtic Park, April 1927

2 CELTIC ROOTS

RACING COMES TO IRELAND

Thomas Aloysius Morris

The Celtic Dog

The fact that Ireland is now the foremost breeder of greyhounds has contributed to the idea that the greyhound is a Celtic breed. Indeed, the Romans knew the dog simply as the Celtic hound. But whether the greyhound was in fact a Celtic dog or just one in which the Celts traded is not clear. Experts, for their part, do not consider the greyhound to be an indigenous Irish breed. Yet, in terms of breeding, owning and training, Ireland is the home of the greyhound.

Coursing

The writing-up of the initial set of rules for coursing in 1576 had been followed, two centuries later, by the establishing of the first formal coursing club at Swaffham in Norfolk. The publication of the rules of coursing and the founding of the National Coursing Club (NCC) took place in 1858. All of the Irish-bred coursing greyhounds automatically appeared in the NCC *Stud Book*.

Commerce and interaction among coursing breeders and trainers throughout Ireland and England was common during the era of Master M'Grath (the 1860s and early 1870s), as evidenced by his whelping and rearing in Waterford, his first courses in Lurgan and his Waterloo Cup debut at Altcar. It was only natural that the Irish would fall in with the British establishment and governing body for coursing: an Irish sub-committee of the NCC ran domestic coursing.

However, in terms of control, Ireland would have been impossible for the NCC to manage if the locals wanted away. While political parallels are obviously now drawn, the split between the Irish coursing fraternity (running fixtures in a myriad of provincial parishes) and the British brass can be put down to nothing more than plain dissatisfaction with certain aspects of the administration and – in the years at the beginning of the twentieth century, which saw the separation of the Irish from many British institutions – the break of the domestic coursing club from its parent body in England was perhaps the least acrimonious of partings.

The Irish sub-committee of the NCC convened a general

meeting in Hayes Hotel in Thurles, County Tipperary – the hostelry had also witnessed the founding of the Gaelic Athletic Association thirty-two years earlier – at which all the issues were addressed. It was decided that a deputation should be sent to England with the view to Ireland ceding from the NCC. Events moved quickly: the Earl of Sefton, the NCC patriarch, greeted the deputation in Liverpool and appears to have been well disposed towards this manifestation of Irish independence.

The Irish Coursing Club

Steering his committee through these potentially tricky waters was Thomas Aloysius Morris, the father of modern Irish coursing. A mark of the energy and organisational and diplomatic ability of T.A. Morris was the fact that the ink had hardly dried on his report of the cordial meeting with the Earl of Sefton when the Irish Coursing Club was founded in 1916.

T.A. Morris became the first secretary of the ICC, and the fact that the present incumbent, D.J. Histon, is only the sixth person to hold the executive role is evidence of the ability and talent of those who have filled the post in the interim. T.A. Morris served as secretary from 1916 to 1952. Between 1948 and 1952 he shared the post with his son Arthur (A.J.), who went on to serve alone between 1952 and 1956.

There followed Kitty Butler (1956–69), Commandant Joseph Fitzpatrick (1969–86), Jeremiah (J.L.) Desmond (1986–2008) and D.J. Histon (2008–). Unlike Irish horse racing – the breeding side of which still relies on the secretariat at Weatherbys, the Northamptonshire-based company that published the first *Thoroughbred Stud Book* in 1793 – Morris had established the *Irish Greyhound Stud Book* by 1923. Thus, the job of keeper of the Stud Book became one of the onerous tasks of the secretary of the ICC.

Horse racing was already up and running at Powerstown Park in Clonmel, County Tipperary, when the ICC came about. Coursing was taking place at Powerstown Park also, and T.A. Morris was one of the organisers of the local club. Indeed, the Irish Cup (under the auspices of the County

A chromolithograph by William Dickes, from *The Gentleman's Journal and Youth's Miscellany*, c.1871.

Limerick Coursing Club) had been run at the Earls of Dunraven's estates at Clounanna, near Adare, County Limerick, since January 1906. After 1916, the ICC officially leased the racecourse for the purpose of running its main competitions, before purchasing Powerstown Park outright in 1932. Future holders of the office of ICC secretary would also become the racecourse manager.

Alongside all his other achievements, T.A. Morris is also credited with the ingenious idea of clubs running trial stakes, the winners of which progressed to the annual national meeting in Clonmel. By 1925, he had put the running of coursing competitions on a national standing and a

'national coursing meeting' took place at Clonmel racecourse seven years before the ICC bought the venue. The original National Breeder and Produce Stakes – the first in 1925 was won by Keen Laddie – would eventually be divided to form the Derby and the Oaks and, together with the consolation T.A. Morris Stake, the Kitty Butler Stake, the Champion Stake and the All-age Bitch Stake, these courses make up the present-day programme that takes place in January and early February. The coursing Classics continue to flourish under the sponsorship banners of countrywide bookmakers Boylesports and the local Hotel Minella.

As if all this was not sufficient, T.A. Morris also began the

publication, in 1924, of the *Irish Coursing Calendar* and became its editor. It was also known as the *Irish Coursing and Racing Calendar* and was a general sports newspaper not confined to greyhound matters. Since 1951 it has been called the *Sporting Press* and, even with the establishment of Bord na gCon in 1958 and its takeover of the control of greyhound racing in the Republic, the ICC weekly publication has remained the official organ of the greyhound industry on an all-island basis. Like all the other instruments of the ICC, it has stood the test of time.

The Advent of Greyhound Racing

The *Irish Coursing Calendar* was to become a national platform, just three years after coming into being, for the great debate about greyhound racing behind a mechanical hare. A decade after the founding of the Irish Coursing Club, greyhound racing (the subject of numerous experiments in Britain) was officially imported from America. The first meeting was staged at Belle Vue, Manchester, on 24 July 1926 and the first race was won by a dog called Mistley.

The coursing fraternity – the county of Lancashire was also home to the Waterloo Cup – scoffed at the poor initial attendances. But the crowds soon exploded. In the next year three tracks in London – Shepherd's Bush (White City), Harringay and Wembley – and one in Liverpool opened. Using the pages of the *Irish Coursing Calendar*, Morris was scathing in his condemnation of the new sport, which he labelled, with disdain, as being an American gimmick. Like his counterparts in Lancashire, Morris predicted that greyhound racing behind an artificial hare would not catch on.

In the meantime, a group of entrepreneurs with the right connections had been invited to Manchester to see the sport for themselves. Belfast bookmaker Hugh McAlinden brought a delegation across to Manchester and, strategically, other members of the ICC from Dublin and further south were included in the party.

McAlinden may have won over some members of the ruling ICC committee but not the secretary. Morris devoted reams in the *Irish Coursing Calendar* to the subject of greyhound racing prior to its introduction. However, he seems to

have modified his views when, unannounced, he went to Manchester in October 1926 to view the spectacle first hand. He still had reservations but appears to have been caught up with the excitement of the evening. He probably came to the realisation that the advent of greyhound racing in Ireland was inevitable. He now turned his concerns to the proper administration and conduct of the sport, should it come to Ireland, while still playing down the chances of it being successful here.

McAlinden's group, in the meantime, had formed the National Greyhound Racing Company Limited and chose the home of Belfast Celtic Football Club, where McAlinden was a director, as the first Irish venue. On Easter Monday, 18 April 1927, Ireland's first greyhound race was staged at Celtic Park in Belfast.

Even so, seven months after the initial Celtic Park fixture, the headline in the *Irish Coursing Calendar* was still about the 'racing crisis'. In the meantime, of course, other sites for the sport had been purchased in Belfast, Cork and Dublin. The ICC 'crisis' was not that the urban-based racing would take away from coursing but that the new branch of greyhound activity was slipping from its control. McAlinden and his cohorts could hardly run the new sport in the face of opposition from the keeper of the Stud Book and the editor of the *Irish Coursing Calendar*.

The ICC and Greyhound Racing

Morris was sensible enough to see that a coursing–racing split would be disastrous. If greyhound racing in Ireland was here to stay, Morris knew that the ICC needed to be the authority. A meeting of all interested parties took place in Dublin on 31 January 1928, at which the ICC assumed control of and became the authority for the sport. It was to remain so for the next thirty years; this was also a period in which the ICC received a poor press. There were accusations that greyhound racing was not being properly and fairly administered.

There are, of course, a number of sides to the story. At this remove, it can be assumed that there were those simply out to blacken the reputation of the ICC. After all, Morris and

Hugh McAlinden, the Belfast bookmaker who introduced greyhound racing to Ireland.

McAlinden's group ... had formed the National Greyhound Racing Company Limited and chose the home of Belfast Celtic Football Club, where McAlinden was a director, as the first Irish venue.

There is also no doubt that the public was flocking to the sport and that the revenue generated was coveted by both the government, who wanted the wealth to work its way down to the grassroots of the sport, and the private track owners, who wanted to keep it for themselves.

his colleagues had achieved so much in the dozen years since the founding of the ICC. It is true that they had a busy schedule with the publishing of the *Stud Book*, a weekly newspaper and the running of the club itself. Yet they had shown themselves capable of successfully running a major sport – as coursing was – on a national basis.

While the ICC was responsible for the administration of greyhound racing, its ownership was in the hands of the National Greyhound Racing Company and the Dublin Greyhound and Sports Association. Greyhound racing had become big business and its conduct and revenue were starting to interest the government of the day in what was still a fledgling state.

The issue that would first see the crossing of the paths of government ministers and greyhound authorities was the establishment of the sport's totalisator (tote) (see chapter 4).

However, the issue of the totalisator was to be merely the sidebar to what was to become the lead story: the government wanting to run greyhound racing. For all its dedication, it is clear from correspondence of the day that the Irish Coursing Club did not enjoy the confidence of the national government. For this reason, it follows that the government would never have contemplated giving a huge financial commitment to tracks that were privately owned, and to a sport run by a club that was not part of the state mechanism.

The state was concerned not just with the control of the totalisator but about governance in the matter of the breeding of greyhounds, which with the demand for the Irish product in Britain especially had mushroomed to be a growing industry and source of export revenue. The ICC days as the authority for greyhound racing in the Republic were numbered.

The first night of racing in Ireland:
Celtic Park, Belfast, April 1927.

Bord na gCon

The founding of Bord na gCon was the inevitable consequence of the success of greyhound racing in Ireland. For all the organisational genius and commercial flair displayed by T.A. Morris in his stewardship, the Irish Coursing Club remained a voluntary body, although only amateur in the sense that many of its members were unpaid for their work on the club's behalf.

Although the club had shown a capability for running a national sport, many would have seen the administration of such a vibrant industry as greyhound racing as being beyond the ICC, and there were problems which some would associate with the ICC management of greyhound racing. Detractors saw the ICC as struggling when having to tackle the rogue element in the ranks of owners and trainers: the whole integrity of the sport was at stake. There is also no doubt that the public was flocking to the sport and that the revenue generated was coveted by both the government, who wanted the wealth to work its way down to the grassroots of the sport, and the private track owners, who wanted to keep it for themselves.

As is the way with matters of state, an advisory committee was set up by the Minister for Agriculture, James Dillon, on 21 February 1951. Dillon picked out Séamus Flanagan as the natural secretary: he was a civil servant with the Department of Agriculture and was delegated to deal with any queries concerning greyhound sport.

Among the assembled committee was Jim Frost from Cratloe, County Clare, whose son Kevin was to sell the John Hayes-trained eventual winner Indian Joe to Belfast bookmaker Alfie McLean in the course of the 1980 English Derby at White City.

Unlike many other arms of government, the Advisory Committee on the Greyhound Industry worked … and worked swiftly at that. The advisory committee heard from a raft of interested parties: the Irish Coursing Club, Irish Greyhound Owners' Association, greyhound racing-track executives, greyhound racecourse bookmakers, Irish Racecourse Bookmakers Assistants' Association, Licensed Greyhound Trainers' Association, Office of the Revenue Commissioners, Racing Board, the National Greyhound Racing Club, as well as getting a flavour of opinion from 146 coursing clubs.

By 18 January 1952 the report had been presented to Dillon's successor at the Department of Agriculture, Thomas Walsh. The name appended to the report was a significant one. As T.A. Morris had been the father of Irish coursing, so Séamus Flanagan would be the patriarch of greyhound racing.

The 1950s was a decade of changing regimes in the Republic and it was 1957 before the now six-year-old document went through the parliamentary process.

The ICC was being edged out of the greyhound racing picture in the Republic, although it did continue to produce the *Stud Book*, a lucrative source of income, to publish the *Sporting Press*, and to organise coursing on a thirty-two-county basis.

The ICC's involvement with track racing did not come to a totally abrupt halt, however, and the new Act allowed for three members of the ICC executive committee to make up, by right, half of the ordinary membership of Bord na gCon. Irish Coursing Club personnel continued as directors of greyhound tracks and horse racecourses.

With its semi-state status, the Bord na gCon sphere of authority did not extend into the six counties of Northern Ireland. And so today – over fifty years after the founding of Bord na gCon, and more than eighty years after the mechanical hare made its debut at Celtic Park – the ICC has retained authority in Northern Ireland, the birthplace of Irish greyhound racing. Northern Ireland may have found itself out of greyhound racing's new order in the South, but its people – whether breeders, owners, trainers or administrators – would continue to have a remarkable influence and impact on both coursing and racing.

C Cigarette Cards

It was not long after the advent of greyhound racing in Britain that the first cigarette cards dedicated to the sport appeared. The first set of fifty was produced by Carreras in Britain in 1926. Ogden and Churchman were other popular tobacco brands to follow. In 1935, Player produced the first set of 'Famous Irish Greyhounds'. A number of reproductions exist but the original sets (made exclusively for the Irish market) in mint condition are highly valued by collectors. The 1935 black bitch Quarter Day, a favourite around Wembley, was the first greyhound to be featured in a set.

Just dandy … At the official opening of the totalisator at Tralee on 7 June 1963: (L–R) Tom McEllistim TD; Dr P.J. Maguire, chairman Bord na gCon; J.J. (James) Collins TD (father of future Bord na gCon chief executive, Seán Collins); Lt.-Col. C.L. Jordan from Biscayne, Florida; Tim O'Connor TD, owner of Spanish Battleship.

3 BORD NA GCON
1958–1968
THE DEFINING DECADE

In the original
office, Flanagan
was flanked by
Pat Holland, a
youthful Seán
Collins and Tony
Fitzgerald. Collins
would succeed
Flanagan as chief
officer and have
as his deputy Pat
Holland, who (with
his wife Monita)
owned Play Solo
and trained him
to win coursing's
Waterloo Cup at
Altcar in 1982.

The Earliest Years

Coming into operation in 1958, the Greyhound Industry Act became the template for decades of history in greyhound racing. Séamus Flanagan, seconded from the Department of Agriculture to be the first chief officer (the chief executive of later years), was supported by a chairman and the six 'ordinary' members of Bord na gCon who were appointed by the Minister for Agriculture. The chairman was there at the will of the Minister for Agriculture, with an open-ended term. The other members were appointed for five-year terms. This would later give way to a rotation system. While based in Dublin, Bord na gCon had addresses at 10 Earlsfort Terrace and at 59 Merrion Square. A government scheme for the decentralisation of agencies saw Bord na gCon move to 104 Henry Street, Limerick, in February 1961.

In the original office, Flanagan was flanked by Pat Holland, a youthful Seán Collins and Tony Fitzgerald. Collins would succeed Flanagan as chief officer and have as his deputy Pat Holland, who (with his wife Monita) owned Play Solo and trained him to win coursing's Waterloo Cup at Altcar in 1982. Tony Fitzgerald would later leave the greyhound industry and become chief executive with the Royal Dublin Society (RDS) in Ballsbridge, home of the Dublin Horse Show.

Others to come on board were Cyril Downes, Noel Drumgoole and Louis McGauran. Downes was the accountant for the new semi-state body and, as a member of the Old Crescent Club in Limerick, went on to become a Munster rugby selector. Drumgoole and McGauran were, like Flanagan, seconded from the Department of Agriculture. Drumgoole was brought in ostensibly to deal with the bookmakers and McGauran to oversee the totalisator. Both would become managers of Shelbourne Park, while Drumgoole and Holland would serve as deputies to Seán Collins during his tenure as chief executive (1989–97). Noel Drumgoole was a fine hurler with his native Dublin and later went on to manage the Limerick county side.

After Jim Frost had helped Séamus Flanagan to put the finishing touches to the blueprint for the landmark greyhound racing legislation, Dr Patrick J. Maguire took the chair. Following his retirement from the Royal Navy, Dr Maguire

Politics and Greyhound Sport

Politics and greyhound sport are regularly intertwined in Ireland. Séamus Flanagan, for example, was 'well got' in both the sporting and political worlds. His brother Seán was both an experienced and astute government minister of the day. He held the important portfolio of Minister for Health from 1966 to 1969. He had also won glory as a Gaelic footballer with his native Mayo. The winner of senior all-Ireland medals in 1950 and '51, Seán Flanagan is generally acknowledged as one of the all-time great players. Seán Collins is a son of James Collins, an Abbeyfeale, County Limerick, member of the Dáil (Irish parliament). Seán Collins had two brothers who served the state in this way: Michael and Gerard, who was Minister for Justice between 1977 and 1981 and Minister for Foreign Affairs in 1982 and, again, in 1989–92. Seán Collins' son Niall was subsequently elected to the Dáil for Limerick West. One of the Bord na gCon members to serve when Collins was chief executive was Luke Kilcoyne from Tubbercurry, County Sligo, whose wife Carmel is a sister of Ray MacSharry, Tánaiste (deputy prime minister) in 1982. Luke Kilcoyne's son Pat was the joint owner (with Terry McCann) of the Ger McKenna-trained Tubbertelly Queen, winner of the Waterloo Cup at Altcar in 1984.

practised as a GP in Clones, County Monaghan. He later lived in Dublin. Dr Maguire served as chairman from 1958 until 27 September 1965.

The other members in the first days of Bord na gCon were Roscommon man Liam Forde who resigned after a year; Thomas Ahern from Celbridge, County Kildare, who retired in 1963; Thomas Fitzgibbon from Askeaton, County Limerick; P.J. Hogan from Miltown Malbay, County Clare, who died in October 1960; John Moriarty from Listowel, County Kerry; and Captain John Ross from Doagh, County Antrim.

The first ever meeting of Bord na gCon was held at the

Department of Agriculture on Friday 11 June 1958. The second gathering was held in room 106 in Leinster House on Monday 28 July 1958, an arrangement facilitated by the Ceann Comhairle (Speaker of the House). Apart from the minutes, there was no need seen to issue an 'annual' report for the second half of 1958. Indeed, Bord na gCon obviously believed that such a report for 1959 would also not be necessary and took the decision on 26 March 1960 to commence the practice at the end of their second full year.

At that point – December 1960 – Bord na gCon had assumed all the greyhound racing functions of the Irish Coursing Club in the Republic. In those days, Bord na gCon members were there for the long haul. Committee member Cornelius Murphy (from Cork city) replaced Thomas Ahern in 1963 and went on until 1972. Thomas Fitzgibbon died in office in September 1968 and was replaced by Patrick J. Leyden from Miltown Malbay,

County Clare, who was another to serve longer than five years. P.J. Hogan died in office in October 1960. He was replaced by John M. Ryan (from Cork city) who also died in office (in September 1962) and was replaced by the venerable Patrick J. Cox.

Based in Newbridge, County Kildare, Paddy Cox was closely involved with both horse and greyhound racing. He was associated with Naas racecourse, much as his son Dermot has been with Punchestown. Paddy Cox's grandson David runs Newbridge greyhound track and is married to Tamarisk Doyle, head of public relations at Horse Racing Ireland, the semi-state thoroughbred authority at the Curragh.

Indeed, it was not until the appointment in 1973 of Seán Henehan (Fethard, County Tipperary), James Lantry (Cork city), Donal J. O'Neill (Tralee, County Kerry) and William Russell (Galbally, County Limerick) that there would be

P.J. Cox (centre), photographed here with his wife Helen, served as a member of Bord na gCon between 1962 and 1982, longer than any other member. Also pictured is Seán Collins, chief executive of Bord na gCon, 1989–97.

a significant change in Bord na gCon personnel. This is underlined by the fact that Séamus Flanagan, on his retirement after thirty-one years as chief officer, had served seven boards, five chairmen and just thirty-eight board members.

With the more rigid regulations, the individuals who owned the tracks found them to be less of a gold mine. They were being made accountable and were no longer just raking the money in.

The Work of Bord na gCon Begins

Flanagan, and those who worked around him, created the pillars on which Bord na gCon was built. Starting from scratch, the original administrators had much with which to deal. The review committee had provided the outline for how greyhound racing would be run going forward, but it was two years after the 1958 Greyhound Industry Act that Bord na gCon assumed total control of the sport.

Almost every aspect of the game altered once Bord na gCon had taken charge. Previously, the racing season closed in early December for a two-month break. Tracks tended not to reopen until the coursing Classics (the Derby/Oaks in Clonmel and Irish Cup in Clounanna) had been completed in February. In the meantime, Bord na gCon compensated coursing clubs for any loss of revenue because of the encroachment of racing dates.

Bord na gCon was keen to move towards year-round racing, although it would be some time before this came to pass. There was obviously much that had to be addressed. There may have been those out to do down unnecessarily the Irish Coursing Club and its ability to administer greyhound racing. In some ways, though, it was true that Irish greyhound racing was in difficulty; for example, the number of litters registered in 1946–47 had been 8,400 (35,000 namings). By 1950–51, there were just 2,900 new litters (13,900 namings).

Bord na gCon wasted little time in undertaking a root-and-branch overhaul. In 1960, more meetings (1,483) had been held at nineteen venues in the Republic than ever before. There are not as many tracks now, but the old six-race cards have made way for eleven-race programmes. The number of meetings staged would also continue to grow. The 10,057 races run in 1960 included a high percentage of sprints, 237 over hurdles and just 57 over 600 yards or more. The organisers of the racing at Lifford were persuaded to stage a race

over 780 yards and Mullingar had one over 810 yards.

In Bord na gCon's first full year of operations, the 725,468 paying patrons were telling Bord na gCon that they wanted hurdle and long-distance races. They did not want sprints. Short-distance races were to prove more popular with the hardened backers in Northern Ireland. When sprints were staged at the Dublin tracks, the takings (particularly on the totalisator) shrank. Bord na gCon introduced a solution: a prize-money grants system that gave higher allocations to tracks willing to stage hurdles and longer races. The board tightened up on disciplinary matters and set up a control committee. The first year saw 410 greyhounds suspended for having 'fighting propensies'.

Bord na gCon dealt with applications to license tracks. Some, including a proposed venue at Boyle, County Roscommon, never got going. Bord na gCon also got tough with the track owners at Tralee, County Kerry, and Youghal, County Cork, over the paucity of facilities.

Bigger obstacles presented themselves, especially the management of the totalisator (covered in detail in chapter 4). There were rows with the bookmakers, the hiatus in the setting up of the totalisator … but, just as it seemed that they were getting on top of everything else, the spanking new semi-state body was to face its greatest challenge yet.

With the more rigid regulations, the individuals who owned the tracks found them to be less of a gold mine. They were being made accountable and were no longer just raking the money in. And these were the 1960s … a time when Europe was not at war and not in a depressed economic state. It was an age of property booms when sites being used as greyhound tracks, especially those in the cities, had become extremely valuable.

In the Bord na gCon chair at this time was Desmond Hanrahan, a member of the Limerick City Coursing Club and former sports editor of the *Limerick Leader* newspaper (Dr Patrick J. Maguire had retired over two years earlier).

Faced with the greatest crisis in the first decade of its existence, Bord na gCon had to take a momentous decision. When the advisory committee reported to the Department of Agriculture in 1952, there were twenty companies

involved in greyhound racing (some no longer exist as venues: Ballina, Clones, Kilrush and Navan).

Confronted with the prospect of Shelbourne Park itself being wiped off the map, Hanrahan put his name to a document that saw the Ringsend track, the home of Irish greyhound racing, pass from the ownership of the National Greyhound Racing Company to that of Bord na gCon. Irrespective of what had gone before or would happen later, 2 January 1968 is the seminal date in the sport's being: the day that Bord na gCon bought Shelbourne Park for the state and the people. The one thing that had never been envisaged by the advisory committee and which had never been

anticipated by the 1958 Act – the ownership of stadiums by Bord na gCon – had become a fact of life.

It may be fair to conclude that had greyhound racing remained in Irish Coursing Club control and had Bord na gCon not existed, then the state would never have countenanced backing the initiative of chairman Hanrahan and his chief officer Séamus Flanagan, and that the sport, as we know it, would be no more.

The Shelbourne crowd witnesses a thrilling climax to the 2008 Paddy Power Derby as Shelbourne Aston lands his last-stride victory. Note how many are turning to the TV monitors for a better view of the finish!

Séamus Flanagan

Dr Patrick J. Maguire

Patrick J. Cox

John Moriarty

Cornelius Murphy

Patrick J. Leyden

Captain John Ross

Desmond Duffy

Members
of Bord na gCon

Ahern, Thomas
Celbridge, County Kildare   1958–1963

Barry, Ann
Limerick city   1997–2000

Brennan, James
Waterford city   1988–1993

Carroll, Patrick   1983–1986
Dundalk, County Louth   *and* 1991–1993

Costigan, John
Cork city   1981–1982

Cox, Patrick J.
Newbridge, County Kildare   1962–1982

Curley, Cathal
Derry city   1996–2006

Delargy, James P.
Belfast, County Antrim   1983–1986

Duffy, Desmond
Loughrea, County Galway   1960–1972

Dunphy, Patrick
Castlecomer, County Kilkenny   1978–1982

Feeney, Pádraig
An Spideal, County Galway   2004–2008

Fitzgibbon, Thomas
Askeaton, County Limerick   1958–1968

Forde, Liam
Roscommon, County Roscommon   1958–1959

Gilbert, Timothy
Dublin city   2008–

Gleeson, Stephen
Limerick city   1983–1986

Griffin, Thomas
Gort, County Galway   2002–2003

Healy, Philip
Listowel, County Kerry   1983–1986

Hegarty, John
Listowel, County Kerry   2003–2006

Henehan, Seán
Fethard, County Tipperary   1973–1977

Hogan, P.J.
Miltown Malbay, County Clare   1958–1960

Kelliher, Eileen
Castleisland, County Kerry   1993–1997

Kilcoyne, Luke
Tubbercurry, County Sligo   1988–1996

Lantry, James
Cork city   1973–1977

Lawlor, Jack
Tralee, County Kerry   1978–1982

Leyden, Patrick J.
Miltown Malbay, County Clare   1968–1977

Lynch, Terence   1978–1980
Crookstown, County Cork   *and* 1988–1990

McKenna, Anthony
Borrisokane, County Tipperary   2004–

Mallon, Séamus
Markethill, County Armagh   2006–2007

Monahan, Pádraig
Roscommon, County Roscommon   1978–1982

Moriarty, John
Listowel, County Kerry   1958–1972

Mulligan, Luke
Department of Agriculture   1994–2002

Murphy, Christopher
Ballinaboola, County Wexford   1988–1993

Murphy, Cornelius
Cork city   1963–1972

Nugent, Helen
Department of Agriculture   2003–2005

O'Connell, Francis
Birr, County Offaly   2005–

O'Driscoll, Noel
Skibbereen, County Cork   1999–2002

O'Dwyer, William
Thurles, County Tipperary   2008–

O'Leary, Cormac
Moyvane, County Kerry   1983–1986

O'Malley, Patrick
Limerick city   1978–1982

O'Neill, Donal J.
Tralee, County Kerry   1973–1977

O'Reilly, Edward
Edgeworthstown, County Longford   1988–1995

O'Sullivan, Richard
Tralee, County Kerry   2006

Quinlan, Ann
Waterford city   1994–2001

Reilly, Daniel J.
Navan, County Meath   2002–

Roberts, Robert
Knocklong, County Limerick   2000–2003

Rogers, Ruth
Ashbourne, County Meath   1995–2001

Ross, Captain John
Doagh, County Antrim   1958–1972

Russell, William
Kilross, County Tipperary   1973–1977

Ryan, John M.
Cork city   1960–1962

Scallon, Oliver
Irvinestown, County Fermanagh   1988–1996

Wall, Teresa
Nurney, County Kildare   2006–

Walsh, William A.
Waterford city   1983–1986

Ward, David
Abbeyfeale, County Limerick   1996–1998

An A–Z of Greyhounds

D Dead Heat

The closeness of the finishes is just one of the elements of greyhound racing that thrills spectators. Everyone has experienced that nail-biting wait for the judge to announce the result of a photo finish. It is not always possible to separate the greyhounds, even with the most sophisticated modern technology. Yet, even in the days before the use of the photo finish, the relevant track officials – the judges – seemed to prefer calling a definite result to a dead heat. That said, the 1968 final of the short-distance Classic, the Irish National Sprint, at Dunmore Stadium in Belfast, saw Dry Flash and Newhill Printer dead heat for first place.

Top men . . . Members of Bord na gCon meeting in late 1988 under new chairman Noel Brassil (front, L–R). Others pictured are (back, L–R): Luke Kilcoyne, Christopher Murphy, Oliver Scallon, Séamus Flanagan (chief officer); (front, L–R): Edward O'Reilly, James Brennan, Terence Lynch.

18 December 1943: telephone operators
at the tote headquarters at White City
Greyhound Racing Stadium, London,
telephoning the odds at the end of a race
to the payout booths.

4 THE TOTALISATOR

GREYHOUND RACING HITS THE JACKPOT

Tote and Dogs: A Perfect Marriage

The tag-line of being able to win 'a lot for a little' was not just appropriate for totalisator betting but was particularly pertinent when it came to greyhound racing. Horse racing, with its big fields, had an appeal for the tote backer who just fancied a flutter and wanted to take a chance on backing an outsider. Horses outside of the first few in the returned odds tend to pay well with the computer-betting system and, regularly, well in excess of the official starting price or those odds offered by the on-course bookmakers.

Many racecourse bookmakers simply chalk up 'win' betting. Especially with a strong market, this appeals to the more dedicated punter backing in bigger denominations. Place-betting, or more exotic forms like forecast betting (naming the first two home), tricast or trio betting (naming the first three in finishing order) or jackpot betting (accumulators over set races) grab the imagination of the smaller punter. But even this kind of punter, faced with large fields in horse racing, might find the task of cracking the correct forecast beyond them.

Greyhound racing – with only six runners and limited permutations – and the totalisator were made for one another. It was little wonder then that, even with bookmakers among their ranks, the member tracks in the Greyhound Racing Association in Britain and the National Greyhound Racing Company in Ireland could not wait to get their hands on the system.

The United Kingdom government of the time was not entirely happy about the computer-betting system falling into private hands. However, racecourses in Britain had been permitted a formal tote, which came into existence in 1929. The totalisator in Ireland had been available to horse racing since Easter Monday 1930, when it cranked into action at Fairyhouse. It was not available on that day at the other meetings at Mallow and Tramore, and it would be some time before the entire horse-racing circuit in Ireland had been switched on.

It was a nervous time for Irish bookmakers, who could only stand by as their futures were debated in the Parliament in Westminster and while their British colleagues did

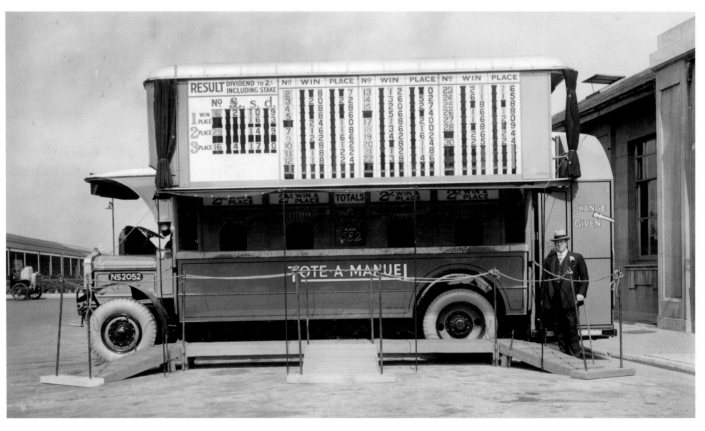

27 June 1929: Mr Howard of the Stadium Club beside his 'Tote-A-Manuel'.

History of the Totalisator

The totalisator was not a 'new-fangled' idea. In 1871, a half-century before greyhound racing was officially run and in an era when Master M'Grath, Honeymoon and Donald were winning coursing's Waterloo Cup for their Irish trainers, York displayed just one example of an early racecourse totalisator.

There was a vital difference between this early machine and what we recognise as the modern totalisator. The early version was ostensibly a 'pool' system, but the eight machines (taking half-crown unit bets that only the rich could afford) were not linked. The result was that every machine paid an individual dividend which had to be calculated manually.

A favourite pastime for race-goers was to tour the various terminals until they found the one that was paying the highest odds on their winning ticket. However, the erratic and unpredictable dividends and the cumbersome nature of the set-up, along with the promoter's refusal to take smaller stakes, would have done nothing to popularise the system.

A Frenchman – the great irony is that he was a bookmaker – Joseph Oller (1839–1922) had first come up with the concept of the totalisator machine in 1864. It would later be perfected to allow for genuine pool betting as we now know it. The Oller invention was the prelude to the French authorities banning bookmakers in 1891 and declaring the tote monopoly, which has existed since as the Pari-Mutuel (PMU).

everything to keep the machines from making them redundant. Political separation came in 1922 and the Irish bookmakers had matters in their own hands.

Horse racing was structured (until 1945) much as greyhound racing would be for its first thirty years (1928–58). The courses were privately owned by wealthy individuals and private companies, while the Turf Club did the regulating, much in the same way as the Irish Coursing Club. The early

governments in the now Free State were under considerable pressure to relax the laws on gambling from all hues of betting interests, as well as endeavouring to defend their plans to those who thought that there were already too many avenues for gambling.

They allowed for the legalisation of off-course bookmaker shops with the Betting Act (1926) and the revised 1928 version. Further regulation came in under the Betting Act (1931) which, although the industry is unrecognisable from that of more than seventy years ago, is still the instrument governing retail betting.

In a fine balancing act and in an effort to placate all parties, the Government introduced the Totalisator Act (1929) and gave the green light for the installation of the betting machines on the racecourses. It was on a short-term agreement with the companies that owned the racecourses. A formal agreement came in the shape of a later, fifteen-year-long licence. But behind the accord lay an unhappiness that such a lucrative source of revenue should be in the private hands of the racecourse owners whose regulators were a club (the Turf Club) and not the politicians.

State Regulation

The experiences of greyhound racing in Ireland and its efforts to introduce totalisator betting would run on parallel lines to those of its equine counterparts. Government unease would be such that when the fifteen-year licence expired, the semi-state Racing Board came into being, the forerunner to the Irish Horseracing Authority and Horse Racing Ireland. The idea was that horse racing and the Racing Board would largely fund themselves from the totalisator profits. The establishment of horse racing's Racing Board in 1945 pre-dated the setting up of Bord na gCon by thirteen years.

But state regulation came at another price, with the reintroduction of an on-course betting levy by the Racing Board and, later, Bord na gCon. Bookmakers at greyhound racing fixtures had largely escaped tariffs up to 1958 until the on-course tax (which Bord na gCon was entitled to impose under the terms of the 1958 Greyhound Industry Act) was introduced at a level of 2.5 per cent. These levies gave the

It was a nervous time for Irish bookmakers, who could only stand by as their futures were debated in the Parliament in Westminster and while their British colleagues did everything to keep the machines from making them redundant. Political separation came in 1922 and the Irish bookmakers had matters in their own hands.

Firm favourites … With no totalisator in operation, these bookmakers – seen cashing-up at the end of racing at Dunmore Stadium, Belfast, in 1987 – enjoyed a lucrative business monopoly.

semi-state horse and greyhound-racing authorities a second stream of revenue towards self-sufficiency.

When it came to the totalisator, it took the legislators longer to get to grips with the intricacies of the greyhound business here. British horse racing had seen the introduction of fully legalised totalisator betting on 2 July 1929, when fixtures took place at Newmarket and Carlisle. British greyhound racing had a legalised tote (under the Betting and Lotteries Act) in 1934, six years after the sport's arrival. This legislation did not extend to Northern Ireland, and the massive betting turnover at Celtic Park and Dunmore Stadium in Belfast was enjoyed solely by the bookmakers.

The Introduction of the Tote

On 25 April 1931, the Irish government received an application from the National Greyhound Racing Company for a totalisator licence under the 1929 Act. In fact, it would be 24 May 1960 – twenty-nine years on from the application and two years after the enacting of the Greyhound Industry Act – that Irish greyhound racing patrons eventually savoured the excitement of betting with the tote. Results on that debut evening at Harold's Cross could hardly have been kinder to the promoters. There was no outright winning favourite and when Small Dash (8/1) beat Mets Champion (5/2), the forecast odds were 97/1. The tote odds returned for the win-pool exceeded those being shouted by the bookmakers in nearly every race.

Jimmy Lalor, a huge bookmaker in those days and the owner of Rough Waters – the dog that had won the Irish Greyhound Derby in 1952 – told curious journalists that night that he believed that he and his colleagues would retain their clients while the machine would be patronised by the smaller backer. Lalor called it correctly. His comments were interesting and, it turns out, crucial to later developments. There was no real decline in bookmaker turnover (but an increase in tax-evasion by some!). The tote was attracting a new breed of backer. On the opening night, there were forty-three terminals in operation and that number proved insufficient to cater for the demand.

The track owners received a percentage of turnover from the bookmakers at their tracks, but did not receive any from the state-owned tote. Consequently, the track owners in Dublin had tried to prevent totalisator staff from coming onto their premises and sought compensation from Bord na gCon for any loss of revenue (from bookmaker levies) attributable to the tote. Such worries were misguided, as much for the bookmakers as for the track owners. Bookmaker numbers were stable and attendances trebled, with more interest generated with every broken record. The tote at Shelbourne Park came into being on 27 June 1960.

In 1959, betting at tracks in the Republic stood at £4,454,100. Two years later, and with the tote up and running, the overall betting figure had gone up to £6,140,932. However, the bookmaker turnover had, on the face of it, dipped, and the bookmakers sought compensation from Bord na gCon which appeared to be doing everything it

In 1959, betting at tracks in the Republic stood at £4,454,100. Two years later, and with the tote up and running, the overall betting figure had gone up to £6,140,932.

Bookmaker Betting Duty in Ireland (%)		
	On-course (racecourse)	Off-course (shops)
Pre-1926	nil	nil
1926	2.5	5.0
1931	nil	5.0
1941	nil	7.5
1945	5.0	7.5
1946	2.5	7.5
1956	2.5	10.0
1964	5.0	10.0
1972	5.0	15.0
1975	6.0	20.0
1980	7.5	20.0
1985	5.0	10.0
1999	nil	5.0
2002	nil	2.0
2006	nil	1.0

E Easter

In 1927, Easter Monday fell on 18 April: the date of the first-ever greyhound race in Ireland. It took place at Celtic Park on the afternoon of 18 April, and not the fifteenth as is sometimes erroneously stated, as that was Good Friday, a date on which greyhound tracks are still forbidden by law to race. The other taboo date is 25 December – Christmas Day. While greyhound racing was imported from Britain in 1927, the export trade in the opposite direction soon took on great importance. The gross value of Irish greyhound exports had already surpassed the one-million-pound mark by 1946.

could to divert race-goers towards the totalisator by introducing, and then increasing, the on-course bookmaker levy. It would rise to a high of 7.5 per cent (this included a separate 1.5 per cent government tax) on 30 June 1980, before the abolition of the on-course levy on 25 July 1999. As much as any tax, the imposition of the on-course levy was universally resented – by the backers who had to pay it and the bookmakers who had to collect it (on behalf of Bord na gCon, as they saw it). With the bookmakers no longer 'tax collectors' in 1999, a new funding system between the state, Horse Racing Ireland and Bord na gCon came into being. The end result of the introduction of zero-tax was a significant rise in betting turnover, both on-course and in the betting shops, the number of which mushroomed to 1,248 in 2008.

Even after the setting-up of Bord na gCon – along with horse racing, greyhound sport was part of the Department of Agriculture portfolio for the greater part of its history – coursing was regarded as an off-shoot of agriculture and retained a renewable tax-exemption status even as the

various administrations tinkered with other betting taxes.

In spite of this hectic activity in the on-course greyhound betting market, the totalisator continued to do brisk business. It was down to the difference in profile of the computer-betting backer and those dealing with the bookmakers. It was reckoned that forecast betting, even in the first year, was accounting for 67 per cent of the totalisator turnover after the immediate introduction of the totalisator at Irish greyhound tracks a half-century ago. A dog at Dundalk – on 26 June 1971 – paid odds of 91/1 for the 'win' alone. On 16 June 1975, a forecast dividend of 787/1 was paid in Cork. Clearly, you did not have to go to Dublin to strike it rich. Enniscorthy and Navan, as well as Dundalk, were noted as places where the tastiest dividends were achieved.

Greyhound racing was striding upsides the bigger, horse-racing boys in terms of turnover, and outstripping the Racing Board in the matter of computerisation. The numbers were the key. And greyhound racing saw an influx of backers who knew virtually nothing about the contestants,

Tax-free betting in operation for the first time at a greyhound stadium in Ireland, at Enniscorthy track, 25 July 1999: (L–R) Larry Byrne, Paddy Sharkey (bookmaker) and Mary Nolan.

their pedigree, their owner or any of the technical stuff, but simply backed numbers and combinations of numbers. The original jackpot was a four-race affair in which those who backed the winners of the first two legs (usually races three and four) then exchanged those tickets and tried to predict two more winners (races six and seven). The bet was a sensation, with a pool of £11,247 recorded a week before Christmas (17 December) at Shelbourne Park in 1975.

The totalisator came to Cork (22 July) and Limerick (1 June) in 1961. Two trends continued to show: a marked increase in attendance due to the operation of the totalisator and, within that, 60 per cent of turnover was going into the forecast pools. Not surprisingly, Bord na gCon rushed in 1962 to set up totalisator operations at Navan (6 June), Dundalk (22 June), Mullingar (3 July), Thurles (21 July), Kilkenny (10 August) and Enniscorthy (23 August). The totalisator units were common to all tracks by 1963, with Clonmel ready by 18 February, Tralee on 7 June, Youghal on 12 July and Lifford on 25 July.

The only tracks now without a totalisator were Ballybunion, Clones, Galway, Newbridge and Waterford. Ballybunion had a licence application refused initially but proposed to race from May 1966. They eventually got the show on the road and Bord na gCon put in the totalisator on 7 August 1967. The seaside track failed to race from 1972 onwards and Bord na gCon moved to purchase Tralee to secure racing in north County Kerry.

On 2 March 1965, Bord na gCon had revoked the licence of Clones to race. Complications pertaining to leasing agreements with Galway, Newbridge and Waterford stalled the introduction there. The new track at Newbridge would eventually get the green light for the totalisator in 1971. By 25 April 1969, the totalisator had also come to Longford, and the track (one of twenty-two tracks on the island in that year) immediately saw attendances double.

Not all the ideas were runaway successes. A 'Quinella' pool came about in 1966 and was certainly less popular than the 'Twin Double' jackpot that hit the Dublin tracks in September of the same year. It was a winner from the word go and really took off at events when it was not won and there was a carry-over until the next night's racing. The

'Twin Double' would lead to the 'Straight Four' jackpot of 1993. This has been retained, but the 'Pick-6' and 'Pick-7' jackpots have since become big draws.

Tote turnover in Ireland rose to €51,272,597 in 2005. A year later, a pool of €256,909 would be achieved in the 'Pick-6' jackpot at Shelbourne Park (9 November 2006). On that night, one race-goer staked €10 and received a return of €76,121. On 7 March 2007, there was just one winner of the 'Pick-6' jackpot, who received €60,104. A 'Pick-7' jackpot pool of €224,274 was realised on 19 December 2008. The single winner walked away with €174,940. At a midweek Shelbourne Park fixture in April 2009, the jackpot pool reached €554,769, with one patron scooping all.

The manual tote was replaced by a French PMU automatic version in 1991 (Shelbourne Park) and 1993 (Harold's Cross), while Bord na gCon achieved a first in Europe with the introduction of hand-held terminals in 1997. Bord na gCon has set up a number of co-mingling totalisator ventures with the US and Sweden, and other avenues are being explored.

Patricia Griffin, the head of wagering at Bord na gCon, who transformed the image of totalisator betting in Ireland.

HAVING A BET

Why not add to the excitement of the evening and have a modest flutter. At each racecourse you have a choice of tote and/or bookmaker betting facilities. Totes at Irish greyhound tracks are modern and some are computerised.

HOW TO BET ON THE TOTE

Tote betting is simple pool betting. The tote collects all the bets on every greyhound and shares out the total collected (after deducting a percentage for the greyhound industry and running costs) to everyone who has a winning bet. On the tote you can have a bet for a small outlay and there are a number of pools to choose from, such as the **Win Pool** (simply select the number of the greyhound you think will win), **Place Pool** (your selection must either win or come second), and **Forecast Pool** (simply select the number of the greyhound that you think will win followed by the number of the greyhound that you think will come second).

N.B. Betting on the tote is by trap number and it is not necessary to refer to the greyhound's name when placing your bets at the tote windows. Betting on the tote commences five to ten minutes before the race starts at windows marked "SELL", and dividends or winnings are paid out immediately after the result of each race at windows where you see a "PAY" sign.

A popular tote pool at some tracks with regular high dividends is the **Twin Double Jackpot Pool**. Patrons must nominate the winners of two selected races, normally 3rd and 4th on the programme and if successful must exchange their tickets and then select the winners of two subsequent races (usually the sixth and seventh races).

Bord na gCon was first to introduce the more 'exotic' type of tote betting to this country such as the Trio Pool.
The **Trio Pool** operates on single races and in this pool patrons must nominate the first three greyhounds past the post in correct order. It is not available at all tracks, but is highly popular where operated.

PHOTOFINISH
THE ANGLE CAN FOOL YOU

A DEAD HEAT VIEW FROM THE LEFT OF THE FINISH LINE

AT THE FINISH LINE

A DEAD HEAT VIEW FROM THE RIGHT OF THE FINISH LINE

BOOKMAKER BETTING

As well as offering an attractive choice of betting to the patrons, bookmaker betting adds to the thrilling atmosphere and excitement of the greyhound racing scene. Whereas tote patrons must await the calculation of dividends to know the return on their bets, patrons who bet with the bookmakers are offered fixed odds, which are displayed on the bookmakers' betting boards. Patrons nominate their selections by name (rather than by trap numbers as with the tote) when placing bets with bookmakers and receive a betting ticket which must be presented to the bookmaker for payment if the selection wins.

A prescribed levy of 5% (5p in the £1) is deducted from each winning bet placed with bookmakers. The deduction applies both to the amount of the bet (the stake) and the winnings.

For example, a £5 bet at odds of, say, 2/1 would result in a net return to the backer of £14.25. (£15 less levy deduction of 75p).

FACILITIES

To add to the exciting night out, many tracks have heated, elevated and glass-enclosed snack and liquor bar facilities from where you can watch all the action and enjoy an atmosphere that's positively electric. Whether you win or lose on the dogs, you'll win on a terrific night out. The majority of tracks have closed circuit t.v. coverage of all races.

Some practical information on betting from a Bord na gCon promotional leaflet

Green card . . . Pat Dalton (left) from Golden, County Tipperary, is licensed to train in America on behalf of Bord na gCon. The photograph, from the archives of the Florida State Racing Commission, shows Dalton signing on the dotted line at the Biscayne Kennel Club in Miami with commission official Max Carey, the legendary baseball player.

5 FLYING THE FLAG

IRELAND'S 'SHIP' COMES IN

Des Hanrahan

Des Hanrahan, chairman of Bord na gCon (1965–83), whose actions saved Shelbourne Park and other tracks from falling into the hands of building developers.

As is the case in all spheres of life, chairmen and chief officers in Bord na gCon were made in all shapes and sizes. They all had the good of the industry at heart, but they tended to have their own ways of getting things done. Some chairmen were more abrasive than others; some seemed happier when overseeing the work of the chief officer and letting the civil servants get on with it. Other chairmen were more hands-on, and impatient to see progress made. As it was in various government departments, so it was in the semi-state set-up.

The first chief officer, Séamus Flanagan (1958–89), played everything by the book. The first chairman, Patrick J. Maguire (1958–65), was a strict disciplinarian in his own quiet way. Des Hanrahan was different. An active member of the County Limerick Coursing Club and a gregarious former sports editor with the *Limerick Leader* weekly newspaper, he came on board in 1965. He was easy-going, on the surface at least. He let Flanagan deal with the bureaucracy while he got on with the business of being the happy-go-lucky face of greyhound racing.

For this reason, Hanrahan's sizeable contribution to the sport is sometimes understated. He saw to it that there was continuity to the Maguire work of putting the industry on a sound footing, as far as finances and integrity were concerned. Two years before Hanrahan took office, sponsorship had come to greyhound racing. The initial benefactors were the brewers, and the sport got a serious lump of the stout-makers' annual promotional budget, notably through the Guinness 600 at Shelbourne Park. Hanrahan, one imagines, would have been in his element at the National Greyhound Awards, which came into being in the year in which he became chairman. It was hardly a coincidence.

The Tracks

Away from the limelight, it was Hanrahan who had to put his seal to the purchase of the first track (Shelbourne Park) by Bord na gCon on 2 January 1968. The purchase of others followed over the next seven years. Bord na gCon purchased Cork in 1969; Harold's Cross in 1970; Youghal in 1971;

National Greyhound Awards

	Racing*	Coursing
1965	Ballyowen Chief	Mourne Monarch
1966	Hairdresser	Rusheen Gallant
1967	Yanka Boy	no award
1968	Russian Gun	Proud Prince
1969	Own Pride	Quiet Dandy
1970	Mark Anthony	Hack Up Fenian
1971	Ivy Hall Flash	Fancy Stuff
1972	Catsrock Daisy	Asdee Stranger
1973	Romping To Work	Move On Swanky
1974	Lively Band	Move On Swanky
1975	Ballybeg Prim	Lusty More
1976	Tain Mor	Quarrymount Riki
1977	Linda's Champion	Master Myles
1978	Pampered Rover	Ashmore Fairy
1979	Nameless Pixie	Gay Comfort
1980	Indian Joe	Ashmore Melody
1981	Parkdown Jet	Knockash Rover
1982	Supreme Tiger	Little Scotch
1983	I'm Slippy	Swanky Star
1984	Moran's Beef	Yolanda Belle
1985	Ballintubber One	Rossa Rose
1986	Storm Villa	Big Interest
1987	Randy	Safety Circle
1988	Make History	Donovan's Ranger
1989	Manorville Magic	Crafty Roberto
1990	Adraville Bridge	Needham Ash
1991	Ardfert Mick	Newry Hill
1992	Farloe Melody	Owens Sedge
1993	Ringa Hustle	Ardnalee Pal
1994	Joyful Tidings	Flashy Flair
1995	Dew Reward	Rebel Blue
1996	Mountleader Peer	Form Of Tender
1997	Some Picture	In The Horrors
1998	Eyeman	Big Fella Thanks
1999	Chart King	Snipefield Glory
2000	Judicial Pride	Micks Magic
2001	Late Late Show	Murtys Gang
2002	Bypass Byway	Multibet
2003	Climate Control	Trajectory
2004	Premier Fantasy	Castle Pines
2005	Droopys Maldini	Boavista
2006	Razldazl Billy	Eoin Rua
2007	Catunda Harry	Castlemartyr
2008	Shelbourne Aston	Sandy Sea

* Greyhound of the Year (1965–95); Dog of the Year 1996 onwards

The last night of racing at Walthamstow Stadium in London in 2008 marked the end of an era.

Tralee in 1972; Clonmel, Galway, Kilkenny, and Waterford in 1974; and Limerick in 1975.

Ireland had a high concentration of tracks, given the population. There were local reasons why all have not survived. Civil unrest and vandalism in Belfast contributed to the demise of Celtic Park in particular. Ballybunion undoubtedly suffered through its proximity to a rival north County Kerry track in Tralee. Add in just Clones and later Navan, and it can be seen that the closure rate in the Republic was low compared to Britain, where closures were rife: Leeds (1982), the original Perry Barr in Birmingham (1984), London's White City (1984) and Harringay (1987), Slough (1987) and Derby (1988) – the casualties of the general economic downturn in the 1980s. Through a combination of difficult trading circumstances (the late

opening of high-street betting shops for one) and the boom in property values, nineteen licensed (National Greyhound Racing Club) tracks have closed since 1995: Cradley Heath (1995), Edinburgh (1995), Norton Canes (1995), Bolton (1996), Dundee (1996), Middlesbrough (1996), Ramsgate (1996), Bristol (1997), Hackney (1997), Spennymoor (1998), Wembley (1998), Canterbury (1999), Swaffham (2000), Wisbech (2000), Catford (2003), Milton Keynes (2004), Rye House (2007), Reading (2008) and Walthamstow (2008).

The difference, of course, was that Britain lacked (and still lacks) the state structure enjoyed by the Irish industry. The Irish, however, were certainly not feeling smug. Of the greyhound racing strength in Britain, the Irish-bred contingent seldom accounted for less than 75 per cent. Every track

F First Races

The first race in Britain was run at Belle Vue in Manchester in July 1926. The runners were Mistley, Parameter, Cryptogram, Old Bea, Air Hawk, Happy Acceptance, and Sudborne Stiff. Mistley (trap one) won the unusual seven-runner affair. The first race in Ireland was run at Celtic Park in Belfast in April 1927. The runners were Master Adams, Calvo, Mutual Friend, Strange Baffy, Gift and Real McCoy. Mutual Friend (trap three) won the race for the record books.

that closed in the United Kingdom meant lost sales for Irish owners, breeders and agents.

The World Greyhound Racing Federation

The quality of the Irish product and the integrity of the export market were issues of which Bord na gCon was always conscious. Generating funds through attendances and betting was just one aspect of the job.

The advisory committee set up by the Irish government in 1951 was particularly concerned about breeding, and the export business, and how it might fall into disrepute. The founding of the World Greyhound Racing Federation (WGRF) in 1971 gave Ireland an avenue through which to acquire and keep a 'quality mark' on the raw material: the greyhound. The first full members were Australia, Ireland and the US. Spain, followed by Mexico and Britain, completed the early line-up.

There was a drawback. Greyhound racing had something in common with its equine equivalent: the need for quarantine when the competitors went outside these islands. With Britain and Ireland enjoying a clean health certificate with regards to rabies, commerce between the islands was, for the most part, possible. There were rabies scares and outbreaks of foot-and-mouth disease, but, by and large, representative competitions like the Waterloo Cup and the English Derby were uninterrupted by these considerations.

The wider international realm was, unfortunately, different: Irish greyhounds taken abroad for competition had to stay abroad. There was simply no other way. The idea of putting a dog in quarantine, racing it in America, and then returning it to quarantine before it could compete again at home was just not an option. And so the vast majority who chose to take Irish greyhounds abroad did so with only one purpose in mind: a profitable sale. The economics of the matter meant that, with good prize money on offer here and in Britain, Irish trainers did not volunteer their charges for races abroad.

Any lack of quality in the Irish greyhounds sent abroad was more than compensated for by Ireland's contribution

to the administration of the sport worldwide. In spite of the insurmountable barrier of quarantine, much has been achieved over the years in respect of the exchange of information on betting, breeding, public relations, veterinary and drugs matters. The WGRF holds a conference every two years, and these gatherings have taken place twice in Ireland: in Dublin in 1994 and in Cork in 2003.

Séamus Flanagan, chief officer/chief executive with Bord na gCon (1958–89), was the president of the WGRF from 1986 until 1987, having previously acted as secretary-general between 1971 and 1972. The WGRF secretary-general for the 1986–87 period was Pat Holland, who would later be a deputy chief executive with Bord na gCon.

An Irish team also came on board in 1993–95 when Seán Collins (then also chief executive of Bord na gCon) was president of the WGRF while his brother-in-law, J.L. Desmond (then secretary of the Irish Coursing Club), was secretary-general. Roles would be reversed in 2002–04 when Desmond (still the top man in the Irish Coursing Club) assumed the WGRF presidency while Collins was secretary-general, a position he filled from 1997 (the year of his retirement from Bord na gCon) until 2009.

Ireland enjoyed a dual mandate in that Bord na gCon members were automatically entitled to be members of the WGRF, as were members of the Irish Coursing Club, because of their established position as the administrators of greyhound racing in Northern Ireland. Since those early days, the WGRF has welcomed many newcomers to the fold: the Czech Republic, Finland, Macao, Morocco, Sweden, Switzerland, United Arab Emirates and Vietnam are among the latest members.

The Anglo-Irish International Race Series

The big no-go area of greyhound racing, however, has been the normal representative interchange that is the stuff of other sports. There was the two-way traffic of competition between Ireland and Britain on the coursing field (Waterloo Cup) and greyhound track (English Derby, Scottish Derby), but actual events in which greyhounds were said to be representing Ireland were limited. There was the Anglo-Irish international race series since the early 1960s, originally designed as two-leg affairs and held with some consistency, but these events became largely sporadic over time. In 1974, the cancellation of that year's series was announced, due mainly to lack of interest, but the series was revived intermittently over the next fifteen years or so.

A contributory factor was again a reluctance shown by the owners and top trainers to commit themselves and their dogs to both legs. In many cases, the owners were happy to be involved with the home leg but felt that there was an insufficient incentive to travel for the away leg. There was also some debate as to what constituted an Irish runner and a British runner. Some were of the opinion that only British-bred greyhounds should represent Britain, but the pool of non-Irish greyhounds was, realistically, of insufficient strength to mount a viable challenge. As early as 1972, the British authorities were questioning the eligibility of Irish-bred greyhounds to represent Britain.

The closure of White City in London in 1984 robbed the Anglo-Irish International of one glamour venue. It continued at other tracks, including one venture north-east to Sunderland, but more often than not just one leg was run. The International at Dundalk remains the one event to truly live up to its billing.

Expansion

Bord na gCon, under Hanrahan, probably knew that the British market was secure. An insufficient number of home breeders meant that the British trainers and tracks were heavily dependent on Irish imports. Bord na gCon had dabbled in the Australian and Spanish markets but clearly identified America as its main target for expansion. The board was certainly not the first to play the Irish-American card in an attempt to grow its industry; it was just that greyhound racing did not lend itself to international outings. Due to the fact that they were dealing with dogs, and the possible menace of rabies, Bord na gCon found itself far more restricted than its horse-racing equivalents.

And even when they got to America, there were other obstacles for the Irish greyhounds. There was the climate, of course: hot in Boston, even hotter in Florida. And there was the fact that the American 'hounds chased a lure situated on the inside of the track. The Irish dogs, creatures of habit and used to the mechanical-hare rail being on the outside of the running track, found it hard to adjust.

On top of that, the Americans were looking for greyhounds to run around 700 yards; their so-called 'middle distances'. The dogs that were used to this kind of distance were marathon dogs in Ireland, where the breeding centred round the classic 525-yards trip. Bord na gCon pushed hard to achieve its American dream, especially in the 1970s, but it was taking three months from the date of arrival for the Irish dogs to adjust. It was this combination of factors that undermined the breakthrough.

There were a number of Irish-American races run since the early days of Bord na gCon. and an American buyer and trainer, Aaron Kulchinsky, brought a team to this part of the world in 1974. Like his Irish counterpart's charges, Kulchinsky's greyhounds struggled to acclimatise in time for their races.

Buy Irish … American trainer Aaron Kulchinsky has his hands full with these Irish-bred pups that he purchased in 1974.

Rocking Ship

The American adventure did, however, bring singular successes for man and beast. Pat Dalton, an owner-breeder from Golden in County Tipperary, had been appointed the international face of Irish greyhound racing. He brought Bord na gCon teams to Spain, Sweden and elsewhere, but, whatever the difficulties of bringing Irish greyhounds to the US, he recognised that an Irish handler could make a lucrative living Stateside.

Dalton and Hanrahan had done much to curry favour with the Americans on behalf of the industry. And a greyhound called Rocking Ship did not realise it, but he was to become Ireland's roving canine ambassador, the greatest advertisement for Irish breeding that Bord na gCon could ever have imagined.

With the system in the US being along the lines of the British arrangement between trainer and track, Dalton established a Florida kennel and employed an Irish trainer, Dubliner Don Cuddy, who had been working at the Shawfield track in Glasgow. Rocking Ship, trained by Cuddy at the Dalton kennels, is claimed to be the greatest marathon runner in the history of the sport.

Some would disagree and put Scurlogue Champ and Ballyregan Bob forward for the accolade. Scurlogue Champ was bought at the Shelbourne Park sales in 1984 and caught the public imagination by weaving his way through the field and winning over extreme distances. English-trained but Irish-bred in the same era was Ballyregan Bob, a dog which possessed more pace than Scurlogue Champ.

There is snobbery when it comes to long-distance racing, and some in Britain and, more particularly, Ireland see it as a sideshow to the true betting heats over middle distances. On the other hand, race-goers tend to have a soft spot for marathon dogs, and the Americans certainly took Rocking Ship to their hearts. Rocking Ship was no 'freak' as far as the Americans were concerned. He was the real deal.

He was bred by James Lyne from Killorglin, County Kerry, and whelped in December 1969. While in Ireland, he ran in Donal Prendiville's name and raced locally in Tralee. He was bought by David Cahill, then based in the US, who much

Lead-out boys dressed for the occasion of the Irish-American International Classic at Biscayne Track, Miami, in 1970.

later retired back to Crecora, County Limerick, and coursed greyhounds under his 'Maryville' prefix. Back in the 1960s and '70s, construction boss Cahill was a prominent and successful member of the Irish community in Chicago.

In Rocking Ship, he and the Dalton/Cuddy team found that they had a greyhound that took different traps, tracks and trips in his stride. He set speed records at the Biscayne, Flagler and Hollywood stadiums in Florida. Rocking Ship ran fifty-four marathons and won forty-four. In keeping with his spine-tingling exploits on the track, he died a dramatic and mysterious death when apparently bitten by a snake.

Dalton and Cuddy went on to establish themselves at the top of the ultra-competitive American greyhound-racing scene. Cuddy moved to the Boston area, which, along with Florida, is a stronghold of greyhound racing in the US. Cuddy later retired back to Dublin and made nightly visits to his hometown tracks. His brother, singer Joe Cuddy, made a considerable name for himself in the showband era. Dalton keeps his County Tipperary range and his transatlantic connections.

Since the Hanrahan days, Bord na gCon teams have made periodic trips to both America and Australia. The trainers have been top-rate, but, just as Irish thoroughbred successes on those continents have been limited, so it has been for our canine standard-bearers. The consolation is that, for the same reasons that have denied them in the wider world, the Irish have had little difficulty in making sure that few have managed to come in and plunder their own prizes.

And, ironically, while encouraging international racing, Bord na gCon also made sure that there was plenty of prize money on the domestic front and that it was worthwhile for Irish trainers and their greyhounds to stay at home.

In fact, it could be said that the most important transatlantic transaction came in the opposite direction, when the sire Sand Man was imported. The American dog's mantle as Ireland's leading sire would then fall to his son, Whisper Wishes. Meanwhile, Australian blood would add considerable dash to the lines in both the US and Ireland.

ABOVE
Bound for Amerikay ... Irish trainer Pat Dalton with one of his early US-bound teams.

Rocking all over the USA ... Irish export Rocking Ship streaks to one of his forty-four marathon successes Stateside.

Saturday night fever . . . Shelbourne Park,
Paddy Power Irish Derby final night, 2006.

6 THE LIFE OF NED REILLY

BORD NA gCON 1969–1994

O'Neill is recorded as the chairman who replaced Desmond Hanrahan in 1983, but, to greyhound followers everywhere, he was 'Paddy O'Brien', the name under which he gave greyhound racing commentaries for the national broadcaster, RTÉ.

A Self-funding Body

For decades, the proud boast of Bord na gCon was one of self-sufficiency: the greyhound authority largely financed operations from its own resources. That limited its horizons going forward. Available funds were swallowed up by prize-money grants for the day-to-day, non-sponsored, ordinary races. The cash was simply not there for anything other than essential track maintenance. Improvements, and certainly capital projects, were not an option.

This was the prevailing climate in the second decade of the stewardship of Séamus Flanagan as chief officer. During this period, in which Bord na gCon could but mark time, the chair at the headquarters in Henry Street, Limerick, was occupied by Patrick O'Neill (1983–88) and Noel Brassil (1988–89).

O'Neill is recorded as the chairman who replaced Desmond Hanrahan in 1983, but, to greyhound followers everywhere, he was 'Paddy O'Brien', the name under which he gave greyhound racing commentaries for the national broadcaster, RTÉ. O'Neill served for five dignified years, blighted by economic recession. Noel Brassil, a member of a north County Kerry family with strong greyhound and bookmaking connections, had hardly settled into the post when his tenure was cut short by ill-health.

On the civil service side, Flanagan was replaced by Seán Collins who, like his predecessor, had been with Bord na gCon from the start. Collins had a good relationship with the media and the former schoolteacher had formidable political connections (see page 28). Collins, the political animal, was adept at keeping the members of Bord na gCon – many of them were Fianna Fáil sympathisers, anyway – on side. Through the Collins connections came, in early 1990, the first drip of the Exchequer funding that would flood through in the second half of that decade and give the sport the magnificent stadiums which it now boasts.

Ned Reilly and the Start of Government Funding

The middleman was the wily and wiry Edward O'Reilly – simply known as Ned Reilly – who lived in Edgeworthstown and who kept the Longford track going through good times and bad. Much like Seán Collins, Ned Reilly was a politician at heart and, crucially, he had the ear of Albert Reynolds. Reynolds had a colourful and varied political career, and was Taoiseach between 1992 and 1994. He headed five other government departments in his time in office and, crucially, had his hands on the purse strings as Minister for Finance between 1988 and 1991.

Fate also ordained that – while born across the Longford border in Rooskey, County Roscommon – Reynolds was the representative for Ned Reilly's constituency and Reilly was a member of Bord na gCon (1988–95). Reynolds, a keen follower of horse racing, was ideally situated to do Reilly a turn. He did, announcing in late 1989 that Exchequer funding would be available for Bord na gCon as well as the horse-racing authorities.

Reilly got on to his chief officer Collins. Collins submitted Bord na gCon's requirements to the Department of Agriculture, the department costed them and sent them to Reynolds, and Reynolds authorised the cheque. There had been a one-off prize money grant in 1986 of fifty thousand punts. The importance of the five hundred thousand punts received in 1990 was that it was the promise and beginning of something far bigger. In the 1991 government budget, the allocation of monies to the greyhound industry had risen to

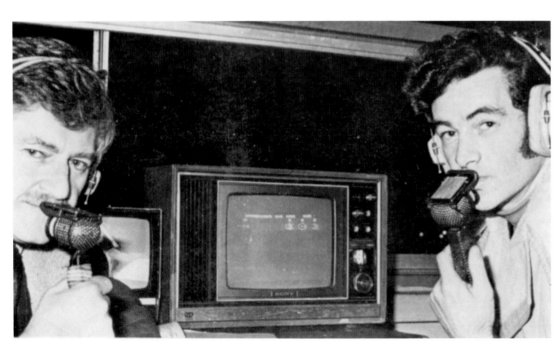

RTÉ commentators Paddy O'Brien (on left) and Des Scahill covering a live television programme of greyhound racing from Shelbourne Park Stadium, Dublin.

seven hundred and fifty thousand punts. Bord na gCon also assisted the farming and greyhound-rearing community in tapping into the European Community's alternative farm enterprise schemes. The same year saw the setting up of the Bord na gCon drug-testing facility in Limerick.

The most important knock-on effect of the money stream from the government was that Bord na gCon could start thinking in terms of track development, starting with Shelbourne Park. The need was urgent. The green light had been given to Sunday racing, but horse racing was seriously encroaching on the evening slot in which greyhound racing had traditionally held a monopoly. Bord na gCon wanted the matter to be addressed by a regulatory fixtures committee; but it never came about.

Controversy

Such are the machinations of politics and sport in Ireland. Ned Reilly seemed an unlikely icon for greyhound racing, but he served it well. It was ironic that, at this time, chief officer Collins had felt obliged to defend the members of Bord na gCon whom he served against charges of cronyism with regard to the manner in which they were appointed.

It may indeed have been the case that some sat on the board in return for political favours, but, ultimately, the 'system' had been seen to work to the sport's benefit. The appointment of Oliver Scallon from Irvinestown, County Fermanagh, in 1988 was clearly a part of the new détente between the north and south of Ireland. In the days when the Irish Coursing Club had a right to three seats on Bord na gCon, Ulstermen Captain John Ross (1958–72) and James Delargey (1983–86) were members.

The appointment of Scallon, however, was more in the way of cross-border co-operation. Politically motivated it may have been, but few devoted more energy to Bord na gCon than did Scallon – a brother-in-law of the singer Rosemary Scallon ('Dana') – in the years 1988–96. Scallon had a keen interest in coursing, and his tenure with Bord na gCon took in the chairmanship of Kevin Frost (1989–94). Kevin was a son of Jim Frost, who had assisted Seán Collins' predecessor Séamus Flanagan in drafting the Greyhound Industry Act

in 1958. Based at Cratloe, County Clare, Kevin Frost was also involved with the management and ownership of the Limerick racecourse, and had owned Indian Joe when he won the 1980 Easter Cup at Shelbourne Park and when he began his challenge for the English Derby at White City, London, in the same year. Frost was succeeded by Kevin Heffernan, whose name will be forever linked to Gaelic football, and who will be always remembered as a player and manager with Dublin.

Board Members as Owners and Trainers

Less successful as a greyhound owner, Heffernan (1994–95) was nevertheless enthusiastic about his track dogs, which he had (and still has) in training with Séamus Graham. Of the Bord na gCon chairmen, Kevin Frost came closest to owning an English Derby winner when selling Indian Joe during the course of the competition in 1980 to Belfast bookmaker Alfie McLean.

And in 1986, two years after Dipmac's Irish Derby win (the dog was partly owned by a future chairman of the

Ned Reilly (left), who was to play a vital part in Bord na gCon developments (1988–95), pictured with Commandant Joseph Fitzpatrick, secretary of the Irish Coursing Club (1969–86).

Kitty Butler, Irish Coursing Club secretary (1956–69)

Family tradition . . . Sisters Joan Spratt (centre) and Ann Quinlan, daughters of renowned Waterford coursing stalwart John Mackey, pictured in 1976 with Joan's son Kevin, and a trio of their greyhounds – Cecil's Delight (trial stake winner New Ross), Quarrymount Honi (trial stake winner Templetuohy) and Quarrymount Riki (winner of the coursing Derby in 1976 and the Irish Cup in 1977).

board, Paschal Taggart), Michael Field, the man who would be chief officer between 1997 and 2002, sent out Kyle Jack, running in the name of his son John, to win in 30.41 seconds the first Irish Derby to be run over 550 yards.

Similarly, Pat Holland – he was deputy chief officer at Bord na gCon under Collins and secretary-general at the World Greyhound Racing Federation in the presidency of Séamus Flanagan (1986–87) – was not averse to getting his hands dirty in the tough field of open coursing. While dedicated to the promotion of greyhound racing, former Irish Coursing Club secretary and artificial lure opponent, T.A. Morris, would have recognised the contradiction in Bord na gCon officials unwinding on Sundays on the coursing field. The richest irony of all was to be found in Holland owning (with his wife Monita) and training the 1982 Waterloo Cup winner Play Solo.

Having Taggart and Field serve the industry together, both having won the Irish Derby, certainly gave the lie to the

assertion that those involved with the industry did not have a vested interest in its well-being. But as Collins was later to point out to the sport's political masters, the majority of those called to be members of Bord na gCon were grounded in the game. Many, naturally, were also members of the Irish Coursing Club and, as such, had an interest in the breeding side of the industry.

Ned Reilly (1988–95) was the backbone of one of the country's smaller tracks at Longford. Patrick J. Cox, the longest serving member of Bord na gCon (1962–82), was the man behind the Newbridge track. Ann Quinlan (1994–2001) had a succession of coursing champions with the 'Quarrymount' prefix. Likewise, Luke Kilcoyne (1988–96) could be seen on track and field with his 'Ougham' greyhounds. Patrick Dunphy (1978–82) bred, owned and trained an English Derby winner, The Grand Canal, which won at White City in 1962. Daniel J. Reilly (2002–) had a son (Ian) who trained an English Derby winner, Droopys Scholes, which won in 2004 at Wimbledon.

Women and Greyhound Sport

Ann Quinlan is one of half a dozen women to have served on Bord na gCon, which did not have a female presence until Eileen Kelliher was appointed in 1993. Eileen Kelliher, who served until 1997, was, like Ann Quinlan, a great coursing devotee.

Another woman to serve was Helen Nugent (2003–05), one of the members to be appointed directly from the Department of Agriculture. Eileen Kelliher and Ann Quinlan were notable for the dedicated manner in which they fought to have their local tracks – Tralee and Waterford, respectively – refurbished, as did Ann Barry (1997–2000) in Limerick. Women have made a considerable impact both behind the scenes and in the public eye in greyhound racing. Apart from the Bord na gCon representation, Kitty Butler (1956–69) served as secretary of the Irish Coursing Club.

The history of greyhound sport is peppered with women as outstanding breeders and owners, and owner-trainers. Ann Barry owned and trained Fire Fly to win her local Classic, the Irish St Leger at the Market's Field, Limerick, in 1997.

Another very successful woman in greyhound racing, who has taken the training of greyhounds to new, fully professional heights, is Dolores Ruth. Her sister Frances has been assistant trainer to one of the country's most decorated handlers, Matt O'Donnell, as well as holding a licence in her own right. Dolores Ruth is the only Irish woman to have won an English Derby, which she did in 1996 with Shanless Slippy at Wimbledon. She subsequently joined that elite Irish-based group of trainers who have had winners of both the English and Irish Derby – Mick Horan, Ger McKenna, Matt O'Donnell, Séamus Graham – when her Razldazl Billy won the Irish Derby in 2006.

Track Improvements

In the Republic, a track could benefit enormously from having representation at Bord na gCon level, not least in securing funding. The authorities did not confine their largesse solely to those tracks, such as Shelbourne Park, that they owned. They also sought a sizeable chunk of equity in private tracks, where improvements were brought about through state aid. After the Bord na gCon-owned Dublin tracks, funding for provincial venues followed. Mullingar is just one example of a privately owned track being assisted in this manner, even though County Westmeath is one of the counties (one-third of those in the Republic) that has never boasted a Bord na gCon member.

If one was to identify three tracks that owe more than others to strong petitioning on their behalf, it would be Longford (Ned Reilly), Tralee (Eileen Kelliher) and Waterford (Ann Quinlan). Then again, every track in the South owes something to Ned Reilly.

Since the Irish Coursing Club ceased in 1990 to have a right to nominate Bord na gCon members from its own ranks, its sphere of greyhound racing influence – Northern Ireland – has suffered. Successive British governments have failed to mark the health of greyhound racing as a priority; and the situation has been no different on a local level with administrations in Northern Ireland. Northern track owners could only look on with envy as Bord na gCon undertook one ambitious project after another in the South. The lack of

investment was a great pity, as Ulster owners and race-goers have always been the mainstay of tracks north of Dublin.

Dolores Ruth is the only Irish woman to have won an English Derby, which she did in 1996 with Shanless Slippy at Wimbledon.

Before they were famous . . . Trainers Frances Ruth (left) and her sister Dolores Ruth, aged five and four respectively, pictured with a family friend in 1971.

Slick-starting He Said So (1) makes his
early pace count to lead the decider in the
Paddy Power Irish Derby, 2005. The final
also featured Droopys Maldini (2), Billy
Playback (3), Droopys Marco (4), Spiral
Citrate (5) and Westmead Hawk (6).

7 'THE DOGS' UPDATED
BORD NA gCON (1995 ONWARDS)

H Handicap Racing

Handicap racing – which gives greyhounds of lesser ability the advantage in the staggered start over faster rivals – is still commonly practised in England and Scotland. It is a tool used by racing managers who have a small pool of greyhounds from which to fashion competitive races. The need never arose in Ireland because of the substantial greyhound population. Bord na gCon discussed the introduction of eight and more runners (a feature in America) in 1971, but this idea never went beyond the discussion stage.

The Officials

It could reasonably be argued that, while some were naturally less gifted than others, all greyhound-sport officials contributed something to the development of coursing and track racing. The discussion could be taken further as to suggest that the administrators in place were appropriate to the times in which they lived and held office.

Cases in point with regard to the field sport are T.A. Morris and J.L. Desmond. Morris (1916–48) organised Irish coursing on a national basis and orchestrated its removal from the yoke of the British ruling body. Initially opposed to greyhound racing, he nevertheless responded to its inevitable advent and ensured the status of the Irish Coursing Club as the regulatory body and guardian of the Stud Book in Ireland. Coursing and the ICC found themselves in crisis again towards the end of the century and, in 1993, Desmond

(1986–2008) had to make the landmark decision to muzzle the competitors at enclosed coursing meetings rather than risk the sport's extinction at the hands of the legislators. But for those men – and those who held the office of secretary in the intervening years – the ICC would look altogether different now. In short, the sport might be no longer.

Séamus Flanagan (1958–89) and Seán Collins (1989–97), the first chief officers of Bord na gCon, were not extravagant characters. The setting-up of a state body to control greyhound racing – it had fallen into disrepute at some levels – was a serious matter, and Flanagan and Collins fulfilled the roles required of them. Money was spent in line with the limited resources available. It was spent well, too, with chairman Desmond Hanrahan (1965–83) putting his name to purchase orders for stadiums in times of financial rectitude in public spending. By the time Kevin Heffernan took

Coursing connection . . . Jerry (J.L.) Desmond, the secretary of the Irish Coursing Club when muzzling was introduced, pictured at Powerstown Park, Clonmel, with his sister Deirdre, whose husband Jimmy Walshe trained the 2003 Waterloo Cup winner Henrietta.

the chair for two packed years (1994–95), the country was starting at least to project a richer image.

Richard O'Sullivan

And when the country was no longer so flush, along came Richard O'Sullivan. A veterinary surgeon by profession, but a man used to handling big budgets in the commercial world, O'Sullivan had a successful career internationally with the Kerry Group and rode to the rescue when the very existence of horse racing at Punchestown looked to be in jeopardy. Greyhound racing is in safe hands with O'Sullivan, who, uniquely, served for a period of months as a member of Bord na gCon before his elevation to the top job later in 2006. O'Sullivan has trimmed much of the Bord na gCon expenditure while advancing stadium development at Limerick and elsewhere.

Paschal Taggart

Preceding O'Sullivan was Paschal Taggart (1995–2006). In Taggart, Bord na gCon had a chairman who was as liberal as the first chairman, Patrick Maguire (1958–65), had been conservative.

Taggart was barely halfway through his tenure when the new Cork track grew up on a green-field site as a monument to his enterprise and imagination. The redevelopment of Shelbourne Park was already advanced when Taggart's appointment was announced at the end of 1994, not by a Fianna Fáil Minister for Agriculture but by Fine Gael's Ivan Yates. Yates would later quit the world of politics and re-emerge as the proprietor of a national bookmaking chain, Celtic Bookmakers.

It can be surmised that while Yates obviously realised Taggart's enthusiasm for greyhound racing, even the minister could not have anticipated the gusto with which the Ulsterman approached what is effectively an honorary and unpaid position. Taggart brought about a seismic change in greyhound racing and the general public's perception of the sport. In its basic demographic, the thrills of the sport were being missed by the bulk of the younger generation, who

Chairmen of the board . . . Paschal Taggart (left), Bord na gCon chairman (1995–2006) and the man who replaced him, Dick O'Sullivan. The latter helped to secure Irish Derby sponsorship from the Kerry Group where he was an executive.

saw it as a pastime for an older, mostly rural, lower-middle-class grouping. Taggart saw greyhound racing as an evening out for all classes, urban as well as rural.

Above all, the emphasis was switched from the 'cloth-cap' generation to a younger set.

The New Meaning of 'Going to the Dogs'

Wining and dining became a major part of the greyhound-racing experience, especially for the newcomers enticed to sample the sport for the first time. The sport was heavily marketed. Those providing the raw material – the greyhound – were not neglected, and prize-money levels were dramatically increased so that the benefits were felt by owners, trainers and breeders. Syndicates of owners – mostly new to the game, young and with disposable income – proliferated.

Such change came at a price. Some older race-goers resented the influx of the younger generation, as well as ruing the disappearance of the grass tracks in favour of the all-sand versions. A sand surface had been initially introduced at Clonmel track, and others – Limerick, Tralee, Waterford, and others – followed between 1995 and 1997. Suddenly, the times achieved by the great greyhounds of the past – Prince Of Bermuda and those from a golden era – meant little as dogs clocked unprecedented speeds on the sand tracks. The seeding of greyhounds had come to Ireland in 1989. This involved wide runners being given wide berths, and was designed to provide trouble-free racing. However, Spanish Battleship won the Irish Derby on three occasions without this advantage. It would have been interesting to compare the modern trackers under the 'free draw' regime. The seeding of greyhounds was actually extended to allow 'middle' runners to occupy their favoured traps.

There were other, more fundamental, changes to the old order. Bord na gCon was now guaranteed a certain level of funding under the government legislation which established Horse Racing Ireland (HRI) in 2000. This system allowed HRI and Bord na gCon to share (on an 80/20 basis) an amount of money equivalent to a percentage of the off-course betting duty. The sums were substantial and rose in tandem with the number of high-street betting offices. By

2008, the Republic was sustaining 1,248 betting shops and turnover had reached a new high at €3.6 billion.

But even public funding at this level did not match the ambition of Bord na gCon in the dynamic decade in which Taggart was in charge. He was determined to change the meaning of 'going to the dogs' from a derisory slogan to a proud boast.

An Antrim man with a myriad of business interests in and around Dublin, where he was now residing, Taggart was not always comfortable working within the constraints of the semi-state set-up. He would have liked a limitless scale of funding, but was forced to sell 1.5 acres of prime Shelbourne Park property to finance developments at the Ringsend track and elsewhere.

By early 1996, the sale of the Western Road track in Cork was on the agenda and, in April 2000, the new venue at Bishopstown had become a reality. Curraheen Park, as it came to be known, encapsulated the Taggart vision of a vibrant industry: race-goers with a young profile, dining in restaurants of the highest standard; new state-of-the-art facilities for both humans and canines; an intensive advertising campaign. Big-name sponsors were courted and inter-track betting allowed those at Cork to wager into the totalisator pools in Dublin. Bord na gCon even underwent a name change and became the Irish Greyhound Board, although it officially retained its Irish title.

It was all happening. With funding from both Horse Racing Ireland and Bord na gCon, the track at Dundalk also relocated. The County Louth management opened the first combined horse-and-greyhound track in these islands. The horses raced on an all-weather surface and under lights.

Barely any track was untouched by this fever of activity, with Harold's Cross and most provincial venues becoming scaled-down versions of Shelbourne Park and Cork. A little later than anticipated, Limerick is now on schedule to get a new stadium on the edge of the city, with Bord na gCon vacating its traditional home at the Market's Field.

Irish Laurels

Cork

500 yards: 1944–60; 525 yards: 1961 onwards

1944	Robeen Printer	28.98	1977	Ashleigh Honour	29.15
1945	Munster Hotel	29.20	1978	Knockrour Girl	29.40
1946	Ballinrea Express	28.80	1979	Knockrour Slave	29.45
1947	Careless Border	28.80	1980	Knockrour Slave	29.00
1948	Double Shadow	28.33	1981	Knockeen Master	29.50
1949	Spanish Chestnut	28.55	1982	The Stranger	28.95
1950	Spanish Chestnut	28.70	1983	Back Garden	29.66
1951	Knockrour Favourite	28.85	1984	Rugged Mick	29.09
1952	Tragumna Dasher	28.70	1985	Follow A Star	29.42
1953	Templenow Rebel	28.55	1986	Big Oran	29.78
1954	Come On Bella	28.90	1987	Yellow Bud	29.28
1955	Spanish Battleship	28.35	1988	Odell King	28.98
1956	Rather Grand	29.00	1989	Airmount Grand	28.82
1957	Kilcasey Streak	28.80	1990	Adraville Bridge	28.78
1958	Brook Prancer	28.43	1991	Terrydrum Tiko	28.86
1959	Celbridge Chance	28.50	1992	Market Rascal	29.58
1960	Last Lap	28.15	1993	Lisglass Lass	28.97
1961	Round Tower Rose	29.80	1994	Clounmellane Oak	29.44
1962	Dark Baby	29.40	1995	Standard Image	29.04
1963	Powerstown Proper	29.75	1996	Deerfield Bypass	29.12
1964	Tanyard Heather	29.20	1997	Mr Pickwick	29.16
1965	Boro Parachute	29.60	1998	Mr Pickwick	29.29
1966	Westpark Ash	29.40	1999	Tigers Eye/Lumber Boss	29.42 (dh)
1967	Philotimo	29.65	2000	Barefoot Ridge	28.69
1968	Flaming King	29.25	2001	Sonic Flight	28.41
1969	Skipping Tim	29.50	2002	Annual Award	28.61
1970	Gabriel Boy	29.25	2003	Nikita Billie	28.34
1971	Ivy Hall Flash	29.15	2004	Boherduff Light	28.14
1972	Dublin Eily	29.70	2005	Tyrur Ted	28.33
1973	Kilbracken Style	29.10	2006	Ardkill Jamie	28.35
1974	Silent Thought	29.50	2007	Catunda Harry	28.18
1975	Moonshine Bandit	29.30	2008	Cashen Legend	28.44
1976	Nameless Star	29.30			

I Identification

Bord na gCon has always been strong on matters of integrity and its enforcement. It was the strong belief of Séamus Flanagan, the first chief officer, that the organisation should not only have the relevant rules in place but should also be seen to enforce them. Greyhounds all have identity cards – or passports – containing descriptions of their physical characteristics. All runners also have unique ear markings. In the old days, the sport abounded with urban legends of coloured dogs having their white spots literally painted over to make them all-blacks.

High Drama in Cork

There was to be high drama on the track before the management team at Cork left for its new track. Greyhound racing on the banks of the River Lee started in 1928 in Ballintemple, out the Old Blackrock Road. It moved to the Western Road, beside University College, Cork, in 1936; and this venue was saved for the sport by its purchase by Bord na gCon in 1969.

Of the established Classics, the Irish Laurels is unique in never having been run anywhere other than its original venue. Since its 1944 start at the Western Road, the Irish Laurels has produced many famous dogs and many famous finishes. Spanish Chestnut won back-to-back runnings in 1949 and 1950, and Spanish Battleship himself clinched the Classic in 1955.

Several trainers carved out little slugs of Irish Laurels history – David Cashman, based at Carrigtohill, sent out Dark Baby (1962), Skipping Tim (1969) and Ashleigh Honour (1977) to win his local Classic.

Paddy Keane – who sent out Faithful Hope to win the Derby at White City in London as an 'English' trainer in 1966 – had returned home. In a purple patch for his Dunboyne, County Meath, kennels, he produced three winners of the Irish Laurels in just four years – Ivy Hall Flash (1971), Kilbracken Style (1973) and Silent Thought (1974).

Ger McKenna did not enjoy quite the same domination in the Irish Laurels as he did in the Irish St Leger at Limerick. However, he won the Irish Laurels on seven occasions, including his 1983–85 hat-trick of Back Garden, Rugged Mick and Follow A Star. McKenna's charge, Knockrour Slave, won in 1979 and 1980, but he was trained by the owners, the Lynch family of Aughabullogue, County Cork, for the initial triumph.

Deerfield Bypass (1996) provided the last of McKenna's domestic Classic wins when triumphant at the Irish Laurels at Cork, just as Concentration (1990) had given him his last British Classic when securing the English Laurels at Wimbledon.

Another Cork credit on the Irish Laurels roll is Christy O'Callaghan who won it when sending out Knockeen Master (1981), The Stranger (1982) and Standard Image (1995) from his Macroom kennels. The Stranger not only completed a quick-fire Irish Laurels double for his handler but went on to win the Irish St Leger at Limerick in 1983. An exceptional greyhound by any standards, fast as well as robustly strong, The Stranger won his Cork final in 28.95, the first time that 29 seconds had been beaten in an Irish Laurels final since the distance of the Classic had changed in 1961 from 500 to 525 yards. Knockrour Slave had run exactly 29.00 in 1980, but it was 1988 and Ned Power's Odell King before that mark was again beaten.

Odell King marked the start of a golden era for the Irish Laurels, won for a second year in a row by a Waterford man in Ger Kiely and his Airmount Grand, which clocked 28.82 in 1989. Trained by Moss O'Connor, Adraville Bridge – the Kerryman won again with Nikita Billie in 2003 – ran 28.78. Prolific trainers were one thing, but multiple-Classic winning canines were another.

Perhaps because of greater opportunities everywhere in the country and increased prize money, greyhounds with established records at certain tracks and in certain events were less plentiful. The Paul Hennessy-trained Mr Pickwick was an exception. He won the Irish Laurels at the Western Road in 1997 and 1998. Hennessy, based at Gowran, County Kilkenny, has sent out three further Irish Laurels winners since the switch to Bishopstown: Barefoot Ridge (2000), Tyrur Ted (2005) and Ardkill Jamie (2006).

Ger McKenna's son Owen – Boherduff Light (2004) and Catunda Harry (2007) – now based at New Inn, County Tipperary, is another to have made a significant impact on the Irish Laurels annals. The year of his second Irish Laurels victory, 1998, also saw Hennessy's Mr Pickwick travel to Shelbourne Park and win the Easter Cup.

But before moving out the road to Bishopstown and a whole new era of racing on sand and consistent sub-29-seconds runs, the Irish Laurels had witnessed one of its most dramatic nights. Matt O'Donnell had mined the Irish St Leger at Limerick and Irish Derby at Shelbourne Park more successfully than the Irish Laurels, but the Killenaule, County Tipperary, trainer got Lumber Boss through to the last Irish Laurels final to be run at the Western Road and to be run on grass. As if to emphasise that the stopwatch is not everything in greyhound racing, Lumber Boss ran a comparatively pedestrian 29.42 in the decider.

The only problem for O'Donnell and the Cork management was that this time was equalled by the Nick Turner-trained Tigers Eye. The pair had dead-heated. This was the first time this had happened in the history of the Irish Laurels, and that it happened in a final of a Classic was very unusual.

The Irish National Sprint had produced not one but two dead heats when run at Dunmore Stadium in Belfast. In 1947, Fair Moving could not be separated from Hockfield Light and, similarly, the judge could not divide the 1968 pair Dry Flash and Newhill Printer. It is interesting to see that the first race meeting ever in Ireland, at Celtic Park in April 1927, recorded a dead heat between Imperial Jimmy and Keep Whistling. Dunmore Stadium in 1929 was the scene of the most bizarre dead-heat episode ever. The bitch Maid Of Devenish and the dog Ballyhenry Lad dead-heated for a race over 600 yards. The owners asked that the greyhounds be allowed to reappear in a 'match' at the end of racing. The management agreed, only for the greyhounds to cross the line again locked together. Thus, an historic double dead heat was declared.

Back in Cork, the 1999 tie between Turner's Tigers Eye and O'Donnell's Lumber Boss aroused considerable interest and there was talk of a later rematch. In fact, the Bord na gCon rules even allowed for such an eventuality, down to specifying which traps should be occupied by the protagonists. It never came about, and, as with so many fascinating aspects of greyhound racing, we are left to wonder what might have happened.

That's close . . . The field cross the line almost in unison in a race at Belle Vue, Manchester, venue for the first ever greyhound race in Britain or Ireland in 1926. The verdict went to Barnacre Boy (2) which won by a short-head from Moon View (1).

Master M'Grath by W. Watson, 1869.
Brownlow House, seat of Lord Lurgan,
is visible in the background.

8 VICTORY AT WATERLOO

MASTER M'GRATH

Weight and Speed

Accounts detailing the history of the greyhound tend to be low in number but high on detail. The consistent omission, however, is any mention of the size of the hounds. That changes with the advent of greyhound racing in 1926 and the regulation that required greyhounds to be weighed before competing.

Weight can have a significant bearing on a greyhound's performance; so much so that the Irish authorities set a standard of three pounds in permitted weight variation.

In other words, a dog that runs when weighed in at, say, seventy-seven pounds cannot be more than three pounds lighter or heavier than this when next competing. In such a way a remarkable consistency in form for the track greyhound was achieved. It was some time after the greyhound trainers came to appreciate this factor that their horse-racing counterparts began the regular weighing of their charges, and gave serious thought to the causes and results of weight fluctuations.

Speed is of the very essence for those involved in greyhound racing. They look to split-second variations to rate one

In the old days . . . there were some easy rules of thumb: a greyhound capable of beating a time of thirty seconds was good; one that could come close to or could better twenty-nine seconds was exceptional.

Master M'Grath by Reynolds, 1868; probably in his kennel at Brownlow House.

greyhound above another. In the old days, when 525 yards was the standard distance and all surfaces were grass, there were some easy rules of thumb: a greyhound capable of beating a time of thirty seconds was good; one that could come close to or could better twenty-nine seconds was exceptional.

For years, there had been a resistance among traditionalists to racing on sand in Ireland. Sand was introduced initially at Clonmel and phased in until the landmark event in January 2001 when Shelbourne Park's turf track was replaced with sand. The cost of employing ground staff to maintain turf tracks was simply too high, and the extensive re-sodding required (largely because of the Irish weather) was another difficulty. The introduction of sand into Irish racing saw the average greyhound run a full second faster than he would have on turf. The sand surfaces were not the only reason for the increase in speed: specialised diets, veterinary care and a larger number of dedicated professional trainers all contributed to the speeding-up process.

Additionally, the fact that greyhounds were getting bigger was clearly not unconnected to the increases in speed – the extra muscle means that the dogs are propelled at a faster speed. We now have track dogs weighing close to eighty pounds and some on the coursing field topping a hundred pounds. It has always been the case that the females of the species weigh significantly less than the males. A measure of the increase in the size of greyhounds is that nowadays the bitches weigh more than the dogs did a half-century ago.

The First Sporting Canine Superstar

In greyhound sport, big does not always mean successful. One problem is that heavier greyhounds are more prone to injury and take longer to recuperate. In fact, the first 'heavyweight' Irish greyhound on the international stage weighed a mere fifty-four pounds, which might partly explain his longevity in the competitive arena. The Romans undoubtedly had their greyhound champions whose names were not recorded. But Master M'Grath was the first sporting canine superstar. He was – unlike others in sport with pretensions to the accolade – a legend, whose achievements became the stuff of song.

Lord Lurgan with Master M'Grath

The object of a course is to test the skill of the two greyhounds against one another rather than to kill the hare. The rules governing every course have stood the test of time, much as the Queensberry Rules have in boxing.

Even to this day, if you ask a non-devotee to name a greyhound, Master M'Grath is the invariable response.

In keeping with the breed's past, Master M'Grath was owned by an Irish peer, Lord Lurgan, who owned considerable estates in Ulster. An interest in coursing was no passing whim for Lord Lurgan: in the 1870s, he had meets staged on his own land. It was Lord Lurgan's associate James Galway who bred Master M'Grath in County Waterford, and the black dog was named for a small local boy who handled him when he was a pup. A monument on the Clonmel–Cappoquin road marks the location of his original kennel.

The Waterloo Cup

In time, Master M'Grath made the long trip north and initially displayed his prowess by winning a couple of stakes at Lurgan. He obviously showed great promise at these initial events, as he was entered for the 1868 Waterloo Cup at the time when the tournament was the blue riband of the sport and at its most competitive. The Waterloo Cup was run at Altcar on the outskirts of Southport, Lancashire, and involved sixty-four greyhounds going up in braces in head-to-head competition that yielded a final pair on the third day. The dogs' ability is judged not by a clock or a finishing line, but by a single person, a judge mounted on horseback. The competitors wear collars of red or white around their necks, and the judge signals the victor by raising the appropriate colour. The object of a course is to test the skill of the two greyhounds against one another rather than to kill the hare. The rules governing every course have stood the test of time, much as the Queensberry Rules have in boxing.

From the founding of the Swaffham club in 1776 up to the 1950s, coursing was a big deal. At the beginning of the twentieth century, it was more important than horse racing at Gosforth Park in Newcastle, Haydock Park near Liverpool and Kempton Park near London. The 'park' in the names of these famous tracks indicates that they were park-coursing venues.

The Waterloo Cup was what every breeder, owner and trainer of a coursing dog wanted to win. It was founded by William Lynn, the proprietor of the Waterloo Hotel in nearby Liverpool, who also organised the first official races at Aintree, which were the precursor to the Grand National. Altcar was what Epsom is to horse racing, Henley to rowing, Wimbledon to tennis and Lord's to cricket. For a greyhound with Irish connections to win the Waterloo Cup was like an Irishman winning the men's singles at the home of the All-England Lawn Tennis Club.

In 1868 Master M'Grath became the first Irish-trained greyhound to win the Waterloo Cup. It was the beginning of a love affair between the Irish and the great tournament, which was to last up to the point when British government legislation halted the Waterloo Cup after the 2005 renewal. Master M'Grath returned to Altcar in 1869 to defend his title. It is estimated that twelve thousand spectators turned up for the second (or middle) day alone. The annals describe the 1869 decider as an epic, with Master M'Grath finally getting the better of the experienced Bab-At-The-Bowster.

By 1870, the Waterloo Hotel had been demolished to make way for Liverpool Central Station. This was not the only upheaval. The entry form for Master M'Grath was late in arriving and there was ill feeling when an objection lodged about the champion competing was overruled by the event's committee (which included Lord Lurgan). The 1870 running proved near-disastrous: Master M'Grath was not only beaten but plunged into the icy River Alt, and had to be rescued by an onlooker. Lord Lurgan vowed never to run Master M'Grath again, and retired him to stud.

Those charged with looking after greyhounds now believe that dogs lose their competitive edge after a spell at stud, and leave their racing form behind. But Lord Lurgan was an enthusiastic gambler and went back on his vow, taking Master M'Grath away from his stud duties for a tilt at the 1871 Waterloo Cup. Lord Lurgan shelled out six thousand pounds in insurance to cover Master M'Grath's boat crossing from Belfast and reputedly pocketed one hundred and fifty thousand when the dog won the Waterloo Cup for the third time in four years.

Master M'Grath died at Christmas in 1871, the same year as his last triumph. He succumbed to tuberculosis of the lung and pneumonia. He had won over two thousand pounds in prize money, a fortune in wagers for his owner, and lost just one of his forty-one courses. He had even been summoned to visit Queen Victoria at Windsor.

Irish Entries at Altcar

The Waterloo Cup worked on an archaic 'nominator' system that still operates at the Irish Cup, the County Limerick all-aged (open to pups and older greyhounds) event that closes the domestic season. The nominator system demands that an owner secures the blessing of one of the committee, who pays the nominator fee but receives a hefty chunk of the purse in return if the dog wins. As a committee member, Lord Lurgan obviously chose to give his nomination to a greyhound running in his own name. Small Irish owners lacked influence in the committee rooms, which meant that their chances of having a runner in the Waterloo Cup were restricted.

Irish owners who wanted to run their dogs at Altcar incurred considerable expense. The Waterloo Cup ran over three days (or more if the weather was bad) and an owner

J Jackets

The colours of the racing jackets worn by greyhounds in Ireland and Britain are now uniform. This only came about in 1989 when Bord na gCon sensibly decided to adopt the British order: trap one (red), trap two (blue), trap three (white), trap four (black), trap five (orange) and trap six (stripes).

Irish backers, who had become confused when watching British races, greatly appreciated this move. The original colours (in trap order) in Britain for seven runners were: red, blue, white, green, black, orange, red/white.

The bronze of Master M'Grath that originally stood on top of a thirty-foot column in Lurgan Park.

K Kennels

Kennel comfort and security for the competitors are now priorities at all tracks. However, many trainers prefer to have someone stay with their dogs in their kennels as a way of relaxing the animals in strange surroundings. An imaginative move by top trainer Matt O'Donnell was to leave a transistor radio in the kennel of one of his runners. The track management took a dim view, fearing the cacophony if all trainers followed – and had the radios tuned to different stations!

had to pay for transport and kennels for the dog, as well as transport and accommodation for the trainer and at least a couple of kennel hands in nearby Southport. In addition, entry fees were high in comparison to the prize money.

Another reason why the Irish fielded few Waterloo Cup entries – and why the chances of success for those that did take part were diminished – was the nature of British coursing. British coursing was open coursing, where the dogs were free to course over endless terrain (hence, Master M'Grath's dip in the river) and where runs could last for minutes. In Ireland, the preferred form was park coursing, where the arena was confined and the courses were decided in seconds. Open coursing depended on an ability to hunt and on stamina. Park coursing was all about pace. At Altcar, the Irish greyhounds were easily faster than their local opponents, but tended not to work too hard.

Irish Winners

Nevertheless, seventeen Irish-trained greyhounds were to bring back coursing's most glittering prize in the years after Master M'Grath's victories. The victories of the bitch Honeymoon (W.F. Hutchinson) in 1875 and the dog Donald (R.M. Douglas) in 1876, both trained by Joe Chestnut, came at the close of the Master M'Grath era. It was not until trainer Michael O'Donovan won with React Robert in 1995 and Dashing Oak in 1996 that this feat of sending out Waterloo Cup winners in successive seasons was emulated. It is now warmly acknowledged that it was Irish owners and trainers who revitalised the Waterloo Cup when it was on its knees in the late 1960s and early 70s.

The aristocratic nominators at the event had always been prejudiced against the Irish. But a lot of theories went out of the window when Dick Ryan brought Old Kentucky Minstrel to slips in 1957. The dog was almost four years old, had won park events through pure pace and had been to stud. After Old Kentucky Minstrel's victory showed that he had a heart to match his speed, Ryan returned to Altcar and had more success with Dubedoon (1961) and Himalayan Climber (1963). Dubedoon was both nominated and owned by Arthur Morris, former secretary of the Irish Coursing

Waterloo Cup Winners

Irish-trained winners of the Waterloo Cup at Altcar (1836–2005)

Year	Winner (Trainer)
1868	Master M'Grath (John Walshe)
1869	Master M'Grath (John Walshe)
1871	Master M'Grath (John Walshe)
1875	Honeymoon (Joe Chestnut)
1876	Donald (Joe Chestnut)
1957	Old Kentucky Minstrel (Dick Ryan)
1961	Dubedoon (Dick Ryan)
1963	Himalayan Climber (Dick Ryan)
1976	Minnesota Miller (Matt O'Donnell)
1977	Minnesota Yank (Jim Ryan)
1982	Play Solo (Pat Holland)
1984	Tubbertelly Queen (Ger McKenna)
1985	Hear And There (Michael O'Donovan)
1988	React Fragll (Michael O'Donovan)
1993	Crafty Tessie (Brian Divilly)
1995	React Robert (Michael O'Donovan)
1996	Dashing Oak (Michael O'Donovan)
1999	Judicial Inquiry (Michael O'Donovan)
2003	Henrietta (James Walshe)
2004	Why You Monty (Michael O'Donovan)

Club in Clonmel, County Tipperary. The dogs trained by Ryan at Goolds Cross, County Tipperary, encouraged English breeders to add a dash of Irish pace to their breeding. Mary Ryan was her father's assistant trainer and went on to breed the legendary park-coursing dog, Master Myles.

The Premier County of Tipperary was to have a remarkable strike rate in the more recent Waterloo Cup history, too. Following Dick Ryan, there came, after a lapse of a decade, Jim and Mary Ryan, who had their kennels at Cashel. The Irish were never again to have a multiple winner like Master M'Grath a century earlier, but Jim Ryan's Minnesota Miller triumphed in 1976 and his Minnesota Yank won the following season. Unusually, the 1976 and 1977 winners were both by matings of Bright Lad and Letesia, although from different litters.

Matt O'Donnell, later to be a much-feared trainer when the English Derby was staged at White City and Wimbledon, was based at Killenaule, County Tipperary, and trained Minnesota Miller in the three weeks prior to his Waterloo Cup win. O'Donnell is one of the few who can be said to have been a successful trainer over track and field. Given the trainer's dual status, then, it is ironic that Waterloo Cup winner Minnesota Miller should have been such a successful sire of track champions.

If the Minnesota victories can be put down to a professional trainer, then the 1982 win of Play Solo revived much of the romance of greyhound ownership. Corkman Pat Holland had held high office with Bord na gCon since its inception in 1958, and was a recognised and respected figure on the international greyhound racing stage. Pat and his wife Monita were enthusiastic coursing supporters. Bought cheaply after winning a minor local event, Play Solo was home-trained and went to slips for the first round at Altcar at 25/1. He won in spite of being the 3/1 outsider of the two finalists.

Two years later and Ger McKenna, Ireland's most successful track trainer, stepped in to win the Waterloo Cup in 1984 for Terry McCann and Pat Kilcoyne from Tubbercurry, County Sligo, with Tubbertelly Queen. She was nominated by Bill Gaskin, an Englishman who knew many of the Irish trainers and who was to figure as owner or nominator with a number of the remaining Waterloo Cup winners. In this, Gaskin would be aided by breeder Tommy Ryan from Murroe, County Limerick, and, above all, Tipperary town trainer Michael O'Donovan.

O'Donovan's list of Waterloo Cup credits began with the Gaskin-nominated and Ryan-owned Hear And There (1985), which defeated another Irish bitch puppy, Morning Lass. Galwayman Brian Divilly – famed breeder and future president of the Irish Coursing Club – made an immense impact on the Waterloo Cup, especially with his bitch Little Shoe. But it was with Crafty Tessie in 1993 that he was eventually to taste outright and overdue success as an owner and trainer.

Michael O'Donovan (trainer, on left) and Tommy Ryan (owner) with React Robert, after his Waterloo Cup victory in 1995.

Corkman Jimmy Walshe sent out Henrietta to win in 2003, but the remaining annals of coursing's greatest competition fittingly belong to an Irishman, and Tipperary man, Michael O'Donovan. In the ten years following Hear And There's victory, he was responsible for no fewer than five more winners: React Fragll (1988), React Robert (1995), Dashing Oak (1996), Judicial Inquiry (1999) and Why You Monty (2004). Like so many fast dogs on track and field with the same prefix, Judicial Inquiry was owned by Pat Daly from Ballinhassig, County Cork.

There were other Irish Waterloo heroes, such as bookmaker Bernard Barry from Dunboyne in County Meath, who became the first sponsor of the cup in 1987, in spite of there being no commercial return for him.

It was left to Pat Loughin, Séamus Neary and a syndicate associated with the Sevenhouses Club in County Kilkenny to be the owners of the last of a score of Irish Waterloo Cup winners, when Why You Monty topped off the Michael O'Donovan sextet.

On the turn . . . Windgap Heresay and
Resolute Time compete in the Oaks
at Powerstown Park, Clonmel, County
Tipperary, in 2009.

9 COURSING IN THEIR VEINS

McGRATH–MATTHEWS–MULLAN

Coursing in Ireland

The founding of the first formal coursing club is recorded as being in 1776 at Swaffham in Norfolk, and the establishment of the Irish Coursing Club took place in Clonmel, County Tipperary, in 1916. Much had happened in the interim. There is evidence that by 1858 regulated coursing fixtures were being run on the Ulster estates of Lord Lurgan, who would become the owner of the legendary Master M'Grath. Lord Lurgan sold his kennels in 1887, but this did not signal the finish of coursing.

At the other end of the country, Lord Fermoy was holding a meet on his estates at Trabolgan in County Cork. Five years after Lord Lurgan's departure from the scene, there were a half-dozen other notable fixtures besides the Lord Fermoy affair at Trabolgan.

A decade later and clubs had mushroomed through the country: along the east coast at Dunlavin, County Wicklow, as well as Dublin and Dundalk. Carrick (both on the River Shannon and the River Suir) had notable gatherings, as did clubs that grew at Borris-in-Ossory and Clonmel/Kilsheelin.

The Irish Cup

Most importantly, the experience of those who had assisted at Trabolgan would lead to the establishment of one of coursing's great institutions, the Irish Cup. First contested in 1905 and won by Peerless de Wit, the Irish Cup had its spiritual home on the estates of the Earls of Dunraven at Clounanna, outside of the village of Adare, County

Part of the packed stand and terraces at the Irish Cup, held at Clounanna, near Adare, County Limerick, in 1969.

Limerick. It would remain there almost until the end of the century: 1998 saw it go to Ballybeggan Park, Tralee, County Kerry, and then revert to another racecourse at Patrickswell, County Limerick.

As with the Irish St Leger on the track, Limerick folk regard the winning of the Irish Cup – run not by the Irish Coursing Club but the County Limerick Coursing Club – as a badge of honour that sets greyhounds and their connections apart. White Sandhills (1933) won the concluding Classic of the domestic season after taking the coursing Derby at Clonmel (1931). Mountain Emperor took the 1944 coursing Derby and the 1945 Irish Cup.

The Irish Cup works on a nominator system: this system also pertained to the Waterloo Cup and involved a notable person deciding on a suitable greyhound and nominating it on behalf of the dog's connections. There is great prestige for the nominator who puts up a winner. That honour fell to the Irish Coursing Club secretary Kitty Butler (1956–69) in 1957 when she nominated Kals Fairy, the Dick Ryan-trained Irish Cup winner. It was a hectic period for the Goolds Cross, County Tipperary, handler as the Irish Cup and Waterloo Cup came in quick succession at the end of February, sometimes just a couple of days separating the finish of one and the start of the other.

The Winners

The year 1957 was to see Ryan complete a monumental double with the Irish Cup win of Kals Fairy and the Waterloo Cup victory of Old Kentucky Minstrel. Given the nature of both fixtures – Altcar being over open terrain and Clounanna being a cross between an open and park fixture – trainers depended on fate for favour in assisting them. It was a combination of the dog's determination, the trainer's talents and fickle fortune that won the day.

Celbridge Chance obviously had all the canine requirements and Jimmy Quigley all the human nous in that Celbridge Chance completed a rare Irish Cup double (1960 and 1961), having already secured the Irish Laurels at the Cork track in 1959.

Altcar ... Dick Ryan (with Frozen Fast on left) on the way to slips at the Waterloo Cup near Southport, Lancashire. Frozen Fast ran up to Latin Lover (pictured here with trainer Norman Farrington, right).

Into his frenetic schedule Dick Ryan fitted the 1973 coursing Derby with Nearly You Sir and the 1974 running with Move On Swanky – the Champion Stakes winner of the following season.

Joe Kenny had a mixed kennel at Borrisoleigh, County Tipperary, and was known for his trackers in more recent years, including Deerfield Sunset, the 1998 Irish St Leger winner at Limerick, as well as a number of top hurdlers. At the outset of his career, Kenny was associated with Simply Terrific, which won both the coursing Oaks at Clonmel in 1961 and the Irish Cup at the end of the same season (which stretched into 1962). Kenny also divided the 1972 coursing Derby (Heathermore King and Newmore King).

Simply Terrific was succeeded as coursing Oaks queen by another speedy sort in Dick Ryan's The Fridge. There have been many such durable champions in the field, and Spring Twilight merits mention for winning the Irish Cup in 1964 and, after a lapse of a year, regaining the title in 1966. Spring Twilight was owned by Paddy O'Sullivan (father of Bord na gCon chairman Dick O'Sullivan) in Tralee, County Kerry, and trained by Tom Thornton.

A significant winner of the Irish Cup in Spring Twilight's gap-year was Mourne Marine, a dog that marked the further emergence of Ronnie Chandler as a trainer. A member of a well-known bookmaking family who also owned Walthamstow track in London, Ronnie Chandler acquired a pupil trainer in Michael O'Donovan, from Tipperary town,

Tom Hayes: the breeder from Killaloe, County Clare, helped everyone identify his greyhounds by giving them his own 'T.H.' initials, as with Tame Hero and Tender Heather.

who would become the most successful handler of Waterloo Cup winners (6), win a coursing Oaks (Bexhill Cottage, 1996) as well as transferring his skills to greyhound racing (Irish Derby with Judicial Pride in 2000).

Chandler added a coursing Oaks with Sparkys Girl (1967) and Little Scotch – owned by Liz Stack, whose husband, Tommy Stack, rode Red Rum to the last of his three English Grand National wins at Aintree in 1977. Chandler savoured Derby success with Gipsy Gem, Mourne Monarch and Dillies Pigalle in the years 1964 to 1966, the second-named pair being in the ownership of Alfie McLean.

Tom Hayes, whose wealth was based on the building business, had an easy-to-identify way of naming his greyhounds. The Killaloe, County Clare, man transferred his own 'T.H.' initials to the 1969 Irish Cup winner Tender Hero and the 1971 winner Tame Hero. The year 1969 is well remembered by coursing devotees as Hayes won the Irish Cup with Tender Hero and the other coursing Classics in the same year, with Tender Heather (Derby) and Tender Honey (Oaks). Tender Heather was followed into the Derby annals by Tame Hero in what was a purple patch for the unassuming Hayes, who came back to win the coursing Oaks with Tender Heartache (1975), Tender Heartrob (1977) and Tender Hillside (2000).

Another breeder-owner-trainer well served by his bloodlines was Tom O'Dwyer, of Cashel, County Tipperary, who had coursing Oaks glory with Smokey Flavour (1978), Smokey Alice (1984) and Smokey Marion (1997), as well as a coursing Derby with Smokey Marshall (2001).

Matt Travers, the Newcastle, County Dublin, trainer, whose Princes Pal won the Scottish Derby in 1987, had sent out Penny County to win the 1979 Irish Derby at Shelbourne Park and his Yolanda Belle would win the coursing Oaks at Powerstown Park in 1985.

In 1970, between Tender Hero and Tame Hero in the Irish Cup, came Felicitas – trained by another Clareman, Gerry Tubridy, who, like Mick Horan before him, had upped sticks and moved to Belfast to train. Felicitas was an early success as an owner for Belfast bookmaker Alfie McLean, who went on to buy Indian Joe in 1980 on the eve of his victory in the

English Derby at White City. Jim Frost, whose son Kevin was the original owner of Indian Joe, nominated Fancy Stuff to win the 1972 Irish Cup. Fancy Stuff was trained by Dick Ryan, as was the 1973 winner Tartan Black.

Another to score a notable success as an owner was Oliver Scallon, who gave such sterling service to Bord na gCon between 1988 and 1996. Scallon owned the Pat McGirr-trained Lusty More, a dual winner of the Irish Cup (1975 and 1976). Another who was to play a prominent role on Bord na gCon, Ann Quinlan (1994–2001) was, in 1977, leading in Quarrymount Riki as the winner of the Irish Cup and her Quarrymount Smut, nominated by her father, John Mackey, would follow in 1981. Riki had already won the 1976 coursing Derby. Denis Lynch, whose family were connected to the Irish Laurels hat-trick of Knockrour Girl (1978) and Knockrour Slave (1979 and 1980), produced Knockrour Tiger to win the Irish Cup of 1979.

Pat Dalton was another who successfully combined track and field activities. As well as operating a kennel in America, being behind Rocking Ship and acting as the roving ambassador for Bord na gCon and the Irish greyhound industry (see chapter 5), Dalton owned a string of good greyhounds, many in training with Ger McKenna. These included Bauhus, which won the 1965 Irish National Sprint, and Lovely Chieftain, the Irish St Leger winner in the same year, as well as the 1970 Irish Laurels winner Gabriel Boy. And, in 1984, Dalton put the name of Hunters Guide on the Irish Cup scroll of honour.

Newry-based Jack Mullan had winners in every other field of greyhound endeavour but was denied in the Irish Cup. But there was to be a remarkable number of Irish Cup winners coming with the 'trained in Newry' tag attached, starting with Noel Mooney's Castleisland Lad in 1978. The man who came to dominate the Irish Cup, and coursing in general, was Brendan Matthews. He had a first Irish Cup winner in Stormy Champ (1982) and there followed Needham Bar (1990), Dunsilly Queen (1992) and Bexhill Drive (1993), as well as Courthouse (2002). Even more impressive is Brendan Matthews' record in the Champion Stakes, the all-aged Classic run at the annual national meeting at Powerstown Park, Clonmel, at the beginning of

February. Needham Wonder (1989), Needham Ash (1991), Newry Hill (1993), Hilltown (1998) and Multibet (2002 and 2003) have won this competition, which requires more pace than the Irish Cup. For good measure, Brendan's son, Paul Matthews, took the 2008 Champion Stakes with Cross Country. The Matthews haul in the coursing Derby reads: Townbrook Bimbo (1985), Newry Hill (1992), Hilltown (1997), Bexhill Eoin (2006) and Razor Ashmore (2008).

Other notable Irish Cup winners have been provided by Eugene McNamara (Ballinaveala Hobo, 1994), who was once the track trainer for hapless owner, Eddie Costello and Tim O'Donovan (Micks Magic, 2001). Tim – the brother of Michael O'Donovan – also won an Irish Derby with He Said So (2005) at Shelbourne Park and handled a coursing Oaks winner at Clonmel in Limousine (2002).

A new reign as Irish Cup king came in 1983 when Ballyduff Bobby won for owner Jimmy Browne – the Ballyheigue, County Kerry, hotelier – and trainer Pa Fitzgerald. Browne's maternal grandfather, Timmy Flaherty, was from the tiny townland of Ahacoora near Lixnaw, County Kerry, and he had bred White Sandhills, which had completed the coursing Derby-Irish Cup double a half-century before Ballyduff Bobby's success. Brendan Fitzgerald and his older brother Pa Fitzgerald had the Irish Cup winner of 1980 (Ballyard Yank) and, after Ballyduff Bobby, Pa Fitz sent out Black Rock (1985), Castle Pines (2005), Castlemartyr (2008) and Sandy Sea (2009). Castle Pines, Castlemartyr and Sandy Sea were in the ownership of Patsy Byrne, who had himself trained the winner of the English Derby in Ballinderry Ash (1991), owned a winner of the Irish Derby (Cool Performance, 2001) and owned a winner of the coursing Derby (Big Interest, 1987).

As it was in the early years of greyhound racing, attributing wins in the Irish Cup to definite trainers is not an exact matter. Pa Fitzgerald himself only claims absolute credit for Ballyduff Bobby and the three Patsy Byrne-owned winners, and modestly admits to having had assistance in the matter of Ballyard Yank and Black Rock.

In coursing, it is common for trainers to stand aside in the latter stages of a competition, and let a more experienced man 'do the dog', as they say. One can only assume that

TOP
Gerard Tubridy: a Clareman drawn to Belfast by the exciting track action there, pictured on the coursing field at Clounanna, near Adare, County Limerick, with the 1978 Irish Cup runner-up Ramona Hiker.

BOTTOM
Jack Mullan, the trainer from Newry, County Down, was master of his art on both track and field.

Patsy Byrne: as an owner or trainer, the man from Duagh, County Kerry, has won the Derby in both coursing and racing.

The 'Master's' Master . . . Trainer Jeremiah Carroll, Listowel, County Kerry, is carried on the shoulders of enthusiasts at Powerstown Park, Clonmel, County Tipperary, after Master Myles had won the coursing Derby in 1978.

Luke Maher, Paulstown, County Kilkenny, stood aside for nobody in the case of his bitch Monologue in the 1932 coursing Oaks. This great bitch proved her worth to the extent of also winning the Irish Derby at Shelbourne Park in 1933.

Champion Stakes

All of the coursing greats – men and beasts – feature regularly in the Powerstown Park records, including the Champion Stakes, which has been run in different guises. When the format had settled to some extent, Dick Ryan sent Move On Swanky to win in 1975, and Brendan Fitzgerald was responsible for So Careful (1980). His brother Pa Fitzgerald had to wait until 2004 before clicking with the Patsy Byrne-owned Mustang Rooster.

Jack Mullan enters the Champion Stakes picture with Ashmore Melody (1981) and Knockash Rover (1982), the latter being owned by Phonsie O'Brien, the brother of racehorse trainer Vincent O'Brien. The realms of canine and equestrian sport have not been entirely separate. Apart from

Vincent O'Brien, Mick O'Toole and Jim Bolger are among those who trained greyhounds before moving on to the larger animals.

Jeremiah Carroll, the owner-trainer of the immortal Master Myles, produced Listowel Laddie to win the Champion Stakes in 1983. Brian Divilly, whose 'Crafty' prefix was inherited from his father, Martin Divilly – he had the 1955 Irish Cup winner Crafty Champion – weighed in with Crafty Roberto (1990). The 2009 addition to the Champion Stakes roll has been a significant one: Catunda Ashmore, trained by Owen McKenna, son of Ger McKenna. As with all dogs with the 'Catunda' prefix, Catunda Ashmore is owned by Dubliner Paddy Byrne.

While he would probably be more readily associated with coursing, Jack Mullan was one of the all-time great dual trainers. He won the Irish Derby with Hopeful Cutlet (1957) and Wonder Valley (1964), and his son Brendan Mullan would win the Irish Derby with Daleys Denis (1993). In between his two track wins, Jack Mullan divided the 1960 coursing Derby (Millers Toast and July The Fourth) and won it outright two years later with Dandy Man. Mullan won another coursing Derby in 1979 with Kyle Guest and, appropriately, he and Ronnie Chandler divided the 1981 renewal with Believe Him (Chandler) and Knockash Rover (Mullan).

The McGraths and Michael Murphy

The year 1975 had already heralded the entrance of the most extraordinary confederacy in the history of Irish coursing. It was all straightforward. When it came to the coursing Derby at Clonmel, Colm McGrath – who is based at Clonoe, outside Coalisland, County Tyrone, and who made his money from fitting out supermarkets and other large retail outlets – would buy a promising pup (the winner of a trial stake, often at an insignificantly small meeting), put the dog in the name of his wife Mary, and send him to Michael Murphy. Murphy had been a sprinter in his younger days and, when he was not operating a petrol pump in Castleisland, he would take the greyhounds off into the County Kerry hills. There, it was said, he had a tract with

Secretaries of the Irish Coursing Club

T.A. Morris	1916–1948
A.J. Morris and	
T.A. Morris (joint)	1948–1952
A.J. Morris	1952–1956
Kitty Butler	1956–1969
Comdt J.M. Fitzpatrick	1969–1986
J.L. Desmond	1986–2008
D.J. Histon	2008–

Presidents of the Irish Coursing Club

Philip O'Sullivan	1916–1924
John Hoare	1925–1926
John Bruton	1927–1929
Thomas Harte	1930
John Griffin	1931–1934
Christopher Kerin	1935–1937
Thomas Ahern	1938–1942 and 1951–1952
M.J. Mulhall	1943–1946
Patrick O'Brien	1947
Revd William Dowling	1948–1950
Bernard Rahill	1953–1956 and 1959
Peter P. Coffey	1957–1958
P.J. Cox	1960–1966
Matthew Sullivan	1966–1972
Lt.-Col. J.P. Kelly	1972–1975
P.J. Chambers	1975–1978
William Russell	1978–1981
A.J. Morris	1981–1983
Michael Fives	1983–1986
Séamus Grady	1986–1993
Matthew J. Bruton	1993–2000
Jack O'Rourke	2000–2003
Anthony McNamee	2003–2008
Brian Divilly	2008–

Englishman Fred Warrell, a close associate of owner Eddie Costello on the track, congratulates Mary McGrath, Coalisland, County Tyrone, on the 1989 coursing Derby win of Donovan's Ranger at Powerstown Park, Clonmel, County Tipperary.

a gradient that replicated the steep incline of the finish at Powerstown Park.

Murphy won his first coursing Derby for Mary McGrath in 1975 (Gayline). Martry Scotch (1982), Autumn Crystal (1983), Sir Lancelot (1986), Pyramid Club (1988) and Donovan's Ranger (1989) followed. The one that got away was 1977 when Boston Point won and the McGrath–Murphy team had his brother Best Man. Some saw Best Man as the fastest dog ever – even greater than 1978 Derby winner Master Myles – and, although knocked out of the Derby at the penultimate stage, he would have an enormous impact on the breeding of future trial-stake winners.

Murphy also had a coursing Derby winner not owned by Mary McGrath in Tullamore (1996) and a coursing Oaks winner in Scotch Lady (1993), while Colm and Mary McGrath had a coursing Oaks winner trained by themselves in Rossa Rose (1986).

Their association with a separate and highly successful trainer of coursing dogs in Murphy, while at the same time being such a feared combination with track greyhounds that they trained themselves to the highest professional standards, merits Colm and Mary McGrath a special place in the history of greyhound sport. Ulster, from where Lord Lurgan had sent Master M'Grath to win his first Waterloo Cup in coursing in 1868, and where racing would be seen on this island for the first time in 1927, is still exerting the hand of influence in greyhound sport.

Murphy had been a sprinter in his younger days and, when he was not operating a petrol pump in Castleisland, he would take the greyhounds off into the County Kerry hills. There, it was said, he had a tract with a gradient that replicated the steep incline of the finish at Powerstown Park.

The centre of attention: Mick The Miller
on the English Derby winner's podium,
White City, London, 1930.

10 AN AFFAIR OF THE HEART
MICK THE MILLER

Most of the other pups from the litter were sold locally but Father Brophy decided to keep Mick The Miller for himself – perhaps seeing something in him. Mick The Miller was put into the public greyhound sales at Shelbourne Park in August 1928, with a reserve price of two hundred guineas.

The First Superstar of the Track

Master M'Grath found fame on the coursing field twenty-nine years before the end of the nineteenth century when he won the Waterloo Cup for a third time; Mick The Miller was the first superstar of the race track twenty-nine years into the twentieth century when he initiated his English Derby double, which has been equalled but never bettered.

Yet, while greyhound generations divided Master M'Grath and Mick The Miller, these two extraordinary dogs had one notable physical characteristic in common: the autopsy of Master M'Grath is said to have shown his heart to be 'twice the size' of an average greyhound's when he died in 1871. Accounts relating to Mick The Miller are more specific still, and say that, on his death, his heart weighed 14.5 ounces when the standard was accepted to be 13 ounces. So it seems that both ability and longevity in the competitive arena may depend on what beats within the greyhound's slight frame.

Mick The Miller was the right greyhound at the right time. His exploits caught the public imagination and catapulted greyhound racing into the headlines. The fledgling sport was only officially born in Britain in 1926, but organisers wasted little time in giving it the trappings and structures enjoyed

Father Martin Brophy

by other sports, especially horse racing. A primary objective was to found a Derby, and as early as 1927 – when the sport was only being conceived in Ireland – the inaugural version was won over 500 yards by Entry Badge. Just two years later, Mick The Miller was on the scene, having progressed from the provincial coursing enclosures to the turf of Shelbourne Park. Now he was about to show how the racing greyhound could be such a reliable betting medium by transferring his form from Dublin to London.

His breeder and owner was Father Martin Brophy, who was born in Paulstown, County Kilkenny, in 1874. He was the Catholic parish priest in the village of Killeigh, County Offaly – a fact that raised few eyebrows in Ireland in those days. Mick The Miller was the runt of a litter whelped on 29 June 1926, and was a sickly pup. His constitution remained less than robust throughout his life, which led to many long lay-offs during his racing career. As is so often the case, the origins of his name are not known for certain, but the most commonly touted story is that he was called after a man named Mick Miller. However, Father W.J. Prendergast, one of Father Brophy's successors as parish priest in Killeigh, contended in the *Emigrant Newsletter* in June 1980 that the great dog was named after a local mill owner, Mick Dunne.

Mick The Miller was initially trained by Father Brophy's neighbour, Michael Greene, and, after trials, they were quick to realise Mick The Miller's potential behind the artificial lure, even though the priest had always been a dedicated follower of the leash in the open-coursing sphere. Most of the other pups from the litter were sold locally, but Father Brophy decided to keep Mick The Miller for himself – perhaps seeing something in him. Mick The Miller was put into the public greyhound sales at Shelbourne Park in August 1928, with a reserve price of two hundred guineas. However, Father Brophy withdrew him from the sale with the best offer of one hundred and fifty guineas – further indication that Father Brophy was more interested in financial gain than trophies. Perhaps with the audacious plan of running Mick The Miller in the 1929 English Derby in mind, he continued to build up the dog's curriculum vitae on the Irish circuit.

To this day, the inhabitants of the County Offaly hamlet

claim Michael Greene of Tullamore as the trainer of Mick The Miller when he won the 1929 English Derby. The record books and a number of official publications actually show Mick The Miller as trained by 'P.' or 'Paddy' Horan. This is incorrect. The dog was trained by Mick Horan, who had a kennel near Trim, County Meath.*

The Greyhound Derby, 1929

What is certain is that Father Brophy, whose presence at White City was remarked and frowned upon by the Church of England hierarchy, was no longer the owner when the final came around. Having settled in to kennels in England and run brilliantly both in trials and in the first round, with a pre-Derby solo trial time of 30.03 seconds, the dog was put up for public auction on the steps of the great stadium and purchased, for eight hundred guineas, by trainer Stan Biss on behalf of Wimbledon bookmaker Albert (A.H.) Williams, in whose name he raced to victory.

In the first round of the Classic, he ran 29.82 for the White City 525 yards, the first greyhound to go below thirty seconds over this distance. He was odds-on favourite for the final. There were just four runners in the 1929 final, and Palatinus won after the other three runners collided at the opening bend. However, the stewards declared the race void – as they could in those days – and ordered the final to be re-run after an interval of just thirty minutes.

Mick The Miller was backed again as if defeat was out of the question. In spite of having so little time to get over his initial exertions, he won the 1929 English Derby in 29.96 seconds – the first ever Irish-trained winner of this race. Even at the remove of eighty years, one can appreciate the feelings of the support-ers of Palatinus, which had won the original running of the 1929 decider. Palatinus led everywhere in the re-run before being col-lared and passed by Mick The Miller close to home. A measure of the effort is that, a year later, Mick The Miller would win again (at first time of asking!) in the slower time of 30.24 seconds.

*Adrian Horan, Mick Horan's son, was a noted coursing slipper and is now attached to Drumbo Park track at Lisburn. He says: 'My father was the trainer of Mick The Miller when he won the English Derby at White City in 1929. There never was a P. Horan nor a Paddy Horan, and my father didn't have a brother of that name. His only brother was Bill Horan, a noted jockey of the time.'

Puppy love: owner Phyllis Kempton with Mick The Miller and two of his offspring.

Photographs of the tall and elegant Phyllis Kempton with Mick The Miller on the lead became some of the most iconic images of chic Britannia between the world wars, and the pair became the inspiration for all manner of art deco *objets d'art*.

The Kemptons

A.H. Williams received just £700 in prize money when Mick The Miller won in 1929 – the smallest purse in Derby history. In 1927, the winner took home £1,000, and £1,500 in 1928. After the win, Williams decided to cash in. In 1929, no greyhound had ever changed hands for more than a thousand pounds, but Arundel Kempton went to an astonishing two thousand guineas to buy Mick The Miller as a loving gift for his wife.

Photographs of the tall and elegant Phyllis Kempton with Mick The Miller on the lead became some of the most iconic images of chic Britannia between the world wars, and the pair became the inspiration for all manner of art deco *objets d'art*. Mrs Kempton could not be persuaded to part with her pet, and refused to countenance her husband selling him to a would-be American buyer who was prepared to double their money and pay four thousand guineas. So, in 1930, it was in Mrs Kempton's name and Sidney Orton's care that Mick The Miller became the first in a small and select list of greyhounds to win the English Derby in successive years.

The story was far from over, however, because Mick The Miller returned for a third tilt in 1931, when, ironically, he was undone by the re-run rule that had helped him two

Canine chic: Phyllis Kempton in a studio portrait with Mick The Miller.

years previously. Mick The Miller was first past the post in the initial race but one of the opposition, Ryland R, was ruled to have fought (or been guilty of 'aggressive interference', as it was called) during the race. A re-run was ordered, and, as he had done before, Mick The Miller started as favourite. There was to be no repeat for the veteran and his old limbs were not up to the second quick run.

Mick The Miller was by no means finished. He won Classic races outside the home of the Derby at such venues as West Ham, White City and Wimbledon, where he would regularly not just win open competitions but race through them unbeaten and record the fastest times en route. He even managed a role in the film *Wild Boy*, starring alongside the British music-hall entertainers Bud Flanagan and

Mick The Miller filming *Wild Boy* at London's Shepherd's Bush in October 1933.

The Duke's dog: The Duke of Edinburgh
(second from right) with Camira Flash,
which went on to win the 1968 English
Derby at White City.

Chesney Allen. The closest that he ever came to returning to his native soil was when Sidney Orton brought him to Cardiff, where he won the Welsh Derby.

The size of his heart aside, the fact that he was a sickly pup, which caused a delay in the start to his serious racing days, can now be put forward as a reason why he could compete at a high level when he was five years of age. A common mistake on the part of anxious owners is to race their greyhounds long before they leave the puppy stage, which often causes injury problems down the road.

Mick The Miller went to stud at a record fifty guineas, but proved to be an expensive flop for the most part. He ended up being mated to bitches whose owners could afford the fee but which did not necessarily have the ideal breeding lines. As with racehorses, the fastest canines do not automatically pass on the winning ability to their progeny, and it can be their lesser-raced siblings that prove the more productive. And so it was with Mick The Miller. His litter brother Macoma – which made his name hurdling and had to be retired prematurely because of injury – left his mark in the breeding paddocks. Mick The Miller had been successfully trialed over hurdles, too. In the early days of the sport, jumps racing was enormously popular, especially at the main British stadiums. In Ireland, it came to be associated with greyhounds thought to be inclined to fight or not regarded as totally genuine, and has largely been discontinued. In the beginning, however, it provided a novel and exciting spectacle, especially for newcomers to the game.

Mick The Miller died in 1939, and predeceased Father Brophy by ten years. The dog's name lives on in greyhound racing history and legend … and in the sport's glossary: to this day, trainers will still refer to a greyhound of ability in their care as a 'Miller'.

Fighting

Long after the Mick The Miller era, the English authorities tended to be more fussy than their Irish counterparts when it came to regulations. It was especially so in respect of interference. The days of the re-run finals to major events were effectively gone, but in-race fighting was still a contentious issue, especially during the 1968 English Derby, when the winner, Camira Flash, was owned by Prince Philip, the Duke of Edinburgh.

In the 1968 semi-finals, Camira Flash finished fourth, and, thus, failed to qualify for the decider. Not Flashing – owned and trained in Ireland by Frank Cavlan – finished third and just in front of Camira Flash. In a hugely controversial move, the stewards deemed that Not Flashing had fought, so disqualified him, and gave his place in the final to 'the Duke's dog' (as he would be immortalised in a song by rock group, The Who). Cavlan accepted the decision in an exemplary and sporting manner, which was not matched by some of the race-goers on final night. There was much jeering but nothing debatable about the decider, and Camira Flash ran his heart out to win. It was later announced that the prize money, which totalled £7,252, had been given to charity.

White City, which had hosted the first greyhound Derby in 1927 and which had witnessed the heroics of Mick The Miller for three glorious years, abruptly closed its doors after the 1984 renewal of the premier English Classic. For the Irish trainers intent of plundering the English Derby still further, all roads no longer led to White City but across London to Wimbledon.

M Match Races

Match races are now a rarity, probably because there is enough really attractive prize money on offer in races proper. Match races harkened back to the origins of horse racing when races were simply the pitting of one owner's horse against that of a rival owner in a match for a specified financial stake and usually over an extreme distance. Greyhound match races came about when an owner, believing his dog to be unlucky when eliminated from a competition, challenged the winner of the final. Match races were popular spectacles at one time but were not pursued by managements because of limited betting revenue. Staying champions such as Scurlogue Champ and Ballyregan Bob were the subject of such challenges in the 1980s.

Full house . . . The magnificent White City,
London, original home of the English
Derby (1927–84).

11 THE GREENING OF
THE WHITE CITY

THE GRAND CANAL ... AND THE BANKS OF THE LIFFEY

For an Irish trainer, going to White City was like the national football team taking on England at Twickenham or Wembley. It was as simple and vital as that.

The English Citadel

White City in London was not purpose-built for greyhound racing, but it became the sport's spiritual home. To the Irish, it was a citadel to be confronted, to be stormed annually … just like Altcar … just like Cheltenham. For an Irish trainer, going to White City was like the national football team taking on England at Twickenham or Wembley. It was as simple and vital as that.

Racing at White City was a new and sometimes daunting experience for the Irish, who were accustomed to tracks that were often basic in their facilities. White City, in contrast, combined Rolls Royce racing and dining on a par with the Dorchester Hotel. White City – originally called the Great Stadium, and built at a cost of sixty thousand pounds for the Olympic Games – was opened on 27 April 1908 by King Edward VII. It was designed to seat sixty-eight thousand and also had an overall terraced capacity for twice that number. In 1927, it was refurbished to be the jewel in the greyhound racing crown and the venue for the sport's Derby.

A race-goer enjoys a night at the dogs, 1943-style, at the White City, London.

The Scottish Derby

Raiding the Scottish Derby at Shawfield – which was first contested back in 1928 – has become a more recent vogue for Irish trainers. It has been secured at healthy intervals since Matt Travers left from Newcastle, County Dublin, and won it with Princes Pal in 1987, one of the years in which the running took place at the old athletics stadium at Powderhall in Edinburgh. With the race back in Glasgow, Gerry Kiely made the trip from Waterford worthwhile with Airmount Grand in 1989, while Francis Murray came from his Crookedwood, County Westmeath kennel and won with Droopys Sandy in 1994. Karl and Ralph Hewitt made the short trip from Ulster profitable in 1999 with Chart King, the same year that this greyhound won the English Derby.

Bonus incentives attracted more Irish trainers, and Paul Hennessy from Gowran, County Kilkenny, became the only Irish handler to win the Scottish Derby twice, with Priceless Rebel (2002) and Tyrur Kieran (2008). Sandwiched in between was the 2005 victory for Droopys Marco, in the care of a true son of Scotland, Fraser Black. He and his family had long since established themselves in Ireland, near Rathangan, County Kildare, with the trainer marrying into the McKenna clan, Ireland's foremost greyhound racing dynasty. The most recent Irish victory here came in 2009 with Cabra Cool, trained by Pat Buckley at Cappawhite, County Tipperary.

The Grand Canal

The official gap in Irish winners since Mick The Miller's 1929 win was credited to 'Paddy' Horan was not bridged until The Grand Canal came home in front of the packed White City stands in 1962 for that most dapper of Irish trainers, Paddy Dunphy. A real old-fashioned gentleman, Paddy Dunphy was seldom seen without a bow tie, and was immaculately dressed, even in private and in failing health and advancing years. His prefix for his greyhounds, 'The

Mick The Miller's 'Irish' win but also set the benchmark for what was to follow.

Other 'Irish' Winners

The Irishness of the 1966 winner was not so straightforward. It may have been 1966 and England may have been hosting the World Cup (which they would, of course, famously win), but the thoughts of greyhound-racing devotees were at White City where Paddy Keane was sending out Faithful Hope for the English Derby. Keane was from Kilmihil, County Clare, along with Commandant Joseph Fitzpatrick, who was one of the cornerstones of the Irish Coursing Club. The rotund Keane was notable for a vast appetite and an enormous intellect, as well as for being an outstanding trainer of greyhounds. He was a formidable figure on the London circuit, and was based at Clapton, when Faithful Hope won the English Derby in the ownership of Sir Robert Adeane and Pauline Wallis. Nightclub-owner Wallis was a glamorous figure who enjoyed the greyhound racing and social limelight in Britain and America. A fearless gambler, she teamed up again with Sir Robert Adeane in the ownership of the great Yellow Printer, winner of the 1968 Irish Derby.

There is an old adage about keeping 'yourself in the best company and your greyhounds in the worst', but Paddy Keane would only tolerate the very best in every respect. He and his wife Olive later returned to Ireland and ran a schooling track in Dunboyne, County Meath, before moving again to Tullamore, County Offaly. Towards the end of the following decade, he won the Irish Derby at Shelbourne Park with Pampered Rover (1978), thereby joining the select few to have trained a Derby winner in both England and Ireland. Keane also had a sharp political mind and he numbered Irish Taoiseach Charles Haughey and his wife Maureen among his owners. Another lifelong Keane patron was Noel Ryan, the former chairman of Dundalk and Drogheda Dairies, who owned Loyal Honcho, the Séamus Graham-trained winner of the English Derby in 2008.

Yet, in spite of Keane's Irish birth and upbringing, the

Paddy Keane, the great trainer from Kilmihil, County Clare, had winners of both the English Derby and the Irish Derby in his kennels.

Grand', was so appropriate. Paddy Dunphy was a one-off in many respects. For the most part, the English greyhound racing scene was dominated by professional trainers. Owners who also trained their greyhounds to win Classics were not unknown, but Dunphy was different again in that he was also the breeder of The Grand Canal. Dunphy, a publican, also broke the mould in that he was the first to benefit from a National Greyhound Racing Club (NGRC) rule change.

There had previously been a stipulation that Irish-based greyhounds entered for the Derby had to be transferred into the care of a licensed trainer in England. This made it impossible to have an Irish-trained winner. So, the victory of The Grand Canal not only came thirty-three years after

ABOVE LEFT
1. Just grand . . . The Grand Canal, the 1962 English Derby winner at White City, London, gets a pedicure from owner/trainer Paddy Dunphy, Castlecomer, County Kilkenny.

2. The Grand Canal (5), winning the 1962 English Derby by a length from Powerstown Prospect (4).

John O'Connor brought Patricias Hope out of retirement to win a second English Derby at White City, London, in 1973.

official records do not count Faithful Hope as an Irish-trained winner of the English Derby. He is not unique. Whisper Wishes – the last winner of a White City Derby – came into the same category in 1984, and so too did Ballinderry Ash in 1991. Owned by Helen Roche (sister of Red Rum's jockey Tommy Stack), Ballinderry Ash was trained by Kerryman Patsy Byrne whose Wimbledon kennel staff were 'imported' from Ireland.

The Irishness of Sand Star (1969) was another indicator of how muddled it could all become. The rules that now allowed Irish owners and trainers to bring their greyhounds across to compete also stipulated that the dog had to stay in kennels licensed by the NGRC and the track owners, the Greyhound Racing Association (GRA). An owner-trainer from Ireland, Hamilton Orr, stuck to the letter of the rules: he went over and deposited Sand Star on NGRC-approved premises with English trainer Barbara Tompkins … and left him there for the duration of the competition. The rules were later amended to the effect that the Irish trainer or his/her NGRC-licensed Irish kennel-hand must remain with the dog.

It was the age of Yellow Printer, and Sand Star appeared to be up against it. Yet he won through. The 'trainer' watched Sand Star from the remove of the White City stands. The British rules had never sat easily with the Irish, and yet they ordained that Hamilton Orr would be recorded as both the owner and trainer of Sand Star, the third Irish winner of the English Derby.

Patricias Hope

A few years after Sand Star's 1969 victory saw the emergence of a greyhound that would grab almost as many headlines as Mick The Miller. Patricias Hope would emulate the first dual winner by winning in 1972 and 1973, and, again, would fit in the category of being British-trained one year and Irish-trained the next.

The first success was straightforward. Patricias Hope landed a massive gamble for his bookmaking connections by winning the 1972 renewal when trained by Adam Jackson. Born in Ballymore-Eustace, County Kildare, Jackson had also sent out Chittering Clapton to win the English Derby in 1965. A gauge of Jackson's ability is that, in 1972, Patricias Hope annexed the Scottish Derby at Shawfield as well as following Mick The Miller by taking the Welsh Derby, then run at Cardiff Arms Park. Patricias Hope was then packed off to stud with John O'Connor, a schoolteacher from Mallow, County Cork. He had bought a half-share in the greyhound owned by bookmaker Brian Stanley.

Patricias Hope, which emulated Mick The Miller by twice winning the English Derby at White City, London, seen in full flight.

In 1973, the English Derby was sponsored for the first time and had a first prize of £12,500 through the backing of dog-food manufacturers Spillers. Patricias Hope had proved particularly enthusiastic and fertile at stud, and had mated sixty-four bitches. But the lure of the prize money and the chance of joining Mick The Miller in the record books was irresistible to his owners. Patricias Hope was entered for the 1973 Derby and soon showed that he had lost none of his dash. He won the final, completing the double, but, like Mick The Miller, was denied in his hat-trick attempt. Similarly, at stud, the quantity of his progeny outweighed its quality.

The other two greyhounds to be twice winners of the English Derby have been the Rapid Ranger (2000 and 2001), trained by Charlie Lister, and Westmead Hawk (2005 and 2006), trained by Nick Savva. Lister won the Classic in four out of seven years; Some Picture (1997) and Farloe Verdict (2003) were his other victors.

Greek Cypriot Savva is the only man to record a hat-trick of winners, with Westmead Lord (2007) following the Westmead Hawk brace. He had earlier won with Toms The Best (1998); this dog was to go on and also win the Irish Derby at Shelbourne Park.

For good measure, it was Savva's brother Theo Mentzis who trained the 1995 English Derby winner Moaning Lad. Leslie Reynolds trained five winners between 1948 and 1954 (Priceless Border, Narrogar Ann, Ballylanigan Tanist, Endless Gossip and Pauls Fun). Ger McKenna (Parkdown Jet, 1981, and Lartigue Note, 1989) is the only Irish trainer to have sent out two winners.

The Irish Versus the Irish

By 1980, the annual trip to White City had become a pilgrimage for the Irish and, as is often the case at the Cheltenham Festival in March, the ones most likely to beat the Irish were the Irish themselves. That was the situation for Limerickman John Hayes when he brought over Indian Joe for Kevin Frost from Cratloe, County Clare, whose family had played such an integral part in the development of horse and greyhound sport on the domestic front. In spite of the presence of experienced compatriot trainers, Hayes'

confidence was such that Belfast bookmaker Alfie McLean came in and bought Indian Joe. There may have been an economic recession on the horizon but there was still plenty of money if the right dog was around. Kevin Frost never revealed how much he was paid, but did say that he felt that he could not refuse McLean's offer. Hayes remained Indian Joe's trainer, and the dog duly won the 1980 Classic.

In the decider, Indian Joe had to beat Fred Flintstone, Matt O'Donnell's first, but certainly not last, Derby finalist. It took another dozen years of trying, but O'Donnell, from Killenaule, County Tipperary, eventually added an English Derby win (with Farloe Melody, owned by John Davis and David Tickner, in 1992) to the Waterloo Cup victory he had had with Minnesota Miller in 1976. Ger McKenna, from Borrisokane, County Tipperary, would do it in reverse, winning first an English Derby in 1981 (the year after Indian Joe) with Parkdown Jet and then his Waterloo Cup with Tubbertelly Queen three years later.

The English Derby had gone from the 500 yards of Entry Badge's win in 1927, to the 525 yards of 1928–74, to the 500 metres of the 1975–84 decade. It had been run during the Second World War at Harringay and revived after the 1941–44 stoppage. It would have to survive yet more turmoil when White City was abruptly sold. The hallowed ground now forms part of the British Broadcasting Corporation, which is ironic given all that the BBC had done to popularise the sport in its infancy. Whisper Wishes' 1984 win brought the curtain down. He was Irish in everything but name – trained in England, but owned by Donegal man John Duffy and handled by Tyrone man Charlie Coyle. He was bought late on the night of his triumph by Kerryman Patsy Byrne and returned to Ireland where he took over the mantle of his father, Sand Man, and sired a whole generation of winners.

To Wimbledon

A new cast of characters at Wimbledon was waiting in the wings, but a couple of the old hands moved to the new set. Ger McKenna's Parkdown Jet was the last Irish-trained winner of the English Derby at White City in 1981, and his Lartigue Note was the first Irish-trained winner of the

Betting was just as crucial a part of the English Derby story as the prize money, and no self-respecting Irish owner would return home without the tale of how much had been taken from the satchels of the English bookmakers.

English Derby at Wimbledon in 1989.

In 1990, Prince Edward found himself with a share of a finalist in the English Derby at its new home. It had been twenty-two years since Camira Flash won at White City. Prince Edward's ownership had come about when owner-trainer Patsy Byrne donated part of his interest in Druids Johno to the victims of a bombing in the Royal Marines Music School. Byrne had wished to give away the entire greyhound but, as an owner-trainer, NGRC rules stipulated that he had to retain a percentage in Druids Johno. All monies won were to go to the victims' fund. There was no on-the-track controversy as there had been in 1968 and, unlike his father Prince Philip, Prince Edward felt comfortable enough to attend the 1990 decider.

Even though the race took place during the FIFA World Cup in Italy – where the Republic of Ireland was competing for the first time on football's global stage – the royal/Irish dog's progress was big news and a considerable publicity boon for greyhound racing. There was to be no royal fairy-tale ending, though, with Druids Johno odds-on but finishing second to Slippy Blue, a winner who received rather less publicity than the runner-up. Still, Byrne is a man who has a stoical approach to such setbacks, and he returned to win the blue riband as a trainer with Ballinderry Ash just one year later, in 1991.

At the same time, the old order was changing. Shanless Slippy (1996), owned by Tyrone man Frank McGirr, had all the traditional early pace of the classic Irish greyhound but was trained by a member of the younger generation, Dolores Ruth. Ruth came from a family with a strong greyhound background even though their kennel was as close to Dublin's city centre as one could get. Her sister Frances was then assistant trainer to Matt O'Donnell, and Dolores Ruth moved away from the quays of the Liffey to somewhere closer to the river's source, and established herself near Fraser Black at Rathangan. This is a part of County Kildare more readily associated with horse racing but which had produced in Shanless Slippy the shortest-priced Irish-trained winner of the English Derby, at 4/9.

Betting was just as crucial a part of the English Derby story as the prize money, and no self-respecting Irish owner would

---

English Derby Winners

Irish-trained winners of the English Derby at White City (1927–84) and Wimbledon (1985–2009)

1929	Mick The Miller (Mick Horan)
1962	The Grand Canal (Paddy Dunphy)
1969	Sand Star (Hamilton Orr)
1973	Patricias Hope (John O'Connor)
1980	Indian Joe (John Hayes)
1981	Parkdown Jet (Ger McKenna)
1989	Lartigue Note (Ger McKenna)
1992	Farloe Melody (Matt O'Donnell)
1996	Shanless Slippy (Dolores Ruth)
1999	Chart King (Karl & Ralph Hewitt)
2004	Droopys Scholes (Ian Reilly)
2008	Loyal Honcho (Séamus Graham)

---

return home without the tale of how much had been taken from the satchels of the English bookmakers. The truth of such stories is borne out by the fact that only two of the dozen Irish-trained winners have not been favourite, either outright or joint. Mick The Miller (4/7), The Grand Canal (2/1), Sand Star (5/4), Indian Joe (13/8), Parkdown Jet (4/5), Lartigue Note (evens), Farloe Melody (6/4), Shanless Slippy (4/9), Chart King (8/11) and Loyal Honcho (5/2) all headed their markets. The exceptions were Patricias Hope in 1973 and Droopys Scholes in 2004. Both were 7/2.

'Droopys' was to become the prefix for a whole generation of speedsters. Droopys Scholes was owned by boxing promoter Brian Peters and trained by Ian Reilly, whose father Daniel had a major stake in the greyhound industry in Ireland. Daniel Reilly has been an administrator, owner and sponsor, and is perhaps best known as the owner of the Navan works where the Dublin tracks' race cards have been printed for many years.

The final English Derby in a millennium spanned by the greyhound breed went, appropriately, to Northern Ireland, where the Irish public had first been introduced to greyhound racing in 1927. Karl and Ralph Hewitt completed the Scottish-English Derby double with Chart King.

If wins for Dolores Ruth and Ian Reilly marked a handing over of the baton, then the older generation of trainers was not quite finished yet. Fifty years after the founding of Bord na gCon, the state agency that had made greyhound racing a matter of national importance, the Irish were to plunder the English bastion once more. Flying the flag this time were Noel Ryan, an octogenarian owner whose interest dated all the way back to the days of Paddy Keane, and Séamus Graham, the man from Ballickmoyler, County Carlow, who had been quietly plotting the 2008 victory of Loyal Honcho since being situated beside Ger McKenna in the GRA kennels at Potters Bar a generation earlier.

The long wait of owner Noel Ryan and trainer Séamus Graham for English Derby glory ended with the 2008 victory at Wimbledon for Loyal Honcho (4). He is seen leading Kryponite (1), Tyrur Kieran (3), Tyrur Laurel (5) and Blonde Dino (6).

Full steam ahead . . . Lartigue Note, named
after a railway system in north County
Kerry, stayed right on track to win the
English Derby at Wimbledon for
Ger McKenna in 1989.

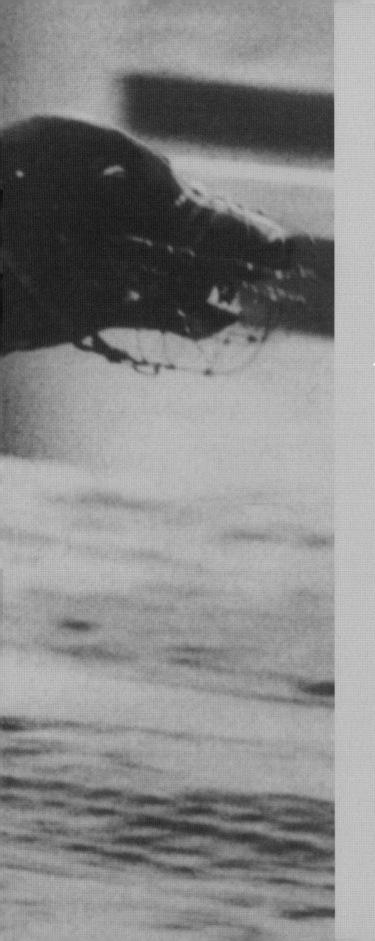

12 THE MAESTRO FINDS THE RIGHT NOTE

GER McKENNA'S ENGLISH DERBY DOUBLE

The registration
of greyhounds
and the licensing
of their handlers
are of paramount
importance to the
English authorities.
It is not that Bord na
gCon was in any way
lax when it came to
matters of integrity;
but there was a
feeling that the English
were overly fussy when
it came to regulation.

Ireland and England

The uneasy relationship that had always existed between the Irish and the English, even outside the political arena, had filtered through to greyhound sport. As in other walks of life, the relaxed Irish approach conflicted with the more bureaucratically minded English way of going. In England, everyone had to adhere strictly to the coursing and greyhound-racing rules. The registration of greyhounds and the licensing of their handlers are of paramount importance to the English authorities. It is not that Bord na gCon was in any way lax when it came to matters of integrity; but there was a feeling that the English were overly fussy when it came to regulation.

Of course, there was always a different system in England: the contract-training system, which saw trainers enter into contracts with individual tracks. The race courses provided kennels and guaranteed that greyhounds would get races. The handlers for their part pledged to supply a certain number of greyhounds in order to keep the course ticking over. In this way, greyhounds and their handlers were attached to a particular track. One advantage of this system is that a database of the form of all greyhounds can be collated and the racing manager can grade them accordingly. This is the basis for the vast majority of greyhound racing, afternoon and evening, in England.

There is a degree of flexibility for 'open' greyhounds – the dogs that attain A1 status in the grading chain. If their trainers want to aim higher, towards events such as the Classics, the dog can move out of the strict contract set-up. In Ireland, every dog is an open performer and, with no contract system, licensed trainers are free to go from one Irish track to another at will.

Irish Trainers and the English Derby

So, when it came to the English Derby, Irish trainers found themselves in highly regulated surroundings. One detected not hostility from the trainers, but rather an underlying resentment that they were unable to come and go as they wished.

For a period after Mick The Miller's win in 1929 and up to The Grand Canal's success in 1962, Irish trainers were not recognised at all in England. Even by 1962, Paddy Dunphy and those who came after him had to get a letter of introduction from Bord na gCon and were forced to stay in the kennels provided by the English authorities.

Ger McKenna, 1981

It seems ironic, then, that when the man who was arguably the greatest trainer of them all came with his raiding party for the 1981 English Derby at White City, he did so to the marching of a British military brass band.

Ger McKenna spent much of his time in Borrisokane, County Tipperary, musing about how to give his charges the edge in the English Derby; probably just as much time as racehorse trainer Vincent O'Brien spent at Rosegreen making similar plans for his horses. Ger McKenna and his greyhounds have been responsible for most of the superlatives in the Irish greyhound record book … most Classics attained, most winners of the Derby, fastest winners. Some of the records may since have been broken; but you can take it that McKenna – or a member of his extended family – established almost all of them in the first place.

Vincent O'Brien and the unrelated Aidan O'Brien did not send out Derby winners from Ballydoyle at their first attempts: neither did Ger McKenna. Training is a business in which one learns and evolves.

Preparing Parkdown Jet

And, in 1981, in the enforced solitude of the English authority's kennel complex at Potters Bar, outside London, McKenna contemplated how to prepare his finalist Parkdown Jet for the Saturday-night decider at White City.

Greyhounds are creatures of habit and soon get into the routine of racing … leaving home, getting into the transporter, stopping off at the same spot for a pee, bedding in at the track kennels for an hour or so, being paraded, put in traps, running as fast as they can, getting a drink … and doing it all in reverse. Some things were different in England: the food and the water for starters. So McKenna began bringing his own over from Ireland. Some of the journeys to the tracks were a little convoluted. McKenna was always highly superstitious and drove in a circuitous manner to ensure that he did not pass a graveyard.

As much as horses, some greyhounds simply seem to take a liking to certain tracks. Perhaps it is just that they are comfortable with the configurations or that they are, for dog reasons, happy there. Many Irish greyhounds, in spite of suffering what in humans would be regarded as homesickness, took naturally to the camber and surroundings of White City.

McKenna himself lived a solitary existence, away from his wife Josie, his sons, John, Ger and Owen, and village life. McKenna never took a holiday and was never, otherwise, away from home.

He would say of the ennui: 'Those days before the GRA kennels at Potters Bar were disbanded were hell: the loneliness. They had a place up the way where you could have a mineral and there was a pool table. But it was not for me. In those days I found it hard to mix.

'Sundays were the worst. There wasn't the normal coming and going. It wasn't like home, where you could salute somebody and get into conversation with them … where you could even pick an argument … give a fella a bollocking, just to liven things up. There was nothing like that.'

As for the greyhounds, what they had not experienced before was the sheer size and noise of the crowds at White City. Even during the English Derby preliminaries, five-figure crowds ringed the racing circuit. The dogs had to become accustomed to the din. And so, in the days leading up to the final of the 1981 English Derby, the silence of a summer evening in the peculiarly rural part of Greater London that was Potters Bar, was broken by the brassy sound of bands belting out 'Rule Britannia', 'The Standard of St George March' or 'Land of Hope and Glory'. By exposing his dogs to the sort and level of sounds (on his kennel system) that they would be faced with at White City, McKenna acclimatised his charges.

Ger McKenna, his wife Josie, and their sons Ger and John after Yanka Boy won the 1967 Irish Cesarewitch at Navan.

The Big Night

Just over twenty-four hours later and the dogs faced the real thing: an atmosphere that the Romans must have savoured during the gladiatorial tournaments in the Colosseum … mixed with the strident strains of the band of Her Majesty's Royal Marines. Parkdown Jet, trained by McKenna for Corkmen Seán Barnett and Robert Shannon, took it all in his stride. He had heard it all before, under greyhound racing's principal conductor, 'The Maestro', as McKenna was known to his admirers and his peers. And

McKenna generates a great deal of affection in the followers of the sport: the man and simply the name. That night at White City – unless you had a serious connection to one of the other finalists – you really wanted Parkdown Jet to win … for McKenna's, the trainer's, sake.

Ger McKenna had been coming to White City since 1974, and had been written about so often in the *Sporting Life* that every race-goer felt they knew him. He had never won the race and was loved for this fact alone. He was part of the English Derby heritage, a stalwart of White City.

As the volume rose to a deafening crescendo on this sweaty June evening, the unfazed Parkdown Jet crouched and sprang forward in the striped jacket of trap six. The ever-superstitious McKenna has, like other trainers, an aversion to blue greyhounds. There is no biological reason for this. It appears simply to be based on the fact that blue dogs (as opposed to black or brindle, the commoner colours) are unusual and attractive and tend to get patted too much. The

result is that they get soft and lose the aggression, drive and urgency needed to beat the other dogs to the quarry. And, in the charge to the opening corner, McKenna must have believed all the old wives' tales and had misgivings about the blue dog.

It was a big night, too, for Joe Kelly. The Wicklowman was a contract trainer at Owlerton, a giant of a track in Sheffield, and having Barley Field in the London final was the pinnacle of a long career and a hard life that yielded few luxuries. Victory for his runner would have meant everything to Kelly. As it happened, Kelly drew trap three and Barley Field was squeezed in a first-bend concertina. Such happenings seem to take minutes but last barely a second. Barley Field was on the ground with four other runners, trying to disengage themselves from the scrum.

The programme for the 1981 English Derby final at White City, London, won by Parkdown Jet.

The Trap Draw

Always a matter for lively debate in the run-up to a major decider is the advantage or otherwise of the trap draw. Traps three and four are not generally favoured as they invite crowding from a brace of dogs on either side. Trap four is called the 'coffin box'. Trap one should be a help because the greyhounds coming from here take, technically, the shortest route. It does not really work that way, though, and trap one has a poorer record in the English Derby final than should, according to the law of probability, be the case.

Trap six enjoys natural favour because having the lure on the outside of the runners is the norm in these islands (as opposed to America where they have an 'inside hare'), and greyhounds, as they were originally bred to do, like to be on top of the hare … to course it.

Being on the outside, of course, means that the trap-six runner only has to worry about interference on its inside. The difference is even greater in a final because, with the crowd baying and the greyhounds unable to hear the bell, and the hare trundling along the rail in the seconds before trap-lift, the gaze-hound in six is quite simply the one to spot the hare first.

AN EMERALD DERBY

From Caherciveen to Limavady they will be glued to their television sets tonight as Irish Television relays the Spillers Derby excitement captured and transmitted to millions by BBC 2's cameras.

Irish eyes have been smiling all the way in this year's Derby. From the second round onwards every runner has been Irish bred and three of tonight's Finalists are also trained in Ireland.

The veteran of the line-up is BARLEY FIELD, nearing four years of age, whose sprightly early pace and railing ability have been a feature of the classic. He is perhaps the key runner for should he again break fast he will make it difficult for RAHAN SHIP and increase the advantage held by the new record holder PARKDOWN JET who is the only seeded wide runner. IN FLIGHT could take off fast from trap five. CLOHAST FLAME can start quickly and finishes well. PRINCE SPY will give them a start but gets every yard of this testing trip.

So with our thanks to Spillers Foods Ltd for their generous sponsorship we look for a great final to start this second half-century of greyhound racing's premier classic.

Display

The Band of H.M. Royal Marines
(Royal Marines School of Music)

under the direction of

Lt.Col. T. R. Mason, M.V.O., L.R.A.M., A.R.C.H., L.G.S.M., R.M.
Principal Director of Music Royal Marines

Prize Money

WINNER £25,000

and Derby Challenge Trophy (to be held for one year) and Trophy

SECOND £5,000;   THIRD £2,500;   OTHERS £1,500

Winning Trainer £500 & Trophy
Winning Breeder £500 & Trophy

Ger McKenna had been coming to White City since 1974, and had been written about so often in the Sporting Life that every race-goer felt that they knew him. He had never won the race and was loved for this fact alone. He was part of the English Derby heritage, a stalwart of White City.

The result of the 1981 English Derby final at White City, London, showing the victory for Parkdown Jet.

10.28—10th RACE - OR   500 Metres Flat

THE SPILLERS GREYHOUND DERBY FINAL

THE SPILLERS DERBY TROPHY WILL BE PRESENTED BY
MRS. CHARLES AULD,
WIFE OF THE MANAGING DIRECTOR, SPILLERS FOODS LTD.

2nd QUINELA POOL—3rd LEG

(race card details of runners: RAHAN SHIP, PRINCE SPY, BARLEYFIELD, CLOHAST FLAME, IN FLIGHT, PARKDOWN JET with their recent form, times and trainers)

ABANDONED MEETING

In the event of an abandoned meeting, retain this race card. If owing to a mechanical breakdown or weather conditions it be decided to abandon a meeting before the fourth race has been completed Patrons will be admitted free to one of the five following meetings on production of the complete race card of the abandoned meeting.
UNDER NO CIRCUMSTANCES CAN ANY MONEY BE REFUNDED.

DUELLA DOUBLE - BOOTHS OPEN AFTER THIS RACE

In a twinkling, Parkdown Jet had rounded the ruck. It was exhilarating to the onlooker, though not breathtaking running from the winner. Parkdown Jet had poached just enough of a lead to hold off Prince Spy, one of the rank outsiders. Prince Spy was owned by Grace Costello, the wife of prominent London-Irish businessman Eddie, who had spent a fortune trying to buy the right dog to win the English Derby. There was much irony in the fact that Costello's 33/1 'no-hoper' would come closer to making his English Derby vision a reality than his much-vaunted favourites.

But if there was ever a hard-luck story, then it was Rahan Ship's. His trainer John Haynes has done so much as an administrator for his fellow trainers in Britain, but back then he was an Irish trainer by virtue of being based near Dublin. Victory for Haynes would have been Faithful Hope or Whisper Wishes or Ballinderry Ash in reverse: Haynes,

Luckless . . . Dublin-based trainer John Haynes with Rahan Ship, which finished third in the 1981 English Derby final at White City.

As a trainer, McKenna had been forced onto the winner's podium on so many occasions. He had never looked comfortable. He appeared particularly ill-at-ease on this night and, one felt, he wanted to be alone with his own thoughts.

The right note . . . Trainer Ger McKenna with Lartigue Note, winner of the 1989 English Derby at Wimbledon.

the quintessential Englishman training an Irish winner of the Derby. The previous Saturday, Parkdown Jet had set a new track record when running 29.09 for the 500 metres. Seasoned observers suspected that he had peaked a week early, but he had enough in reserve – just – to win the final in a slow 29.57.

The Win

At the end of the race, 29.57 seconds of pent-up emotion gave way to pandemonium. McKenna was overwhelmed, lost in a sea of ecstatic people celebrating: many were family members, others simply well-wishers, and the rest just strangers who had backed his winner.

As a trainer, McKenna had been forced onto the winner's podium on so many occasions. He had never looked comfortable. He appeared particularly ill-at-ease on this night and, one felt, he wanted to be alone with his own thoughts. He looked shocked by the frenzied nature of the reception, and numbed by the sudden realisation of a long-held dream fulfilled.

Back in Borrisokane, most homes had a single television channel: Radio Telefís Éireann. The odd aerial in Borris, and ten miles away in Nenagh, indicated those who could get the BBC. However, most of the extended McKenna family did not see the final on television: they had decamped to London. They had been there in previous years to commiserate with McKenna on his disappointments and, in 1981, they were there to share in the celebrations. As far as Ger McKenna was concerned, the wild parties were for others, whether in London or back at home. His quiet satisfaction would be in the next week, on his return to the County Tipperary village, walking up the main street and recounting with neighbours what had happened in the capital of England.

Ger McKenna's first English Derby was always going to be special, and sportsmen tend to treasure that kind of breakthrough more than their other achievements

Lartigue Note

Eight years on from his victory with Parkdown Jet, and five years after achieving his other remaining major ambition – winning the Waterloo Cup, with Tubbertelly Queen – McKenna returned to London. The kennels at Potters Bar but a memory, McKenna was based at the village of Tiddington, near Oxford.

One would need to know almost nothing about the ideal conformation of the racing dog to recognise that Lartigue Note was a near-perfect specimen. He was owned by Cathal McCarthy, who has a serious interest in fast dogs and has an equine stud farm near Navan, County Meath. Lartigue Note was bred by Tom Moore, a dreamer whose dreams had been fuelled when he sat at home in Ballybunion, County Kerry, and watched on television Parkdown Jet win the English Derby at White City.

Lartigue Note was named after a prototype monorail system that the French engineer Charles Lartigue had built to travel between Listowel and the seaside village of Ballybunion in north Kerry. During the build-up to the final, one sensed an uncharacteristic confidence in the McKenna camp: after the dog's semi-final defeat, McKenna was moved to say that he would win the final no matter what box the trap draw handed him. In the final itself, Lartigue Note might himself have been on the monorail. He barely moved off a straight course. Coming from trap two, he careered down the second lane as if programmed to do so, and won in a blue blur. There was no veering to either side. His was among the most facile of wins.

By the time of Lartigue Note's win, coverage of greyhound racing, as with so many sports, had passed from the BBC to satellite television. Back in Borrisokane, the owner of one of the public houses had ordered a newfangled dish that enabled the village to watch the live action from Wimbledon. Come the Saturday in 1989, the dish had not been delivered. And so, illuminated by streetlights, villagers gathered outside Slevin's electrical store and watched through the window as Lartigue Note, via satellite, put Borrisokane back on the map.

The last Irish trainer to win the Derby at White City, McKenna had beaten his colleagues to be the first Irish trainer of a Derby winner at Wimbledon; and he remains the only handler to have trained winners of the Derby at the two tracks.

Times

Irish dogs have tended not to run particularly fast finals. Mick The Miller was good on his day but his 29.96 for 480 metres in 1929 was easily bettered (29.72) by Wild Woolley just three years later. The Grand Canal (1962) was clocked at 29.09, but every winner thereafter would cover the 480 metres in faster times. Indian Joe (1980) ran 29.68 and Parkdown Jet (1981) did 29.57. The latter had set a track record at the penultimate stage, but Balliniska Band had recorded 29.16 in the 1977 decider, again over 500 metres at White City. Lartigue Note (28.79), Farloe Melody (28.88), Shanless Slippy (28.66), Chart King (28.76), Droopys Scholes (28.62) and Loyal Honcho (28.60) were by no means the swiftest winners since the switch to Wimbledon.

It underlines the fact that – while many set store by the clock and some see it as the sole indicator – stopwatches are merely a gauge of ability. The evidence of your own eyes, the manner in which a greyhound wins rather than a winning time or distance, is a more reliable yardstick.

As far as the English Derby (and Irish Derby, too) is concerned, it may be a case that Irish-trained greyhounds are prepared so that nothing is left to chance in the semi-finals. Getting to the final in a week's time is all that matters. You can take your chances then. Perhaps it was this that McKenna had in mind when he sent Parkdown Jet out to break the White City track record in 1981. He had gone back 0.48 of a second in a week, a substantial amount in race terms; but he still won the final.

With Lartigue Note, it was not his times but the manner of his running that had persuaded McKenna to buy the dog from Tom Moore on Cathal McCarthy's behalf.

Guinness is good for you ... A packed
Shelbourne Park, Dublin, on one of the
early nights of sponsored racing.

13 THE IRISH DERBY 1932–1952
HEADING FOR 'ROUGH WATERS'

Two Dublin Tracks

The Irish Coursing Club took control of greyhound racing in Ireland at a meeting in Dublin on 31 January 1928. The meeting was attended by members of the ICC executive committee and by the owners of the greyhound tracks then in existence: Celtic Park in Belfast and Shelbourne Park in Dublin. Some of the personnel involved were on the ICC executive committee and were also directors of the National Greyhound Racing Company, which had bookmaker Hugh McAlinden at the helm.

If the ICC thought that the rest would be smooth sailing, it was sadly mistaken. Later in the same year, a company called the Dublin Greyhound and Sports Association went into business in Harold's Cross. The early history of greyhound racing in Ireland is overshadowed by the poor relationship between the two Dublin tracks.

The National Greyhound Racing Company had been incorporated in December 1926, the directors having been inspired by what they saw in Manchester, where greyhound racing in Britain had got underway in July of that year. April 1927 had seen the inaugural greyhound race in Belfast and the same National Greyhound Racing Company Limited that organised racing in Belfast repeated the success in Dublin in May of that year. The racing in Dublin, of course, was at Shelbourne Park. Dealing with two tracks, both under the same management, had made matters straightforward for the ICC.

The First 'Irish Derby' and the Classics

Enter the Dublin Greyhound and Sports Association and its stadium at Harold's Cross. The management here immediately set about copying the English format and staged an 'Irish Derby'. Entry Badge won the inaugural English Derby, over 500 yards, at White City in London in 1927. A greyhound called Tipperary Hills won what Harold's Cross dubbed the Irish Derby, or National Derby, when the track was but a year old. The trainer, Billy Quinn, came from Killenaule, County Tipperary, a hamlet from where Matt O'Donnell would later send out a Waterloo Cup winner at Altcar (Minnesota Miller, 1976) and an English Derby

winner at Wimbledon (Farloe Melody, 1992). Billy Quinn won subsequent runnings of the Harold's Cross event, but the annals have been unkind to Tipperary Hills – history and the ICC do not recognise him as a Derby winner, as the Harold's Cross race was never deemed to be a Classic.

The status of competitions and whether they should be regarded as Classics would continue to be a contentious matter. It appears that the ICC did not address the Classics question until August 1931. A year later, it released the list: the Derby would go to Shelbourne Park; the Oaks to Clonmel (the ICC's home track); the St Leger to Celtic Park; the National Sprint to Dunmore Stadium; and the Grand National to Harold's Cross. There are now fourteen Classics on the calendar; and, of the original quintet, only Shelbourne Park still holds the Derby and Harold's Cross has the Grand National. The others have moved. Both the Derby and the Grand National have, however, been elsewhere in the meantime. The other Classics are the Irish Cesarewitch (Mullingar), Easter Cup and Ladbrokes '600' (both Shelbourne Park), National Breeders' Produce Stakes (Clonmel), Corn Cuchulainn and Puppy Derby (both Harold's Cross), Irish Laurels (Cork), Golden Jacket (Galway) and Unraced Classic (Tralee).

Harold's Cross vs Shelbourne Park

Back in 1932, the owners of Harold's Cross were miffed that they were not getting the Derby, as they had started it! Worse still was the fact that the glamour event was going to their Dublin rivals at Shelbourne Park. In retaliation, Harold's Cross decided that it would go its own way by refusing to stage the Irish Grand National – the race it had been allocated.

Regardless of the squabbling behind the scenes, the fact that there were two tracks operating in the capital was a huge bonus for owners in the south. Before Shelbourne Park was opened, owners, trainers and greyhounds had to endure a long and uncomfortable journey to Belfast. The first race at Celtic Park was the curtain-raiser to a Monday-afternoon meeting at Easter, and owner Jim Tuite and his winning four-year-old, Mutual Friend, had to travel to Belfast from

Oldcastle, County Meath. The following month, Tuite would have had the luxury of only having to journey 'down the road' to Dublin for the opening Saturday-night fixture. Mind you, the winner of the first race at the Ringsend circuit, Morning Prince, had come from the townland of Caherelly, County Limerick.

To break the impasse, what now seems a sensible compromise was proposed and adopted. The Irish Derby would, from 1934, alternate between the two Dublin tracks. There were two exceptions – a 1939 running in Limerick and a 1942 running in Cork. In 1970, the Derby found a permanent home at Shelbourne Park.

The Early Years of the Irish Derby

Before this happy state of affairs, Guidless Joe had won in 1932 what is now officially regarded as the first Irish Derby, this one having been afforded Classic rank by the ICC. As would so often be the case in the early history of the great event, Guidless Joe came fresh off the coursing field. The dog was owned by the jockey Jack Moylan – grandfather to one of the all-time great jockeys, eleven-times British champion, Pat Eddery. Moylan was to win horse-racing's Irish Derby at the Curragh in consecutive seasons on Slide On (1944) and Piccadilly (1945). Guidless Joe was trained by Mick Horan, who was the trainer of Mick The Miller in 1929 when he won his first English Derby at White City.

Even in an age of dual-purpose greyhounds, Guidless Joe was obviously an exceptional performer on track and field. The same was undoubtedly true of Monologue, the second winner of the Irish Derby at Shelbourne Park. While Moylan was a Munster man, the home province of Leinster had the trophy in 1933 through Monologue's owner Luke Maher, who hailed from Paulstown, County Kilkenny. The connection between greyhound sport and the hurling stronghold of Kilkenny has always been strong, and Derby crowds were swollen by the simple expedient of having the final coincide with the horse show at the Royal Dublin Society grounds in Ballsbridge or the all-Ireland finals in Gaelic games at Croke Park. Coinciding with the Croke Park deciders is something to which Bord na gCon has successfully reverted in more recent years for the staging

History-maker . . . Proud owner Jim Tuite, Oldcastle, County Meath, with his four-year-old, Mutual Friend, winner of the first greyhound race to be staged in Ireland.

of the Paddy Power-sponsored Irish Derby. The record of Monologue shows that she won the 1932 Easter Cup at the Dublin track and the coursing Oaks at Clonmel.

The management at Harold's Cross finally found favour in 1934, and the Irish Derby of that year went to Tim Fennin from Athy, County Kildare, and his Frisco Hobo. The success of Minstrel Rover at Harold's Cross in 1936 had an even bigger audience in that it was the first broadcast on what is now RTÉ radio.

P Prefix

In greyhound racing, it is possible to buy your own prefix to clearly identify your runners. In this way, a number of greyhounds have become synonymous with their owners and breeders. A prime example is the 'Westmead' prefix, which marks out the greyhounds bred, owned and – in this case – trained by Nick Savva. Corkman Denis Lynch had the famous 'Knockrour' prefix, and Brendan Matthews, a great breeder-owner-trainer in both coursing and racing, has had a number of prefixes, including 'Townview'.

The Irish Derby on the Move

There has always been a certain incongruity in the fact that two Dublin tracks had the monopoly of the Irish Derby. It did, of course, make obvious commercial sense to hold the race in the country's largest centre of population; but most of the competitors were coming from outside 'the Pale'. For all its size and the fact that it is the centre of government, only current appointee Tim Gilbert has (of fifty-three members to serve so far on Bord na gCon) a Dublin address. Since most of the greyhounds were bred in the provinces, it was natural that there would be lobbying among Irish Coursing Club delegates to allocate an early running of the Derby to a track outside Dublin. With the influence exerted by

major centres of greyhound-rearing in Counties Cork and Limerick, it was axiomatic that their voices would be heard.

An effort to calm tensions may have been the reason why the Irish Coursing Club sanctioned the removal of the Irish Oaks from its local Clonmel track to Harold's Cross. The first Irish Oaks was won by Queen of the Suir over 550 yards at Clonmel in 1932. The bitch Classic was next run over 525 yards there in the following season. However, it then took on a pattern similar to the Derby by alternating between the Dublin tracks until 1970. Cork and Limerick hosted renewals of the Oaks on three occasions between them, the last winner crowned outside Dublin being Mad Printer, in Cork in 1943.

Lilac's Luck upset the odds to win the 1945 Irish Derby at Harold's Cross.

The deal was also done that the first Irish Derby to be run outside Dublin would go to Limerick, and that Cork would get the Classic at a later date. Limerick got the top competition in 1939, but did not get the trophy. It went to Roscommon man J.J. Doran and his Marchin' Thro' Georgia. The Derby went from Shannonside, via two more runnings at Shelbourne Park, to Leeside, Cork, in 1942. This time the locals did prevail when Uacterlainn Riac, owned by Jerry Crowley, Ovens, County Cork, was successful.

Tanist and Western Post

There had been an even greater significance to the 1940 result when the winner was Tanist. Greyhound racing in Ireland had by this point been going for thirteen years. In the early years, the track runners had all come straight from the coursing fields. Even Irish Derby winners were required to earn their keep outside of the racing season, and they reverted to the winter code. It was, however, inevitable that the rising level of prize money on the track would make racing ever more attractive to owners. It made sense that owners and trainers would now specialise in the track game. Trainers of racehorses were in a similar position, and Vincent O'Brien and, later, Aidan O'Brien both gave up National Hunt racing – both were highly decorated in the field – to concentrate on the more lucrative Flat racing.

Tanist arguably marks a line in this respect. He was bred by a 'W. Twyford', which – with shades of Mick The Miller – was the pseudonym of a Catholic priest. Tanist was trained in Killenaule, County Tipperary, by Billy Quinn whose Tipperary Hills had been denied by the bureaucrats the accolade of first winner of the Irish Derby. The exceptional ability of Tanist on the track was underlined by his winning of the 1940 Derby in 29.82 for the 525 yards. Eight winners before him had failed to beat the thirty-second barrier, and it would be another eight before Western Post went inside that mark. Times were gradually getting faster, and would continue to do so. Yet it would be 1950 (Crossmolina Rambler's 29.70) before an Irish Derby finalist ran faster than Tanist. The first greyhound to run faster than thirty seconds in any event at Shelbourne Park had been Tanist's full brother by an earlier mating of Inler and Tranquilla, a dog called Talis.

But even before Crossmolina Rambler could lower the Tanist time in a decider, something even more remarkable occurred: less than a score of years since the first running of the premier Classic, a winner (Tanist) had sired a future winner (Daring Flash). That was by no means the end of it, and Tanist also sired Mad Tanist, which became the next prolific sire of Classic winners. Mad Tanist was destined not to win the Irish Derby of 1944 or 1945, but he was responsible for the 1951 Irish Derby winner Carmody's Tanist and the English Derby winner of the same season, Ballylanigan Tanist. The feat of Tanist – winning an Irish Derby before siring another winner – would not be repeated until the 1966 winner Always Proud produced a worthy son in the 1969 winner Own Pride.

Another notable Irish Derby winner of the period was Western Post, in 1948. The prize had now increased to £1,000 and the winner was trained by Paddy Moclair, who was a noted footballer with his native county of Mayo.

Flapping

Greyhound racing was still a private business under Irish Coursing Club control; but, as the Irish Derby moved into the 1950s, there remained a grey area beyond anyone's control. 'Flapping' is to the greyhound game what pony racing is to the world of the thoroughbred horse. It is an unlicensed sub-culture in which many young jockeys learn their trade

Daring Flash, a son of the 1940 winner Tanist, won the Irish Derby at Harold's Cross in 1947.

There were unlicensed gatherings in Ireland, known as rag meetings; but the fear of being discovered and reported to Bord na gCon and then getting suspended from mainstream racing was such a disincentive that they died out.

before they come into regulated stables and into the strict regime of the Turf Club. The Turf Club takes a dim view of licensed trainers running horses there (under false names, of course), but there is a benign understanding that it is a breeding ground for the young riding stars of the future.

The same sort of stance was taken with regard to the flapping of Irish dogs in Britain, where unlicensed tracks have always been a big part of the scene. There were unlicensed gatherings in Ireland, known as rag meetings; but the fear of being discovered and reported to Bord na gCon and then getting suspended from mainstream racing was such a disincentive that they died out.

Jimmy Lalor

Jimmy Lalor was one of the most colourful characters in greyhound racing at the time. He was both a fearless bookmaker and an intrepid backer. So, when he bought a dog called Rough Waters at the Shelbourne Park sales, he was not inclined to enlighten his fellow bookmakers as to the true identity of the owner. Lalor registered Rough Waters as owned by Patricia Cummins, which was his wife's maiden name. He was summoned by the Irish Coursing Club and instructed to register the dog correctly as being owned by Mrs Patricia Lalor

The dog then disappeared … while he did a tour of Scotland's 'flaps', assuming a different name for every outing. Come 1952, Rough Waters was back racing under his own name and listed as being officially trained by Jimmy Lalor's brother Henry. It had rained cats and dogs in the twelve hours before the 1952 Derby final. Rough Waters made the fastest start, and he was away and clear, turning for home. However, the heavy ground took its toll and he held on by only a neck in a desperate finish. Rapidly closing was Dismal, a dog owned by one of Lalor's great rivals, fellow bookmaker Paddy Meehan. The Irish Derby trophy had pride of place in the front room of Jimmy Lalor's home off Dublin's Navan Road.

The Lalor household was one of bookmakers. Three of Jimmy's four sons – John, Jim and Gary – followed in his footsteps. The Lalor house was less than four miles from the city centre. About the same distance further out the Navan Road is Blanchardstown. That village had become home to a Kerryman, Tom Lynch, and a kennel of greyhounds that had become the bane of the bookmakers, and whose 'Spanish' prefix would forever resonate through the sporting world.

All smiles . . . Owner Jimmy Lalor (second from left) receives the Irish Derby trophy from Dublin Lord Mayor Andy Clerkin after the 1952 victory of Rough Waters at Shelbourne Park. Also pictured are (extreme left) trainer Henry Lalor and (extreme right) track manager Paddy O'Donoghue.

Irish Derby Winners

Run at Shelbourne Park, except in the asterisked years

* Harold's Cross, **Cork, ***Limerick

525 yards: 1932–85; 550 yards: 1986 onwards

Year	Winner	Time	Year	Winner	Time	Year	Winner	Time
1932	Guidless Joe	30.36	1960	Perry's Apple	29.55	1988	Make History	30.26
1933	Monologue	30.52	1961	Chieftain's Guest*	29.45	1989	Manorville Magic	30.53
1934	Frisco Hobo*	30.45	1962	Shane's Legacy	29.58	1990	The Other Toss	30.14
1935	Roving Yank	30.18	1963	Drumahiskey Venture*	29.60	1991	Ardfert Mick	30.18
1936	Minstrel Rover*	30.48	1964	Wonder Valley	29.30	1992	Manx Treasure	30.53
1937	Muinessa	30.83	1965	Ballyowen Chief*	29.42	1993	Daleys Denis	30.30
1938	Abbeylara*	30.09	1966	Always Proud	29.44	1994	Joyful Tidings	30.35
1939	Marchin' Thro' Georgia***	30.05	1967	Russian Gun*	29.44	1995	Batties Rocket	30.19
1940	Tanist	29.82	1968	Yellow Printer	29.11	1996	Tina Marina	30.20
1941	Brave Damsel	30.64	1969	Own Pride*	29.20	1997	Toms The Best	30.09
1942	Uacterlainn Riac**	30.22	1970	Monalee Pride	29.28	1998	Eyeman	30.09
1943	Famous Knight*	30.26	1971	Sole Aim	29.12	1999	Spring Time	30.00
1944	Clonbonny Bridge	30.53	1972	Catsrock Daisy	29.20	2000	Judicial Pride	29.68
1945	Lilac's Luck*	30.12	1973	Bashful Man	28.82	2001	Cool Performance	30.01
1946	Steve	30.20	1974	Lively Band	29.11	2002	Bypass Byway	29.42
1947	Daring Flash*	30.04	1975	Shifting Shadow	29.35	2003	Climate Control	29.71
1948	Western Post	29.90	1976	Tain Mor	29.35	2004	Like A Shot	29.87
1949	Spanish Lad*	29.87	1977	Linda's Champion	29.52	2005	He Said So	29.66
1950	Crossmolina Rambler	29.70	1978	Pampered Rover	29.23	2006	Razldazl Billy	29.49
1951	Carmody's Tanist*	29.64	1979	Penny County	29.28	2007	Tyrur Rhino	29.73
1952	Rough Waters	29.95	1980	Suir Miller	29.18	2008	Shelbourne Aston	29.83
1953	Spanish Battleship*	29.78	1981	Bold Work	29.32			
1954	Spanish Battleship*	29.64	1982	Cooladine Super	29.34			
1955	Spanish Battleship*	29.53	1983	Belvedere Bran	29.65			
1956	Keep Moving	29.18	1984	Dipmac	29.15			
1957	Hopeful Cutlet*	29.60	1985	Tubbercurry Lad	29.14			
1958	Colonel Perry	29.79	1986	Kyle Jack	30.41			
1959	Sir Frederick*	29.30	1987	Rathgallen Tady	30.49			

Tom's the best . . . Trainer Tom Lynch (right) with his 1967 Irish Derby winner Russian Gun, the dog's owner Hugh Marley and his wife.

14 TOM LYNCH
THE ARRIVAL OF THE 'SPANISH' ARMADA

The Greatest Greyhound

After all the twists and turns, in greyhound sport as much as in any other, you arrive at one destination, which is the inevitable question: who or what was the best? An impossible poser, of course. After all, most of the legendary names have never been seen by the current generation of experts, pundits and devotees.

Greyhound sport invites ready comparisons with horse racing. Arkle is often cited as the best of all time in this sphere. Many commentators who saw Arkle win the Gold Cup in Cheltenham in 1964, 1965 and 1966 are around today. These wins were an outstanding achievement for the Tom Dreaper-trained gelding, and while, occasionally, other horses get mentioned in the same breath, nobody really believes that there has ever been a match for Arkle, before or since. The feeling that Arkle was the greatest is based not on speed or prize money won, because neither is a satisfactory gauge a half-century later. Prize money now bears no comparison to what was available in the 1960s, and, like humans, the racing animal just gets faster. The only satisfactory markers at this remove are the contender's achievements and the quality of the opposition.

Before time became a factor in greyhound racing, the arguments raged over the respective merits of coursing dogs. The principals in open coursing are the Waterloo Cup winners Master M'Grath and Fullerton. Master M'Grath won three times in four years (1868–71). Amazingly, even that record was bettered by Fullerton, which won in four straight years (1889–92). In their outstanding literary and pictorial history of the Waterloo Cup, Charles Blanning and Sir Mark Prescott make the bald statement, 'Fullerton was the greatest greyhound that ever ran.' Yet, it is fair to say that almost everyone in these islands with no intimate knowledge of greyhounds will have heard of Master M'Grath. Few will know of the exploits of Fullerton.

Twenty-seven years into the next century, and away from the variables associated with coursing behind the hare, Irish greyhound fanciers would have a yardstick by which to mark one dog apart from others: the clock. But even time itself would be overtaken. Through improved diets and training techniques, greyhounds would become faster than those of the previous generation. And even as everyone became accustomed to what would be mean time for the standard distance of 525 yards (or 500 metres), the running ground changed from grass to sand and the times became unrecognisable from the old days.

Overall achievement is the only reliable barometer, something to which Blanning and Prescott would subscribe since neither saw Fullerton other than in his stuffed state at the Natural History Museum at Tring, Hertfordshire.

The Greats of the Early Years

There was an array of outstanding racing greyhounds in the first score and more years of the sport's existence in Ireland. Old Blade won the Easter Cup in 1928 and 1929 at Shelbourne Park. Astra won the Easter Cup in 1945 and 1946 as well as the second running of the Irish Puppy Derby at Harold's Cross in 1944. The bitch Chicken Sandwich won an Irish Oaks at Harold's Cross in the twilight of her career in 1936, but is also recorded, two years earlier, as winning an early Irish St Leger, one of the few to be run at Shelbourne Park. Monologue was another bitch from the upper echelon to annexe the 1932 Easter Cup and 1933 Irish Derby (both at Shelbourne Park) to her coursing credits. Monarch Of The Glen has to be right up there, too. He won the Irish St Leger in 1942 at Harold's Cross and retained that trophy at Celtic Park in 1943 while also adding the Easter Cup in 1943. Derby winners did not necessarily reproduce their form elsewhere. However, that comment did not apply to Abbeylara. The winner of the Irish Derby at Harold's Cross in 1938, Abbeylara won an Irish St Leger (1938) and Easter Cup (1939), both at Shelbourne Park.

Tim O'Connor

Another twenty-seven years into the now established sport, a greyhound emerged that would be the Irish track's first indisputable canine superstar. In terms of track racing, Spanish Battleship certainly eclipsed all that had gone before. Many would contend that his credits have never been matched since. Perhaps, they never will be …

Mick and the Miller . . . Golden Miller, which was owned by the eccentric Dorothy Paget and which dominated the Cheltenham Gold Cup (1932–36) and also won the Aintree Grand National (1934), pictured with Mick The Miller, which won the English Derby at White City, London, in 1929 and 1930 when he was owned by the elegant Phyllis Kempton.

Q Question Mark

Ever since it was first published under Irish Coursing Club secretary T.A. Morris in 1923, the *Irish Greyhound Stud Book* has maintained an unchallenged status of great integrity. There have, however, been isolated incidents that have demanded investigation. In one celebrated case, Commandant Joseph Fitzpatrick (ICC secretary 1969–86) put a question mark over the parentage of one litter of pups. When Fitzpatrick could not be satisfied, he included a footnote to the effect that either of two sires could have fathered the litter. The humorous response of the breeder was to name one of the pups Who's Me Da?.

The making of Spanish Battleship was in the marrying of two talents. Tim O'Connor and Tom Lynch were Kerry-men, the former from Killorglin and the latter from Cahirciveen. That seems unusual now in that Killorglin and Cahirciveen are in the south of the county, and north Kerry is regarded as the county's greyhound stronghold. Yet, it was surely inevitable that the two would become confederates.

O'Connor was a Teachta Dála (TD), a member of the Irish Parliament in Dublin. He mated his bitch Cordial Moonlight to Shaggy Lad and produced a dog called Spanish Lad. The next time that she came into season, Cordial Moonlight was brought to Rebel Abbey and threw Spanish Chestnut. Trained by the owner-breeder, Spanish Lad and Spanish Chestnut clashed in the final of the Irish Laurels at Cork in 1949, and it was the pup Spanish Chestnut that beat his older half-brother. Spanish Chestnut returned to Cork in 1950 and retained his Laurels crown.

But, in the meantime, O'Connor aimed to capitalise on this purple patch. He headed north to Dublin and won the 1949 Irish Derby (held at Harold's Cross) with Cork runner-up Spanish Lad. That other Kerryman, Tom Lynch, was already showing that he possessed the same deadly eye as a trainer as O'Connor had displayed as a breeder. In a demonstration of his ability to keep a greyhound 'right' over a period of months and years, Lynch sent out Peaceful Lady to win the Irish Oaks at Harold's Cross in 1952 and repeated that achievement with the same bitch at Shelbourne Park in 1953.

Meanwhile, the O'Connor breeding fortunes were holding good. He leased a Tralee bitch called Ballyseedy Memory for mating purposes and put her to his dual Irish Laurels winner Spanish Chestnut. They produced the 1951 litter of which Spanish Battleship was a member. The dog showed limitations, but O'Connor still recognised the potential and sent the youngster to Tom Lynch.

Simply the best . . . The great Spanish Battleship pictured with owner Tim O'Connor.

Tom Lynch

Lynch was a heavy man with an enormous heart and a gentle soul. He had come to Dublin in 1932, the year of the first running of the Irish Derby, won by Guidless Joe, at Shelbourne Park. His initial job was at the rival track at Harold's Cross, where he supervised the starting traps. In 1933, he joined the staff at Joe McKenna's kennels near Templeogue. He married his former boss's daughter, Peg McKenna, in 1946. Joe and Peg's home was in Blanchardstown, County Dublin – on the road to Navan and on the border with County Meath. The Lynch family lived in the Main Street and the Lynch kennels were behind what is now The Greyhound Bar. The pub was run then by the Cleary family, and one of the sons was later a Catholic priest of national note, Father Michael Cleary. As a youngster, he was one of the Lynch kennel-hands.

Lynch had almost made a sensational start to his solo career when his charge Down Signal nearly won the 1944 Irish Derby final at Shelbourne Park. The dog was, in fact, deemed to have been beaten by Clonbonny Bridge in 30.53 for the 525 yards. The only Irish Derby won in a slower time was that of 1937, which fell to the bitch Muinessa in 30.83. The 30.53 of Clonbonny Bridge was equalled by Manorville Magic in 1988 and Manx Treasure in 1992, but, at that stage, the race was being run over 550 yards!

Peg Lynch always believed the 'head' verdict against Down Signal, trained by her husband-to-be, to have been the wrong call. In those days, there were no photo-finishes, and track officials, especially those at Shelbourne Park, seemed reluctant to call a dead heat. One of the leading bookmakers at Shelbourne Park, Séamus Farrell, recalls how there was actually an official line at the Ringsend track that there was 'no such thing as a dead heat'. When the photo-finish came into being in the early 1960s and a dead heat was actually called, there was a prolonged chorus of derisory cheering from those present.

Lynch won his first bona fide Classic in 1948 when Lovely Louisa took the Irish Oaks at Harold's Cross. Another early star of the Lynch kennels was Imperial Dancer, which won the 1950 Irish Cesarewitch, although the event's 'Classic' status at that time is unsure. There was no doubting the fact that Tom Lynch had arrived when Peaceful Lady won the 1952 Irish Oaks at Harold's Cross, and in the following year at Shelbourne Park.

Spanish Battleship

And, so, it was under the sympathetic care of Tom Lynch that the talent was coaxed out of Spanish Battleship. He won the 1953 Irish Derby at Harold's Cross, an extraordinary coincidence in as much as the owner of the Irish Derby winner of the previous year, Jimmy Lalor, lived down the road and regarded the The Greyhound Bar as one of his 'locals'. Spanish Battleship was sent down to Cork in an effort to emulate his sire by winning the Irish Laurels. This time, Spanish Battleship simply emulated Spanish Lad by finishing second. He returned to the fray in 1954, winning the Easter Cup at Shelbourne Park, while also contesting an established competition (Corn An Tostal) at Harold's Cross, which he also won. Many would now regard this as unthinkable, but, just as greyhounds were competing in both coursing and track meets, so it was common then for them to run in track events that overlapped.

The Easter Cup was a significant credit to have on your record. It marked the traditional recommencement of the Irish racing campaign after the closed/coursing season. It had been the immediate target of Mick Horan and Father Martin Brophy before they went to win the English Derby in 1929 with Mick The Miller, the dog with which Spanish Battleship is most readily compared.

The track that Mick The Miller had regarded as 'home' would see another remarkable chapter in the Spanish Battleship story. Indeed, it is interesting that when Mick The Miller won his first English Derby, trainer Mick Horan was given as based at Shelbourne Park because the British were employing a contract-training system where trainers were attached to specific tracks. Mick Horan was, in fact, based near Trim, County Meath, but there is some evidence that dogs like Mick The Miller were kennelled overnight at the track at which they would be racing (obviously to cut back on travel).

There was no confining Tom Lynch and Spanish Battleship.

There was no confining
Tom Lynch and
Spanish Battleship.
Not only did Spanish
Battleship become the
first greyhound to win
the Irish Derby twice,
but he emulated his
kennel companion,
the Oaks-winning
Peaceful Lady, by
retaining his title at a
different track.

Spanish Battleship: a fine study of the
three-times winner of the Irish Derby.

Not only did Spanish Battleship become the first greyhound to win the Irish Derby twice but he emulated his kennel companion, the Oaks-winning Peaceful Lady, by retaining his title at a different track. His coming back a year after taking his first Derby at Harold's Cross and winning twelve months later at Shelbourne Park is the mark of greatness. Even greater things were to come. He took the Tipperary Cup at Thurles, and returned to action in 1955, a year of unprecedented achievement.

The Easter Cup annually saw the established stars clash with the rising stars, and its winning was for greyhounds of substance. And Spanish Battleship was back and winning it at Shelbourne Park for a second time, as well as the Irish Laurels in Cork. His crowning glory came at Harold's Cross. Spanish Battleship not only won the Derby for a third time but did so by running faster than before. His 29.78

for 525 yards at Harold's Cross was followed by a 29.64 at Shelbourne Park and a 29.53 back at Harold's Cross. The times do not matter as much as the three wins in three years; and even that is less important perhaps than the fact that he won the premier Classic at two tracks, another Classic (Irish Laurels) at yet another track (Cork) as well as the Easter Cup (twice) at the premier venue of Shelbourne Park, and the McCalmont Cup (also twice) at Kilkenny. Even by the following year (1956), Keep Moving had won the fastest-ever running of an Irish Derby final (29.18). And, at that stage, a greyhound called Prince Of Bermuda had rewritten all the rules pertaining to the speed at which the racing greyhound was expected to travel when he ran the Shelbourne Park circuit in 28.98.

Spanish Battleship had a constitution in keeping with the greyhound greats, such as Master M'Grath and Mick The

Miller. He was a handy size and appears never to have raced beyond a weight of sixty-four pounds; and he never did pass on his ability to a later generation. It is one of the quirks of the sport – in coursing and racing, and in both the male and female of the species – that the longer the dogs race at a high level, the less likely they are to be successful in the breeding paddocks.

Russian Gun

The Tom Lynch story did not end with Spanish Battleship. A dozen years on from the legendary canine's final Irish Derby appearance came Russian Gun. He won the 1967 Irish Derby at Harold's Cross, and only the brilliant Yellow Printer denied him the double at Shelbourne Park in 1968.

Back at Harold's Cross in 1969, Lynch turned out Monalee Gambler to run up to Own Pride. The latter was to be a first Irish Derby winner for Ger McKenna, trainer of Prince Of Bermuda. Tom Lynch sent out a fourth winner of the Irish Oaks in Gallant Maid in 1957 at Shelbourne Park, Springvalley Grand to win the 1960 National Breeders' Produce Stakes at Clonmel, and the last of eleven Classic winners came from the Blanchardstown kennels when Mark Anthony took the 1970 Irish St Leger in Limerick.

Tom Lynch and Spanish Battleship have both carved out for themselves a huge niche in the history of greyhound sport. The dog's legacy did not come through his offspring, but Tom Lynch would be the inspiration for those to come, including a son of the same name, his brother-in-law Gay McKenna and the McKenna dynasty.

R Racing Terms

Greyhound racing has a glossary all to itself, plus an abundance of abbreviations that are to be found in the programme:

ep	=	early pace
fa	=	fast away
sa	=	slow away
d	=	dog
b	=	bitch
bd	=	brindled
bk	=	black

Yellow Printer, which beat Russian Gun in the Irish Derby decider at Shelbourne Park in 1968, was sent by his joint-owner Pauline Wallis (later Pauline O'Donnell) to America where he made a lasting impact in the breeding ranks. He is pictured here with one of his handlers in England, Paddy Milligan.

JAMES
FARRELL

BLACK PoLo		1
PETER the TAILOR		2
BLADE SHADOW		3
LARKS WING		4
TYRUR RACHEL		5
SIEM REAP		6

James A. Farrell.

Like father . . . Bookmaker Séamus Farrell
supervises his son, also Séamus, as he
marks up the odds at Shelbourne Park.

15 SÉAMUS FARRELL

TRIUMPHS AND TRIBULATIONS OF A BOOKMAKER

In the early 1940s, when he was hardly fifteen years of age, Séamus Farrell started as a 'runner' for the Molloy family. The runner carried cash and messages from one bookmaker to another.

The Farrell Family

Séamus Farrell is almost as old as greyhound racing itself. In fact, he was born in October 1927, just six months after the sport came to Ireland. The Farrell family ties are strong – to one another and the greyhound-racing game.

Séamus was the youngest of three Farrell boys who grew up in a household in the Liberties, near Dublin's city centre. There was Charlie Farrell, whose son Raymond has worked as a bookmaker himself and is versed in the newer world of betting exchanges. Then came Paul, who is part of book-making culture. In his younger days, Paul was a tic-tac man, fluent in the mute language of the racecourse. His fleeting hands signed the odds from one end of the bookmaking line to the other. Made redundant by the walkie-talkie, even before the mobile telephone came along, Paul still goes nightly as a spectator to the Dublin dog tracks.

Séamus goes, too. Remarkably, he is still working. With his son of the same name, he alternates between making the 'book' and clerking. Another son, Paul, has a restaurant in New York but his father still renews Paul's bookmaker's licence annually in case he should ever come back. The family does not end there. Philomena Farrell, Séamus's sister, married Albert Sharpe, a nephew of the actor of the same name. The original Albert Sharpe was from Belfast and was a top-of-the-bill name in a number of productions, includ-ing the film of *Darby O'Gill and the Little People*, when he played opposite Jimmy O'Dea and Seán Connery. There was a great demand in cinema for the 'stage Irish' characters – a type epitomised in Hollywood by Barry Fitzgerald – and Albert Sharpe was much sought-after.

Philomena Farrell's sons, Albert and Paul Sharpe, are involved in the bookmaking business, too. Albert Sharpe runs the gaming side of Dublin businessman Dermot Desmond's empire, while Paul works for bookmaker Bernard Barry, the one-time Waterloo Cup sponsor whose family are also steeped in greyhound history.

Séamus Farrell's direct line of contact to the sport came through his father, Paul, who worked for the McAlinden family. The patriarch here, of course, was Hugh McAlinden, the bookmaker and Irish Coursing Club member who had gone to Manchester to see the first greyhound races at Belle Vue and who brought the sport to Celtic Park in Belfast in April 1927, in the face of opposition from the ICC secretary T.A. Morris. The McAlindens were the big bookmakers on the rails at Irish racecourses, and old Paul Farrell could hardly have had a stronger employer.

Séamus Farrell's Career

In the early 1940s, when he was hardly fifteen years of age, Séamus Farrell started as a 'runner' for the Molloy family. The runner carried cash and messages from one bookmaker to another. He took out his first bookmaking licence in his own name in 1950, a lifetime ago. After all, it was three years before Spanish Battleship's first Irish Derby and eight years before the formation of Bord na gCon. It was also a decade before the introduction of the totalisator onto Irish greyhound tracks.

His brother Charlie had already made a book at Navan, and Séamus Farrell also set up his first pitch there. The track was owned by the Cantwell family and Harry Barry, uncle of Bernard Barry, was both the leading bookmaker and grey-hound owner of the period.

There were seven races on the programmes in those days, and anything up to thirty bookmakers at every meeting at the County Meath venue. Bookmaking was highly competi-tive. On week nights, Séamus Farrell bet at Navan and, on Sundays, he moved to the flapping track at Santry for the afternoons and Chapelizod for the evenings. The flapping tracks involved greyhounds competing under assumed names and these races were obviously outside the Irish Coursing Club's regulatory net. There were many around the country, with the greyhounds chasing various ingenious artificial lures. Apart from the track at Santry, near Dublin Airport, there was a rare one on the banks of the Royal Canal – between Phibsboro and Glasnevin – which was a straight run, as opposed to a four-bend affair. Chapelizod survived until the advent of Bord na gCon, when its fixtures clashed with those at Harold's Cross. Bookmaking was strong but the appetite in the city for greyhound racing still had its limits. They were reached with three regulated tracks in the city, and so Chapelizod closed.

Apart from the evening racing during the week at Harold's Cross and Shelbourne Park, there were the morning trials at the public greyhound sales. Greyhounds with no known form were backed with substantial sums, the sessions attracting the big buyers and the bigger bookmakers.

Jimmy Lalor

Séamus Farrell now lives in the County Dublin village of Castleknock, equidistant between the places where his old bookmaking colleague Jimmy Lalor and the bookmaker's nemesis of the time, trainer Tom Lynch, had their homes. Farrell recalls: 'It is almost impossible to describe Jimmy Lalor at the time. He won the Irish Derby, of course, at Shelbourne Park in 1952 with Rough Waters which was trained by his brother. But he had greyhounds with every trainer. I remember that his brother and others used to protest that they had no room in their kennels; but once Jimmy put his eye on a dog at the sales, he decided that he would have to have it and the dog had to be accommodated. The easiest way to say it is that Jimmy Lalor was to greyhound racing then what J.P. McManus is to horse racing now. He must have had forty or more dogs on the go at the one time. It was hard to keep up.'

Farrell was not a bookmaker in Jimmy Lalor's life but a backer: 'I put on the bets for him and we would meet in The Greyhound Bar in Blanchardstown after racing. In those days, the pubs in Dublin had to close at ten o'clock in the evening and, after the dogs, Jimmy Lalor headed outside the city boundaries to Blanchardstown.'

Lalor was invariably accompanied by his bookmaker's clerk, Harry Allen, who later turned his hand to journalism and furnished the national newspapers with reports and results – a function in which he was assisted by his son Michael, who is still *in situ* in Harold's Cross and Shelbourne Park. Jimmy Lalor and Harry Allen were two highly opinionated men when it came to greyhound racing and the late-night sessions in The Greyhound Bar must have been pretty lively affairs.

Séamus Farrell recalls: 'Jimmy Lalor used to get in touch

and I would put on the bets. Just to give an example: I remember him giving me £1,000 (huge money in the 1950s) to have a double for him at Navan. I went there and the double came up. The arrangement was the usual one of meeting up in the pub in Blanchardstown to give him the winnings. But when I got there, Jimmy Lalor was pacing up and down and waiting for a phone call from Belfast. In those days, the telephone system was such that you had to pre-book long-distance telephone calls in advance. So, this

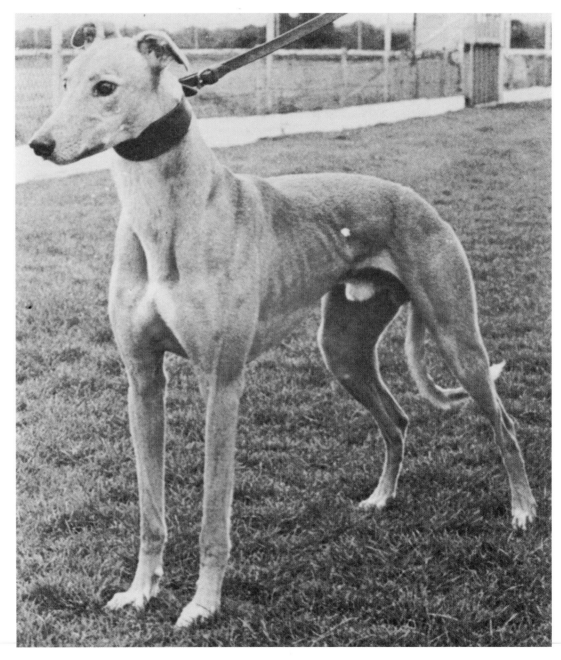

Top of the charts ... Lively Band, which was trained by Corkman Jack Murphy at Kilmessan, County Meath, hit the headlines in 1974 by winning the Irish Derby at Shelbourne Park and Irish St Leger at Market's Field.

Few would argue
other than that
Yellow Printer was the
fastest English-based
greyhound to win the
Irish Derby, and few
would contradict the
assertion that he was
the greatest non-Irish
greyhound to contest
the Irish Derby.

call had been booked the night before; and here we were waiting for the call. I had come in with the winnings from a £1,000 double in Navan but it seemed that the *real* money was on another dog altogether running in Belfast. Suddenly, the phone rang … Jimmy knew at this time that it was his call from Belfast. The dog had won and there was a big sigh of relief.'

Russian Gun, 1967

Not all of Séamus Farrell's evenings had happy endings. Into the affluent 1960s he decided to stick his neck out. The betting market on the night was incredibly strong. There was the average bookmaker on the 'outside' – the side of the

Bunny girl … Sarah's Bunny, which won the 1979 English Derby at White City, pictured at the Playboy Club, London. Sarah's Bunny was trained by Geoffrey DeMulder at Hall Green, Birmingham. By coincidence, the Irish Derby of the same year at Shelbourne Park was also won by a bitch, Penny County, which was trained by Matt Travers at Newcastle, County Dublin.

track opposite the grandstand – and those 'inside', who were prepared to lay the heavier bets. Overall, there were usually about 130 bookmakers in attendance at Shelbourne Park on a Saturday night.

Séamus Farrell felt sufficiently confident to bet on the inside. Yet, even here, nobody had really given much thought to the idea of making a long-odds book. This was the simple procedure of marking up the odds on all the runners in advance of the first round of a Classic. With the price of some greyhounds going to 100/1 and beyond, there was an obvious attraction for the backer. But it could leave the bookmaker badly exposed in the final if there had been an insufficient number of upsets during the earlier rounds. In this way, a bookmaker could end up with big liabilities on four or five of the six greyhounds in the decider. Sometimes, the burden of bets on one dog outweighed all others. A classic case in point came in 1967 when Séamus Farrell's other neighbour Tom Lynch came up with a black dog called Russian Gun. The Irish Derby took place at Harold's Cross in that year and Hugh Marley had paid £3,000 to Frank Muldoon from Dungannon, County Tyrone, for a black son of Pigalle Wonder, which had sired the 1964 Irish Derby winner Wonder Valley. It was a huge outlay, even for a man of means like Marley, who was a building contractor in Portadown, County Armagh. Like many others in that part of the country, Marley 'liked a bet'. In his case, it was something of a euphemism.

Farrell was up to his neck with Russian Gun, which he had laid at 20/1 before the start of the competition; but he had the right to believe that he could get him beaten in the final as the black dog was unfavourably drawn in trap three. The other bookmakers obviously believed that it would be the undoing for a normally poor starter. It was felt that Russian Gun would struggle to get a clear run round the bend at Harold's Cross, a track tighter than Shelbourne Park. Having been 20s ante-post, Russian Gun was still 5/1 on final night, an indication of his outside chance.

It was just the respective fortune of Farrell and Marley that the decider was the one occasion on which Russian Gun chose to bolt from traps. Russian Gun was a powerfully built greyhound at seventy-four pounds, and was still a puppy. He motored on down the back straight as his opponents got in each other's way. There were only two Irish Derby finals run subsequently over 525 yards in a slower time than the 29.44 of Russian Gun in 1967. That was of little consolation to Farrell, who had his worst Irish Derby result in sixty years as a licensed bookmaker.

The next season produced the result that he wished he had had in 1967. The year 1968 heralded a greyhound of exceptional quality. Few would argue other than that Yellow Printer was the fastest English-based greyhound to win the Irish Derby, and few would contradict the assertion that he was the greatest non-Irish greyhound to contest the Irish Derby. In the first round, John Bassett's charge clocked an astonishing 28.83 on the turf at Shelbourne Park, and shattered the 28.98 of Prince Of Bermuda's run over a decade

earlier. Russian Gun ran with credit in a decider that also included Leslie McNair's 1969 Irish Oaks winner Itsamint.

At least Séamus Farrell never needs to be reminded of the pain of 1967. The mammoth painting in The Greyhound Bar of a strapping black greyhound, bearing a striking resemblance to Russian Gun, has disappeared.

Also gone are Navan and the unlicensed tracks. In the wake of Ronnie Delaney's 1956 gold medal for the 1500 metres at the Olympic Games in Melbourne, middle-distance running became all the rage, and a Dublin optician, Billy Morton, created Santry Stadium as the home, not of unofficial greyhound racing, but of Irish athletics.

S Seeding

This system was designed with the intention of minimising the degree of trouble in races, especially immediately after the start and in the dash to the first turns. It was originally introduced in Britain in 1971. Greyhounds that show a preference for the rails are given inside draws; those with a preference for the outside are assigned the letter *w* to signify that they are wide runners. The system has since been expanded so that those who run down the middle of the track are given the letter *m* as middle runners. A race, therefore, may line up as: trap one, trap two, trap three (m), trap four (m), trap five (w) and trap six (w).

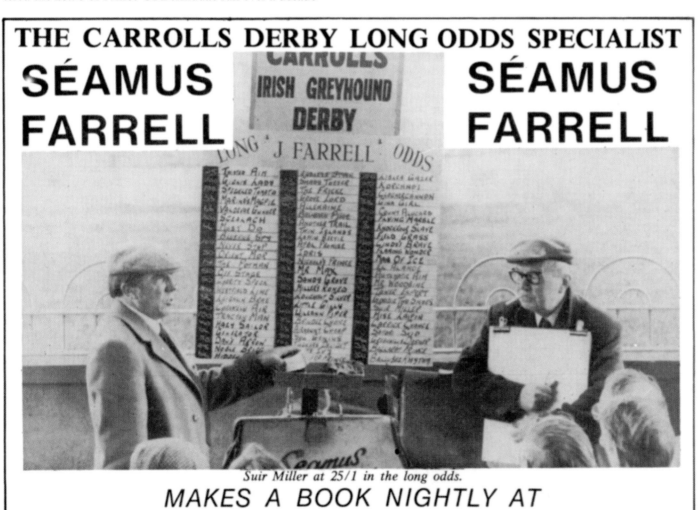

THE CARROLLS DERBY LONG ODDS SPECIALIST
SÉAMUS FARRELL SÉAMUS FARRELL
CARROLLS IRISH GREYHOUND DERBY
Suir Miller at 25/1 in the long odds.
MAKES A BOOK NIGHTLY AT HAROLDS CROSS AND SHELBOURNE PARK.

Sticking his neck out . . . Bookmaker Séamus Farrell prices up the long odds in a 1981 advertisement for the Irish Derby at Shelbourne Park.

Even now, the passing of the old track is lamented by trainers and bookmakers. Being beside the River Liffey, the running surface was regarded as being particularly safe by the latter, and some of the fastest greyhounds of the period were raced there.

Sideshow . . . A 1953 programme for midget car racing at the Chapelizod Greyhound Stadium.

Chapelizod

Changes were also coming about in another Dublin suburb where Séamus Farrell had made a pitch. The greyhound track at Chapelizod owed its existence to the entrepreneurial spirit of James Tallis Dixon. Born in 1888 and named after the sixteenth-century church composer and musician, Thomas Tallis, Dixon made his fortune (along with Eric Craigie of the still-famous auctioneering family) in buying and selling horses for the British army in Ireland. The profits allowed him to purchase a stately home and lands from Sam Broadbent in the County Dublin village of Chapelizod.

It was at the suggestion of a London businessman, Ike Geller, that Dixon decided to build the greyhound racing venue there. His company traded as the Dublin Greyhound Stadium Limited – a venture always opposed by Paddy O'Donoghue and the management at Shelbourne Park.

Chapelizod was immensely popular both for greyhound racing under lights on Sunday evening and as the home ground of St Patrick's Athletic AFC, a League of Ireland team then attracting massive support. The track was well regarded by the greyhound community, with Ger McKenna and all the major trainers among its patrons. This was resented by the management of Shelbourne Park, which would have opposed Chapelizod being granted official status.

The end result of the acrimony was to be heavy with irony. In spite of the opposition, Chapelizod was finally recognised by Bord na gCon. However, this meant that they were racing not on Sunday but in midweek opposition to the other Dublin track at Harold's Cross. Forced to close almost a half-century ago, the traps and other effects at Chapelizod were removed and used at a schooling track at Ashbourne, County Meath.

Even now, the passing of the old track is lamented by trainers and bookmakers. Being beside the River Liffey, the running surface was regarded as being particularly safe by the latter, and some of the fastest greyhounds of the period were raced there. Some of the most colourful bookmakers worked here, too. Séamus Farrell apart, there was the incomparable Terry Rogers. Rogers had recommended the young Ger McKenna as private trainer to his business partner Bill Cutler in Britain, the platform from which McKenna launched his brilliant career.

Rogers was regularly at odds with officialdom in both horse and greyhound racing. It was Rogers who introduced 'first past the post' payouts in betting shops, which ignored the sometimes inconsistent deliberations of the stewards. And, at Chapelizod, Rogers was a familiar figure as he stormed off to complain about something or other – often the speed of the artificial lure being driven by Denis Dixon, the owner's son.

Many years later, the litigious but highly likeable Rogers acquired a top-flight solicitor to deal with his expanding business, property portfolio and plethora of complaints. In that wonderful way in which the world turns in cycles, the solicitor appointed to his account was Terence Dixon, another son of James Tallis Dixon, the man who established the track at Chapelizod.

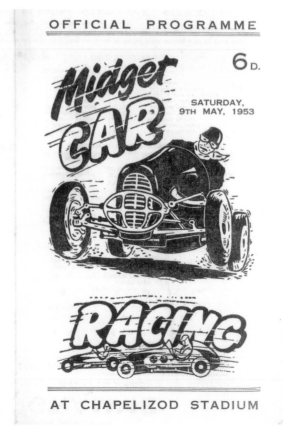

OFFICIALS OF THE MEETING

Held under the International Sporting Code of the A.I.A.C.R., the R.I.A.C., and the Supplementary Regulations of the Midget Racing Car Club of Ireland, Ltd.

R.I.A.C. STEWARD	J. C. Millard
PRESIDENT OF THE CLUB	G. D. P. Colley
SCRUTINEER	N. Flynn
CHIEF MARSHAL	A. A. Morrissey
ASSISTANT CHIEF MARSHAL	D. O'Kennedy
JUDGE	W. E. MacArthur
SCOREKEEPERS	J. McEvoy and O. Shiels
TIMEKEEPER	W. E. MacArthur
STARTER	E. T. Gaskin
SECRETARY OF THE MEETING	P. Torphy
PADDOCK MARSHAL	J. P. Coogan
COMMENTATOR	M. O'M.O'Donohue
M.R.C.C.I. STEWARD	P. J. Barry, PC.

Hon. Secretary: P. Torphy, 89 Celtic Park Avenue, Whitehall, Dublin.

FOR CHAPELIZOD STADIUM

Manager	J. T. DIXON
Track Manager	P. G. GYLL
Medical Officer	DR. C. MURPHY

The Irish Red Cross in attendance.

*

NO BETTING ALLOWED

GREYHOUND TRIALS
ARE HELD AT THIS STADIUM, MONDAY–FRIDAY, 10 a.m. till 1 p.m., 2 p.m. till 5 p.m. SATURDAYS, 10 a.m. till 1 p.m.

NIGHT TRIALS Each Tuesday
From 8 p.m. till 9.30 p.m.

PRINTED BY ARDIFF, THE PROGRAMME PRINTER, DUBLIN—D1330

OFFICIAL PROGRAMME

Midget CAR RACING

6 D.

SATURDAY, 9TH MAY, 1953

AT CHAPELIZOD STADIUM

ST. PATRICK'S ATHLETIC A.F.C.

SEASON 1955-56

LEAGUE OF IRELAND SHIELD

St. Patrick's Athletic

v.

Shamrock Rovers

CHAPELIZOD STADIUM

SUNDAY, 23rd OCTOBER, 1955

KICK-OFF 3.30 P.M.

EDITORIAL

With three series of fixtures yet to be completed in the Shield Competition, the honours must go to Shamrock Rovers, Waterford or ourselves as with 14 points each from 8 games we have a 5 points advantage over our nearest rivals, Cork Athletic and Sligo Rovers, who meet to-day at the Mardyke.

FREE DRAW

Draw at half-time for, 1st £1, 2nd 5/-.
Prizes may be claimed after the game from Mr. Blythe.

Nº 787

CHAPELIZOD STADIUM

IN CONJUNCTION WITH DALE MARTIN PROMOTIONS LTD.

PRESENTS ALL-IN

WRESTLING

Doors Open 7.30 p.m.	Friday, July 17th	Commence 8 p.m.

A SUPER SENSATIONAL INTERNATIONAL HEAVYWEIGHT CONTEST
6 Ten Minute Rounds   2 Falls, Subs or K.O.

The Dazzling Irish-American

Pat Curry

BOSTON, U.S.A. The most spectacular and colourful Irish-American ever to appear in Europe. First appearance in Dublin. Thrill-a-minute ring personality. Has drawn with Assirati and defeated most of the best in Europe

v

Twenty Stone Red Bearded

Man Mountain Benny

CALIFORNIA, U.S.A. The powerful red-bearded Goliath of the ring. One of the biggest and strongest heavyweights in wrestling. 20 Stone of phenomenal strength. The Film Star wrestler

A SPECIAL JUNIOR HEAVYWEIGHT CONTEST
6 Ten Minute Rounds   2 Falls, Subs or K.O.
India's Famed   England's Ex-Amateur

ARJIT SINGH   V   LEN BRITTON

LAHORE, PUNJAB—Clad in the traditional garb of his country   LONDON—Winner of many trophies and medals

A SUPERB WELTER-WEIGHT CLASSIC
4 Ten Minute Rounds   2 Falls, Subs or K.O.
Welterweight Champion of England   The No. 1 Contender

JACK DEMPSEY   V   JACKIE PALLO

of Wigan   Highbury, London—A former Amateur who is building a great reputation

AN ANGLO IRISH JUNIOR HEAVYWEIGHT CONTEST
5 Ten Minute Rounds   2 Falls, Subs or K.O.
The Uncrowned Champion of Europe   Dublin's Pride

ARTHUR BEAUMONT   V   BILL FOLEY

of Manchester   of Clondalkin

Referee for all Bouts the World Famous Mr. 'Tiny' Carr of London

Prices 2/-, 3/6 *Unres.* 5/-, 7/6, 10/- *Reserved*

— Rights of Admission Strictly Reserved —

BUSES: SPECIAL SERVICE. 25, 26, 66, 67 FROM ASTONS QUAY
For Advance Bookings Phone or visit—CLERYS, ELVERYS OR
CHAPELIZOD STADIUM

ARDIFF, KILMAINHAM

Two further examples of the versatility of Chapelizod Greyhound Stadium as a sporting venue.

Racing's green jacket . . . The Owen
McKenna-trained Like A Shot, winner
of the 2004 Paddy Power Irish Derby,
takes a breather after his exertions at
Shelbourne Park.

16 CLASSIC CONNECTIONS

THE McKENNA CLAN

T Triple Dead Heat

Although the odds are heavily against such an event, a number of triple dead heats for first place have been recorded. At Shawfield in Glasgow in March 1972, Turkish Maid, Thurles Queen and War Girl could not be separated by the judge.

The Greatest Trainer

There are grounds for debate on the subject of the 'greatest greyhound'. The normal criteria of prize money won and times achieved are not reliable yardsticks because of changing monetary values and different running surfaces. The whole topic is subjective. Actual achievement is the only true gauge.

In the case of Spanish Battleship, he won the Irish Laurels and the Easter Cup (twice). Above all, there is his winning of the Irish Derby on three occasions. It is the fact that his Classic wins came at different tracks rather than the fact that he continued to run faster that sets him apart.

Parallel problems are encountered when it comes to deciding about the greatest trainer – the most important human element in the story. Tom Lynch had the good fortune to be given Spanish Battleship to train … and Russian Gun. These dogs were brilliant speedsters, but it does not follow they would have succeeded to the same extent, or at all, with another handler. Horse-racing enthusiasts have mulled over the same question: does the jockey win the Classic because of being 'given' the ride on the good horse by a trainer; or do the horse and jockey succeed because of the trainer?

Such quandaries contribute to the fascination of human and animal sport. And, by coincidence, the Spanish Battleship era was followed by the emergence of a man whose status is on the same level as that of this canine immortal.

The Classics

Born in February 1930, Ger McKenna took the matter of winning with greyhounds to unimagined heights. The money, whether through the purse or the wagering, was in the Classics – the prestige, too. The Classic list, devised by the Irish Coursing Club in 1932, numbered just five: Derby, Oaks, St Leger, Grand National and National Sprint. In 1939, the first running of the National Sapling Stakes took place and, under the new title of the National Breeders' Produce Stakes, this Clonmel event was added to the Classic calendar. Five years later, the Laurels became a part of the Classic roll and, in the early days of Bord na gCon (and for four decades later), the domestic Classic list was extended to read: Derby, Oaks, St Leger, Grand National, National Sprint, National Breeders' Produce Stakes, Laurels and Cesarewitch.

In the forty years after Prince Of Bermuda became his first major winner (Irish St Leger, 1956), Ger McKenna was a colossus on the greyhound scene in Britain as well as Ireland. Based at Borrisokane, County Tipperary, he won thirty-one domestic Classics. These were vintage days for the sport, and the only Classic that Ger McKenna did not win was the Irish Grand National.

Ironically, it was the jumps event that prompted Bord na gCon to examine the whole Classics question. By 1959 the Irish Grand National had become devalued to the extent that it was shunted from one track to another. There were years when it was not run at all, its monetary value had plummeted, and the Irish trainers' interest in hurdling had hit a low. The Irish Grand National retained its Classic status (and still does), but it obviously could not be seen in the same light as other, richer and more prestigious Classics.

Bord na gCon went further, and the Classics list has undergone a drastic change in the past decade. The number of events now extends to fourteen. The original quintet is intact, as are the three original additions of the National Breeders' Produce Stakes, Laurels and Cesarewitch. The further inclusion of an unraced event at Tralee and the Golden Jacket at Galway is partly in recognition of the contribution of the greyhound racing community that supports those tracks. In the case of the other four events – Easter Cup, Ladbrokes '600', Corn Cuchulainn, Puppy Derby – it could be argued that they should have been considered Classics before now.

Irrespective of whether or when their Classic mark was awarded, there are five core competitions in the calendar: Derby, Oaks, St Leger, Laurels, Easter Cup. The level of prize money for these races, the betting on them and their popularity with the public has been consistently high. There has also been continuity in the running of these established events. Above all, the Classics have maintained prestige for the connections of the winners, and held on to their importance in the overall scheme.

The great greyhounds, by and large, contested the Easter Cup at Shelbourne Park, the Laurels in Cork, a Derby or Oaks at Harold's Cross or Shelbourne Park, and ended the season running in the St Leger in Limerick.

Mick Horan, the coursing slipper who also had an English Derby winner (Mick The Miller, 1929) and Irish Derby winner (Guidless Joe, 1932) died in 1962. What number of Classics would his Trim, County Meath, kennels have accrued eight decades later? Or Billy Quinn at Killenaule, whose Tipperary Hills won an 'Irish Derby' before the event was afforded Classic status by the Irish Coursing Club? Quinn's sympathetic handling coaxed that ground-breaking 29.82 Irish Derby final run from Tanist in 1940. What might Quinn have achieved in simple terms of Classics won in the modern era?

In the case of Ger McKenna, there would have been an almost endless list if the feature races won had already been converted into Classics (as they were subsequently). As it stands, McKenna's official list of wins is impressive enough: the English Derby (2), English Laurels (1), Irish Derby (3), Irish Oaks (1), Irish St Leger (12), National Breeders' Produce Stakes (2), Irish Cesarewitch (4), Irish National Sprint (2) and Irish Laurels (7).

The Origins

There is an irony in the fact that the one missing Classic, the Grand National, is where it all began for the McKenna clan. Gerard McKenna's father Malachy was a cattle dealer who had six brothers and thirteen children. He remarried after the death of his first wife, and Gerard (Ger) was the first child of the second family. Those in the many-branched McKenna tree all liked to keep 'a dog or two'; but Ger went the whole hog. His intention was always to be a full-time trainer, and you could detect the same determination in his youngest son Owen when he was growing up. Through the good offices of Irish bookmaker Terry Rogers, McKenna had an educational spell in England, at kennels near Wolverhampton, when he was still in his early twenties.

The McKenna Classic connection had already been established. In 1935, Ger's uncle Joe (his father's brother) sent

Ger McKenna's Classic Count (34)		
English Derby (2)	Parkdown Jet 1981	
	Lartigue Note 1989	
English Laurels (1)	Concentration 1990	
Irish Derby (3)	Own Pride 1969	
	Bashful Man 1973	
	Rathgallen Tady 1987	
Irish Oaks (1)	Nameless Pixie 1979	
Irish St Leger (12)	Prince Of Bermuda 1956	
	Swanlands Best 1960	
	Apollo Again 1962	
	Lovely Chieftain 1965	
	Yanka Boy 1967	
	Own Pride 1969	
	Time Up Please (2) 1971, 1972	
	Ballybeg Prim 1975	
	Nameless Star 1976	
	Red Rasper 1977	
	Moran's Beef 1984	
Irish Laurels (7)	Gabriel Boy 1970	
	Nameless Star 1976	
	Knockrour Slave 1980	
	Back Garden 1983	
	Rugged Mick 1984	
	Follow A Star 1985	
	Deerfield Bypass 1996	
National Breeders' Produce Stakes (2)	Big Kuda 1973	
	Cill Dubh Darkey 1976	
Irish Cesarewitch (4)	Butterfly Billy 1965	
	Yanka Boy 1967	
	Ballybeg Prim 1975	
	Oughter Brigg 1987	
Irish National Sprint (2)	Bauhus 1965	
	Move Gas 1969	

Irrespective of whether or when their Classic mark was awarded, there are five core competitions in the calendar: Derby, Oaks, St Leger, Laurels, Easter Cup. The level of prize money for these races, the betting on them and their popularity with the public has been consistently high.

out Druze to win the Irish Grand National. Joe McKenna was originally based not in Borrisokane but in Birr, in the adjoining county of Offaly. Joe was the first McKenna to graduate above having a couple of greyhounds to supplement his income, and he moved to Templeogue in Dublin in 1933, where the big track action was starting to take off. Joe McKenna died in 1942, his successes to be eclipsed by later family members, but he remained an inspirational figure. His son, Gay, trained nine Classic winners from his base at Cabinteely, County Dublin.

One of the early kennel-hands employed by Joe McKenna was Tom Lynch, from Cahirciveen, County Kerry. Tom went on to marry Joe's daughter Peg, move to Blanchardstown and produce eleven Classic winners.

Happy families . . . Ger McKenna (second from left) pictured with his father Malachy and his brother Joe. On the right is kennel-hand Joe Gleeson.

Ger and Gay McKenna

The 1960s and 1970s were dominated by Ger McKenna and his cousin Gay. Joe McKenna came close to sending out the Irish Derby winner in 1934 when Buzzing Dick ran up to Frisco Hobo in the first renewal to be held at Harold's Cross. Tom Lynch, who would marry into the family in 1946, ran up the premier Classic in both 1944 (to Clonbonny Bridge at Shelbourne Park) and 1951 (to Carmody's Tanist at Harold's Cross). A year after the third of the Spanish Battleship Irish Derby wins, Ger McKenna came second with Prince Of Bermuda when Keep Moving set a new standard for a decider in winning in 29.18.

There were other near-misses before Gay's Ballyowen Pride became the first McKenna name on the Irish Derby credits in 1965. From then until 1973 – just nine runnings – the McKenna/Lynch kennels provided thirteen greyhounds that either won or ran up the final. Gay's reign was to be crammed into this glorious period, although his success had begun earlier, when Skip's Choice won the 1960 Irish National Sprint. Gay won the Irish Cesarewitch twice (Postal Vote in 1970 and Rita's Choice in 1973), and recorded a brace in the Irish Oaks (Drumsough Princess in 1965 and Rosmore Robin in 1970). His Irish Derby quartet was made up of Ballyowen Chief (1965), Always Proud (1966), Monalee Pride (1970) and Catsrock Daisy (1972).

As a trainer, Ger McKenna enjoyed longevity at the top four times greater than his cousin Gay, who had been a friend and rival in equal measure. Prince Of Bermuda put Ger on the map when he ran up the Irish Derby at Shelbourne Park in 1956 and then won the Irish St Leger at Limerick in the same year.

Ger's earliest greyhound memory was of going to Limerick with his father to trial a bitch called Charity Maid. The younger McKenna was only eight years of age but by this point had already made up his mind where life's road was going to take him. Perhaps it is for that reason that Limerick has always held a special place in his heart, and he has returned to win the Irish St Leger there on an incredible twelve occasions. His first win was with Prince Of Bermuda in 1956 and the last with Moran's Beef in 1984. Prince Of Bermuda won the 1956 Irish St Leger in 30.66 for the 550 yards, a final time not bettered until McKenna's Time Up Please (30.56) won for the first time in 1971. Prince Of Bermuda had run an astonishing 28.98 in a heat of the Irish Derby and became the first greyhound to break 29 seconds for the 525 yards at Shelbourne Park in 1956. He also ran 27.95 for 500 yards – the distance of the Irish Laurels until 1960 – at Cork.

Own Pride, Ger's first Irish Derby winner in 1969, doubled up and also won the Irish St Leger in that year. Time Up Please won the Irish St Leger in both 1971 and 1972. Nameless Star completed the Irish Laurels–Irish St Leger double in 1976. Both Yanka Boy (1967) and Ballybeg Prim (1975) won both the Irish Cesarewitch and the Irish St Leger. Amidst all this frenetic activity, Ger still made time to undertake his annual pilgrimage to the English Derby, at White City and then Wimbledon. He won at the former with Parkdown Jet (1981) and at the latter with Lartigue Note (1989). This pair of winners was related three generations back as Parkdown Jet was by Cairnville Jet, a son of the McKenna 1969 Irish Derby winner Own Pride, out of Gabriel Ruby. Cairnville Jet and Gabriel Ruby, the 'parents' of Parkdown Jet, appear in the breeding of Lartigue Note three generations back. Gabriel Ruby was by Peruvian Style out of Gabriel Blue, whose sire was the McKenna 1967 Irish Cesarewich–Irish St Leger winner Yanka Boy.

Six Ger McKenna-trained dogs have been named as recipients of the National Greyhound Awards since their inauguration in 1965: Yanka Boy (1967), Own Pride (1969), Ballybeg Prim (1975), Nameless Pixie (1979), Parkdown Jet (1981) and Moran's Beef (1984).

Missing from that list is a greyhound that McKenna considered to be one of the fastest that he had ever trained: Lovely Chieftain. This greyhound, which was the 1965 Irish St Leger winner, was owned by Pat Dalton, who was pioneering the Bord na gCon export bid in America but was not neglecting the home front. Dalton, a shrewd judge himself, obviously considered McKenna to be the best. Coincidentally, the Dalton range in Ireland is at Golden, just miles from where Ger's son Owen is based at New Inn, County Tipperary. Dalton also owned Bauhus, which McKenna trained to win the Irish National Sprint at Dunmore Stadium in 1965, and Gabriel Boy, another McKenna winner of the Irish St Leger in 1970.

A greyhound great ... Gay McKenna, cousin of Ger McKenna, brother-in-law of Tom Lynch, father of G.J. McKenna and father-in-law of Fraser Black, pictured at his Cabinteely, County Dublin, range.

The sand that has replaced the turf at Ireland's venues has wiped away most of the track speed records established by greyhounds prepared by Ger McKenna, Gay McKenna, Tom Lynch and their extended families. But the memories not only remain but stay vivid. Like the mental pictures of Back Garden, Rugged Mick and Follow A Star; the greyhounds that gave McKenna a hat-trick of Irish Laurels wins in 1983, 1984 and 1985.

The old Cork track on the Western Road was in a tight situation, its back up against a busy road. In such a confined arena, viewing space on a final night was at a premium ... as was the running ground for the greyhounds. A dog not in front, and with yards to spare, when hurtling to the first bend in the Irish Laurels decider was going to encounter serious spatial difficulties. The place to be was in the vanguard. Rugged Mick, arguably the fastest starter of any McKenna runner, was ... cheered on by a boy looking the spitting image of his father a half-century earlier.

... the most decorated of the McKenna offspring to this point has been Ger's son Owen. Even allowing for the increased opportunities of the past decade, Owen McKenna's start as a licence-holder in his own right has been impressive.

RIGHT
That's my girl ... Paula McKenna, daughter of trainer Gay McKenna, with Postal Vote, winner of the 1970 Irish Cesarewitch at Navan and runner-up (to Sole Aim) in the 1971 Irish Derby at Shelbourne Park.

The Next Generation

And it is with this boy, Owen McKenna, and his cousins, that the story continues. There were already fifty-five Classics on the board before this next generation – the sons of Tom Lynch, and Ger and Gay McKenna – came along. And, again, it was the Irish Grand National that was to prove the route to more Classic success. Joe McKenna's grandson G.J. (Gay's son also known as Ger) won his first Irish Grand National with Yacht Club (1991) when based at Cabinteely. At that time, another grandson, Thomas Lynch (Tom and Peg Lynch's son), had sent out Handball to win the Irish Grand National twice (in 1988 and 1989) from his kennels near Dunboyne, County Meath.

To add to the remarkable story, Gay McKenna's daughter Paula married Fraser Black in 1977. Black has consistently supplied feature race winners since his first Classic (Droopys Jaguar) on the domestic front in the National Breeders' Produce Stakes in 1987. He travelled from his base in Rathangan, County Kildare, to his native Scotland in 2005 to lift the Scottish Derby in Glasgow with Droopys Marco.

However, the most decorated of the McKenna offspring to this point has been Ger's son Owen. Even allowing for the increased opportunities of the past decade, Owen McKenna's start as a licence-holder in his own right has been impressive. He secured the premier Classic, the Irish Derby, with Like A Shot in 2004. His father's influence was seen in his preparation of Lughill Jo to lift the Irish St Leger in 2007, and also in his Irish Laurels victories with Boherduff Light (2004) and Catunda Harry (2007). Catunda Harry carved out a special niche for himself in Irish greyhound-racing history when he became the first dog to better 28 seconds for 525 yards, running 27.99 at Limerick in June 2007.

Ger McKenna, his races won, has passed the baton on to Owen.

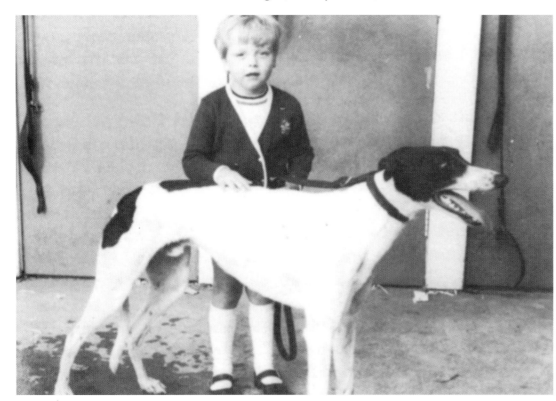

Star in the making ... Owen McKenna with his father's 1974 Irish Puppy Derby winner Shamrock Point at Harold's Cross.

'Like' a McKenna winner . . . A familiar scene at Shelbourne Park in 2004 as Like A Shot becomes another McKenna-trained winner (Owen – Ger's son – this time) of the Paddy Power Irish Derby.

Farloe Melody winning the 1992 English Derby at Wimbledon for Matt O'Donnell. The dog and trainer rank among the sport's greats.

17 MATT O'DONNELL AND
THE NEXT GENERATION

RAISING THE BAR

O'Donnell and his dogs put the County Tipperary hamlet of Killenaule back at the centre of the greyhound racing world.

The Vocation of Training

Anatomist, dentist, herbalist, pedicurist, pharmacist, psychologist, veterinary surgeon … there is more to training greyhounds than the mere title suggests. Apart from the variety of skills required, the time allocated to the job is enormous. Professional trainers will rise at perhaps 7.30 in the morning, be kept busy by the chores of a busy kennel until 6.30 that evening … and then have to turn around and drive to the track.

The vet is only called in for the most serious of injuries and the handler is required to know everything from head to toe about the longtails of the canine species, with regard to health and safety. The racing dog demands round-the-clock, day-to-day attention. Holiday is a foreign word to the handler. Training is a vocation, and the number of man-hours that go into the job is hardly reflected in the bills in the way it would be for other services.

In terms of displaying a work ethic and a single-minded determination to win, few have matched Matt O'Donnell. Ger McKenna, the only trainer to have surpassed O'Donnell's level of achievement, came from a greyhound-training-and-rearing tradition. O'Donnell's link to the sporting world lies solely in the fact that his maternal uncle, Patrick Anglim, had been an Irish high-jump champion.

Starting a kennel from scratch, O'Donnell was known as a fair employer who demanded of his staff a level of dedication that few but the trainer possessed. O'Donnell and his dogs put the County Tipperary hamlet of Killenaule back at the centre of the greyhound racing world. It is the village from which Billy Quinn hailed. He was the man who won the first 'Irish Derby' at Harold's Cross, an event the authorities of the time at the Irish Coursing Club refused to recognise as a Classic. It would not be until 1932 that Guidless Joe would win the first official Irish Derby at Shelbourne Park. Eight years later, Quinn returned to the capital in triumph when bringing one of the truly great greyhounds, Tanist, to Shelbourne Park where he won the 1940 Irish

The best of rivals … Matt O'Donnell (left) and Ger McKenna pictured at the 1978 Irish St Leger final at Limerick. O'Donnell trained the winner, Rhu, to break McKenna's domination of the Classic.

Derby in the phenomenal time of 29.82.

O'Donnell would have treasured Tanist, as Quinn must have done. O'Donnell-trained dogs live in pristine luxury, are fed the best and travel in style. At the time that O'Donnell started to make his mark, many greyhounds travelled in mobile kennels tied to the bumpers of estate cars, their proximity to the exhaust pipe doing nothing for the lungs needed to propel them around the track at over thirty miles per hour. O'Donell's dogs travelled in air-conditioned luxury.

Matt O'Donnell and Ger McKenna

O'Donnell was a professional trainer in every sense and a real challenge to the domination of Ger McKenna. They followed much the same paths to an extent. Because one notable thing about greyhound trainers is that they take time to mature. Ger McKenna, for all the expertise gleaned in his early career, did not unlock the secrets of winning the English Derby until he was fifty-one (Parkdown Jet, 1981); and it was another three years until he finally won a Waterloo Cup with Tubbertelly Queen. O'Donnell – of the same generation as Ger McKenna – got off the mark in the Irish St Leger in 1978, but it would be another dozen years before he won his first Irish Derby with The Other Toss and 1992 before his English Derby victory with Farloe Melody.

The Ger McKenna–Matt O'Donnell paths converged at the Market's Field in Limerick at the Irish St Leger. Soon, the Market's Field will be but a fond memory for the proud sporting public of Limerick when they move to their new home. Ostensibly, all greyhound circuits are the same: four bends and a circumference of around 500 yards. They were built to a tried-and-trusted formula of racing left-handed, which the greyhounds find safe and familiar. They are not all exactly the same. Dunmore Stadium in Belfast was a bigger circuit than any other in these islands before its closure a decade ago. It and the other tracks in Northern Ireland had sand surfaces long before those in the Republic. Galway and Mullingar tended to be among the tracks returning slower times. Cork and Dundalk were tight tracks that took knowing.

Limerick was idiosyncratic for a couple of reasons. The

Nap hand . . . The six finalists for the National Breeders' Two-Year-Old Produce Stakes at Clonmel in 1978 with handlers (L–R) Steven Gleeson, Geraldine Christopher, P.J. Tynan and Matt O'Donnell who supplied five of the sextet including the winner Always Kelly (black dog on left).

finishing line was so close to the first bend that greyhounds could prop (slow down) at the end of a race. The traps were also slightly out from the rails, and, for this reason, the runners tended to move to the middle of the track in the run to the opening corner. Given these quirks, it is remarkable that the two most successful trainers should have dominated the local Classic to such an extent.

Nothing gives a Limerick greyhound enthusiast more pleasure than a local concern winning the Irish St Leger. The event was originally allocated to Celtic Park in Belfast in 1932, and there have been renewals at Harold's Cross (1935, 1937 and 1942), Clonmel (1933) and Shelbourne Park (1934, 1936, 1938 and 1939). As the Irish Laurels came to Cork in 1944, so the Irish St Leger found its permanent home in Limerick in that year.

Owen McKenna was following in the footsteps of his father Ger when Lughill Jo won in 2007 and there were great celebrations when Ann Barry, later a Bord na gCon member (1997–2000), sent out Fire Fly to win in 1997, just

U Unlucky

The number of hard-luck stories in greyhound racing is legion. One that springs to many minds is that of the John Haynes-trained Rahan Ship, which had to vault a stricken opponent in the 1981 English Derby at White City – a race won by the Ger McKenna-trained Parkdown Jet. The irony is that the winner was a blue dog – thought by the greyhound racing fraternity to be an unlucky colour for a dog's coat.

Yale Princess, trained by Matt O'Donnell, wins the Irish Oaks at Harold's Cross in 1987. A further victory in the bitch Classic eluded the Killenaule, County Tipperary, kennel until Skywalker Queen's success at Shelbourne Park in 2009.

as Christy Daly had done with Randy a decade earlier.

Limerick folk always insist that it takes a special dog to win the Irish St Leger, and while they always wish that the winner has Shannonside connections, they took bragging rights out on the fact that giants of the game like Ger McKenna and Matt O'Donnell judged the success of a season on whether the kennel won the Limerick Classic. Just how seriously the race is regarded is driven home by the fact that between McKenna's Prince Of Bermuda winning in 1956 and O'Donnell's Batties Spirit scoring in 1995, the pair won nineteen of the forty finals. In those four decades, of course, they also provided runners-up and a host of finalists. This domination was tantamount to the Ger McKenna–Gay McKenna–Tom Lynch axis in the Irish Derby between 1965 and 1973, when thirteen of their charges filled first or second place in the premier Classic.

O'Donnell did not arrive on the track scene until Rhu won the Irish St Leger in 1978. He posted seven winners of the race in an eighteen-year period in which McKenna won just once, with Moran's Beef. O'Donnell had come late to track glory because he was a coursing man at heart. However, without family to help out on a daily basis and employees needing to be paid – apart from the shortness of the winter season – it would have been impossible for someone in O'Donnell's position to run a fully professional kennel on the prize money available in coursing. O'Donnell had won a Waterloo Cup with Minnesota Miller in 1976, and his Whiteleas Tim had run up the coursing Derby to Hack Up Fenian at Powerstown Park in 1971.

O'Donnell and the Classics

He did not have to travel far with Always Kelly for his first track Classic, the National Breeders' Produce Stakes at Clonmel in 1978. His first Irish St Leger at Limerick followed in the same year and, as befits the nephew of Paddy

Anglim, he added the jumps Classic – the Grand National at Thurles – in 1979 with Keeragh Sambo. The narrow and disputed – O'Donnell was never shy about voicing his opinion – verdict by which Whiteleas Tim was beaten in the final of the coursing Derby would be mirrored in many Derby finals on the track. Sorties to White City and Wimbledon in London and Shelbourne Park in Dublin failed to find a Derby winner. O'Donnell greyhounds racing in England tended to run exceptionally well in the opening rounds but fail in the finals.

When O'Donnell unlocked the formula, the winners came in a torrent. Beyond the age of fifty-one at which Ger McKenna won his first English Derby, Matt O'Donnell was flooded with winners. The Irish Derby was secured in 1990 with The Other Toss. At this stage, O'Donnell had also gone into the breeding business, and 'The Other' was his prefix, the way in which the public recognised O'Donnell's own stock. O'Donnell won the Irish Derby again in 1991 with Ardfert Mick, so called because the owners Noel and Kathleen Clifford came from Ardfert, County Kerry.

As with horse racing, it was an era when many Irish training successes were achieved with British-owned animals. O'Donnell was especially well served by English patrons such as Alice Swaffield, whose greyhounds carried the 'Batties' prefix, and whose Batties Rocket gave O'Donnell a third Irish Derby in 1995. The Derby final was also contested by the winner's sister Batties Spirit, which went on to win the Irish St Leger in the same year. After Rhu in 1978, Supreme Tiger (1982), Ballintubber One (1985), Storm Villa (1986), Dereen Star (1989) and Barefoot Dash (1992) came good in the Irish St Leger before Batties Spirit. 'Barefoot' became another familiar prefix. These dogs were owned by Bryan Murphy who lived in the Cayman Islands. Murphy won the Irish St Leger again in 1993, but the trainer on this occasion was Gay McKenna's son-in-law Fraser Black.

The 2002 running was won by Larking About, part-owned by Shane Taggart (son of the then Bord na gCon chairman Paschal Taggart) and trained by Paul Hennessy, whose work rate was reminiscent of a younger Matt O'Donnell.

O'Donnell won a second Clonmel Classic in 1985 with

Kansas Rebel taking the National Breeders' Produce Stakes. This period also marked the coming of Frances Ruth into the O'Donnell set-up, and the Dubliner undoubtedly influenced the trainer's later success. Frances's sister Dolores won the Irish St Leger in 2000 with Extra Dividend, owned by Liam Garrahy, father of veterinary surgeon John Garrahy who was Bord na gCon's regulations manager at the time.

Yale Princess (1989) gave O'Donnell success in the Irish Oaks and, coincidentally, he shared the record with Ger McKenna of having just one winner of the bitch Classic and three winners of the Irish Derby. However, the Killenaule kennel added a second Irish Oaks in 2009 with Skywalker Queen. Many professional trainers tended to steer clear of bitches at this time as they were prone to upset the day-to-day kennel routine when coming into season. Arrancourt Duke (1989) completed the O'Donnell treble in the National Breeders' Produce Stakes while Lumber Boss put him on the Irish Laurels roll of honour.

More than most events, the Easter Cup has thrown up a share of dual winners. The very first was Old Blade, in 1928,

Diarmaid (left) and Eoin Garrahy, grandsons of the owner Liam Garrahy, with the Dolores Ruth-trained Extra Dividend, winner of the Irish St Leger at Market's Field, Limerick, in 2000. The boys' father, John Garrahy, was regulations manager wth Bord na gCon and did much to maintain the good image of the sport.

which came back to Shelbourne Park to retain the title in the following year. The Irish Puppy Derby winner of 1944, the durable Astra won the Easter Cup in both 1945 and 1946. The name of the great Spanish Battleship was added in 1954 and 1955. And, of course, Spanish Battleship went on to win the Irish Derby on three occasions. That was an honour denied to Farloe Melody, owned by John Davis and David Tickner, not once but twice when he reached the domestic decider in both 1991 and 1992. He stamped himself as a greyhound of exceptional ability and one with a special place in his trainer's memory by winning the English Derby of 1992 at Wimbledon. Just as a number of candidates can be put forward as the greatest greyhound trained by Ger McKenna, so there is no shortage of material in O'Donnell's case. Although the name of Farloe Melody will not be found on the credits at Cork or Limerick, he was the sort of greyhound that owners and trainers dream about.

O'Donnell added Spartacus (1984), Spartafitz (1987) and Lassana Champ (1990) to his Easter Cup haul. O'Donnell and Ger McKenna represent a link with the old order of the sport, as did Paddy Keane. He had the winner of the 1966 English Derby in Faithful Hope, the 1978 Irish Derby in Pampered Rover, three Irish Laurels winners – Ivy Hall Flash (1971), Kilbracken Style (1973), Silent Thought (1974) – and many more outstanding greyhounds in between. Keane left England in 1968, had a brief sojourn in America and returned to Ireland in 1969. He died in April 1992.

The Next Generation

Greyhound racing was changing. Many will argue over the respective ability of the greyhounds but there was no denying what was happening at the turnstiles and in the betting ring. The year 2004 saw Séamus Farrell and the rest of the bookmaking fraternity turn over €93,500,740.

This was the year in which Ger McKenna's son Owen won the Irish Derby at Shelbourne Park for the first time, with Like A Shot. The licence to train was being handed on. Ger McKenna had his last Classic win with Deerfield Bypass (Irish Laurels) in 1996. That year saw Dolores Ruth train Shanless Slippy to win the National Breeders' Produce Stakes at Clonmel and, in direct succession to McKenna and O'Donnell, the English Derby at Wimbledon. Dolores Ruth has enjoyed a remarkable strike rate with a comparatively small kennel of greyhounds. Her other Classic successes have been with Extra Dividend in the 2000 Irish St Leger, Sonic Flight in the 2001 Irish Laurels and with Razldazl Billy, which produced some electrifying performances to win the 2006 Irish Derby.

Owen McKenna is a long way off his father's tally of thirty-four Classic wins but he has hardly begun to chase that total and has already won the Irish Derby (Like A Shot, 2004), Irish Laurels (Boherduff Light 2004, Catunda Harry, 2007), Easter Cup (Ahane Lad, 2006) and Irish St Leger (Lughill Jo, 2007). And he has already fulfilled one ambition that eluded both his father and Matt O'Donnell. In February 2009, Owen McKenna sent out Catunda Ashmore – owned by that great Dublin track and field stalwart Paddy Byrne – to win an Irish coursing Classic, the Champion Stakes, at Powerstown Park, Clonmel.

Trainer Dolores Ruth with her bitch Unsinkable Girl at Shelbourne Park.

Irish St Leger

Run at Limerick except in the asterisked years * Harold's Cross,
**** Clonmel, ***** Celtic Park, ****** Shelbourne Park
550 yards

Year	Winner	Time	Year	Winner	Time	Year	Winner	Time
1932	Castle Eve*****	32.08	1965	Lovely Chieftain	30.92	1998	Deerfield Sunset	30.03
1933	Brilliant Bob****	31.53	1966	Movealong Santa	30.92	1999	Frisby Flashing	29.64
1934	Chicken Sandwich******	31.59	1967	Yanka Boy	30.77	2000	Extra Dividend	29.79
1935	Carra's Son*	31.82	1968	Pools Punter	30.88	2001	Droopys Kewell	30.37
1936	Moresby*****	31.68	1969	Own Pride	30.95	2002	Larking About	29.73
1937	Cheers For Ballyduff*	31.42	1970	Mark Anthony	31.02	2003	Mountleader Rolf	30.01
1938	Abbeylara******	31.61	1971	Time Up Please	30.56	2004	Never Give Up	29.88
1939	Negro's Crown*****	31.77	1972	Time Up Please	31.05	2005	Redbarn Panther	29.72
1940	Cherrygrove Cross	31.82	1973	Romping To Work	31.04	2006	Indesacjack	29.66
1941	not run		1974	Lively Band	31.20	2007	Lughill Jo	29.37
1942	Monarch Of The Glen*	31.28	1975	Ballybeg Prim	30.44	2008	Boherash Gaoithe	29.71
1943	Monarch Of The Glen****	31.48	1976	Nameless Star	30.62	2009	Bar Blackstone	29.62
1944	No Relation	31.48	1977	Red Rasper	31.15			
1945	Dark Shadow	31.37	1978	Rhu	31.44			
1946	Star Point	31.55	1979	Airmount Champ	31.20			
1947	Pouleen Boy	31.48	1980	Rahan Ship	30.72			
1948	Beau Lion	31.52	1981	Oran Jack	30.60			
1949	Ballybeg Surprise	31.45	1982	Supreme Tiger	30.44			
1950	Maddest Daughter	31.55	1983	The Stranger	31.04			
1951	Ella's Ivy	31.08	1984	Moran's Beef	30.06			
1952	Silver Earl	31.25	1985	Ballintubber One	30.42			
1953	Gortaleen	31.26	1986	Storm Villa	30.65			
1954	Mount Nagle Surprise	31.10	1987	Randy	30.23			
1955	Doonmore Dreamer	30.98	1988	Local Kate	31.04			
1956	Prince Of Bermuda	30.66	1989	Dereen Star	30.24			
1957	Kilcaskin Kern	31.05	1990	Alans Judy	30.42			
1958	Firgrove Snowman	31.28	1991	Castleland Dream	30.22			
1959	Ocean Swell	31.18	1992	Barefoot Dash	30.40			
1960	Swanlands Best	31.60	1993	Barefoot Marty	30.54			
1961	Jerry's Clipper	31.10	1994	Kilvil Skinner	30.84			
1962	Apollo Again	31.26	1995	Batties Spirit	30.42			
1963	General Courtnowski	31.12	1996	Airmount Rogue	29.89			
1964	Brook Jockey	31.66	1997	Fire Fly	30.36			

Spot the winner: Slip The Lark (5) heads
the field early on in the Paddy Power
Irish Derby at Shelbourne Park in 2008.
He leads from Advantage Johnny (6),
Ballymac Ruso (2), Machu Picchu (4),
Headleys Bridge (1) and the eventual
champion Shelbourne Aston (3).

18 THE EASTER CUP

GATEWAY TO GREATNESS

Early Days at Shelbourne Park

Other tracks in the country may now boast big-city facilities and big-money purses, but Shelbourne Park remains the proving ground for man and beast. For a trainer to show evidence of his or her worth against his or her peers, and for a greyhound to begin to have pretensions to greatness, the winning of races and competitions at the main Dublin stadium is an imperative. It has always been so, since Shelbourne Park opened its doors literally weeks after greyhound racing had been introduced to Ireland in 1927.

The maiden meeting at Shelbourne Park was staged on Saturday 14 May 1927. The track's manager Paddy O'Donoghue was destined to be the dominant figure in greyhound racing in the capital right through to the point when the running of the sport passed into the hands of Bord na gCon over thirty years later.

The first race was over 500 yards and was won by Morning Prince, the joint favourite, which was owned by Jeremiah Ryan from Caherelly, County Limerick. Eleven months later, the first of the canine track-racing superstars made his appearance. Mick The Miller – and his brother Macoma – made their Dublin debuts in April 1928, after their owner-breeder Father Martin Brophy travelled from his Killeigh, County Offaly parish and entrusted the promising pups to trainer Mick Horan who had his kennels at Trim, County Meath. Both were trialled, Mick The Miller being highly

The Cassidy Family with Clogher McGrath, winner of the Easter Cup in 1951.

impressive. Father Brophy valued him at two hundred guineas but Mick The Miller only attracted a top bid of one hundred and fifty guineas in the August sale.

Easter Cup Winners

The sickly Mick The Miller did not return to action until the following March and ran up the final of the 1929 Easter Cup. The winner was Old Blade, which was defending the title won in the inaugural Easter Cup. By 1932, the Easter Cup had established the reputation that it retains: of being the pointer to future champions in England and Ireland. The 1932 winner was Monologue, the heroine of the coursing Oaks at Powerstown Park in Clonmel. Monologue then came back to Dublin in 1933 and won the second Irish Derby at Shelbourne Park. Abbeylara won the 1939 Easter Cup and had, in 1938, already won the Irish Derby at Harold's Cross and a rare running of the Irish St Leger at Shelbourne Park. Monarch Of The Glen had already won the Irish St Leger – this renewal being at Harold's Cross – in 1942 before capturing a second Irish St Leger at Celtic Park and an Easter Cup at Shelbourne Park in 1943. The 1944 Irish Puppy Derby winner Astra proved a hardy sort, with Easter Cup wins in 1945 and 1946.

The most durable of them all would be Spanish Battleship, which annexed two Easter Cup successes (1954 and 1955) to his Irish Derby hat-trick (1953, 1954, 1955) spread between Harold's Cross and Shelbourne Park.

In 1993, General Courtnowski showed his worth in the Easter Cup before going south to Limerick and victory in the Irish St Leger. Catsrock Daisy remained at Shelbourne Park in 1972 and won both the Easter Cup and Irish Derby.

The unmistakable link between the Easter Cup and the Irish Derby was replicated in the penchant of Easter Cup winners for the English Derby, whether at White City or Wimbledon. Trained by Mick Horan, Mick The Miller had narrowly failed to complete the double in 1929 when runner-up in Dublin to Old Blade before his London win. The second Irish-trained winner of the English Derby was Paddy Dunphy's The Grand Canal, and he arrived via a win in the Easter Cup. John Hayes' Indian Joe was the 1980

Top trio . . . (L–R) Trainer Séamus Graham, and joint owners Paschal Taggart and Noel Ryan, with Dipmac, winner of the Irish Derby at Shelbourne Park in 1984. Graham went on to train the 2008 English Derby winner Loyal Honcho for Ryan, while Taggart was a later chairman of Bord na gCon (1995–2006).

Easter Cup winner and he would triumph at White City just months later.

The cachet of the Easter Cup would be even more strongly enhanced when the dual winner Farloe Melody (1991 and 1992) went on to claim an English Derby victory at Wimbledon for Matt O'Donnell. Chart King won the 1999 Easter Cup and English Derby for brothers Karl and Ralph Hewitt, and the most recent trainer to use the Easter Cup stepping stone to English Derby glory is Séamus Graham. Graham is based at Ballickmoyler, on the border of Counties Carlow and Laois, and has made a considerable impact at the Dublin tracks in spells that have seen him initially operating as a private trainer (or agent), when he just

V Veterinary

If a dog is man's best friend, then his vet is the greyhound trainer's best buddy. There are a number of veterinary surgeons whose practice is taken up almost entirely with the care of racing greyhounds. In 1979, and for a number of years afterwards, the vets were helpless when trying to deal with the epidemic of parvovirus, which had a devastating effect, especially on the puppy population in Ireland.

handled greyhounds for himself. Unlike Paddy Dunphy – the publican from across the Kilkenny boundary in Castlecomer – Graham moved on to the fully professional ranks. He shares with Dunphy the distinction of sending out a winner of the English Derby, which he finally did for the first time at Wimbledon in 2008, with the Noel Ryan-owned Loyal Honcho.

It was Ryan – a patron of Paddy Keane, who won the English Derby in 1966 (Faithful Hope) and Irish Derby in 1978 (Pampered Rover) – who set Graham on the Classic trail. Ryan owned the Graham-trained Dipmac in partnership with Paschal Taggart (who went on to be chairman of Bord na gCon (1995–2006)). Graham, who also trained for Taggart's predecessor, Kevin Heffernan (1994–95), has run his greyhounds almost exclusively in his home province of Leinster, and the bulk of his successes have been achieved at Shelbourne Park. Dipmac won the Irish Derby of 1984; there was a hiatus before his 1995 Irish Oaks win with Cool Survivor. He claimed the bitch Classic at Shelbourne Park in 2000 and 2001 with another outstanding performer, Marinas Tina. He completed an Irish Derby treble with Tina Marina (1996) and Climate Control (2003). He has lifted the Easter Cup thanks to Premier Fantasy (2004) and Mineola Farloe (2005).

Paul Hennessy

Trainer Paul Hennessy made an even greater impact on the Easter Cup. Based at Gowran, County Kilkenny, Hennessy has not garnered an extraordinary personal haul of credits but his kennel has housed a number of multiple award-winning greyhounds. For a number of reasons, modern greyhounds tend not to accumulate as many honours as those in the past. It has become rare to see a Spanish Battleship-type going from one big event to another and mopping up the prizes. This is down to the more competitive nature of the calendar and the availability of lucrative purses outside of the Classics.

Hennessy has bucked that trend with a string of greyhounds, including Ardkill Jamie, Late Late Show and Mr Pickwick. The achievements of Mr Pickwick elevated Hennessy from the ranks of run-of-the-mill trainers, and, in 1997, Mr

Pickwick had an Irish Laurels win to his credit. In the following season, Mr Pickwick retained his Cork Classic after annexing the Easter Cup. After the Mr Pickwick double, Hennessy captured the Irish Laurels on another three occasions (with Barefoot Ridge in 2000, Tyrur Ted in 2005 and Ardkill Jamie in 2006). The trainer has claimed the Easter Cup six times in all (with Mr Pickwick in 1998, Mr Bozz in 2000, Late Late Show in 2001 and 2002, Ardkill Jamie in 2007 and Tyrur Kenny in 2008).

The Scottish Derby has also been a regular target for Paul Hennessy and the Glasgow Classic fell to his Priceless Rebel in 2002 and Tyrur Kieran in 2008. He fulfilled the ambition of every trainer when taking Tyrur Rhino to Shelbourne Park and winning the Irish Derby of 2007. Hennessy's Irish St Leger came through Larking About (2002) and his Irish Oaks win with April Surprise was a significant fillip for one of the younger trainers.

The Irish Oaks

The Irish Oaks shares with the Irish St Leger the distinction of having been contested at five different venues. The bitch Classic is often won by some of the smaller kennels or by owners with an eye to future breeding potential. The Spanish Battleship kennels of Tom Lynch housed the dual winner Peaceful Lady (1952 and 1953), while Séamus Graham's Marinas Tina (2000 and 2001) was another outstanding winner over two campaigns. A truly top-drawer winner from a typical Oaks 'household' was Romping To Work, owned by Helen and Larry Kelly from Cappawhite, County Tipperary. Romping To Work won the Irish Oaks (then run at Harold's Cross) in 1973. She then moved closer to home and took the Irish St Leger. In this golden greyhound age, Lively Band – trained at Kilmessan, County Meath, by Jack Murphy – completed the Irish Derby–Irish St Leger double in 1974. Murphy then won the Irish Oaks with Main Avenue in 1975.

The Irish Oaks of 1983 fell to the incomparable Quick Suzy, owned by Mary McGrath from Coalisland, County Tyrone. Airmount Jewel's success in 1985 heralded a purple patch for breeder-owner-trainer Gerry Kiely who had his kennel

One would imagine that there should not be a great difference between winning the Derby on track and field. However, the litany of those who have tried and failed tells another story.

'Rhino' on the charge . . . Trainer Paul Hennessy finally won the Paddy Power Irish Derby at Shelbourne Park in 2007 with Tyrur Rhino (5), seen here disputing the lead with Express Ego (2), with Ardkill Jamie (1) close up.

just outside Waterford city. Among a roll of honours, Kiely also claimed the 1989 Scottish Derby with Airmount Grand and the 1996 Irish St Leger with Airmount Rogue.

The 1991 Irish Oaks marked something of a departure for G.J. McKenna, the son of Gay McKenna. G.J. McKenna is more readily associated with his preparation of Irish Grand National winners, but his sending out of Gentle Soda to win the Irish Oaks was a notable achievement.

Fraser Black, who married Gay McKenna's daughter Paula, had the 1996 Irish Oaks winner in Fossabeg Maid. But while some trainers have been blessed with Irish Derby success at a young age and in a short space of time (Michael Barrett had Linda's Champion in 1977 and Suir Miller in 1980), the sport's main prize has eluded Black. For all his disappointment in the track Derby, Fraser Black holds the distinction of being the only top-flight Classic-winning trainer to have also won a coursing Derby. Black won the Derby in his native Scotland with Droopys Marco in 2005, the 1988 Easter Cup with Joannes Nine, the 1993 Irish

St Leger with Barefoot Marty and – apart from his 1996 Irish Oaks with Fossabeg Maid – there was a decade's gap between his wins in the National Breeders' Produce Stakes with Droopys Jaguar (1987) and Clashaphuca (1997). Arguably, his proudest moment came with Owens Sedge winning the 1993 coursing Derby at Powerstown Park, Clonmel.

The Derby on Track and Field

One would imagine that there should not be a great difference between winning the Derby on track and field. However, the litany of those who have tried and failed tells another story. Ger McKenna won thirty-four track Classics in his decorated career, including two renewals in the English Derby (Parkdown Jet in 1981 and Lartigue Note in 1989) and three in the Irish Derby (Own Pride in 1969, Bashful Man in 1973 and Rathgallen Tady in 1987), but just one open coursing Classic in the Waterloo Cup (Tubbertelly Queen in 1984). Matt O'Donnell also won the

Irish win . . . Joint-owner Terry McCann with his bitch Tubbertelly Queen, winner of the 1984 Waterloo Cup at Altcar, near Southport, Lancashire, when trained by Ger McKenna.

Irish Derby on three occasions (The Other Toss in 1990, Ardfert Mick in 1991 and Batties Rocket in 1995) as well as an English Derby (Farloe Melody in 1992) and a Waterloo Cup (Minnesota Miller in 1976). However, he fell at the last hurdle when Whiteleas Tim went under to Hack Up Fenian in the 1971 coursing Derby.

Dolores Ruth (Shanless Slippy in 1996 and Razldazl Billy in 2006) and Séamus Graham (Loyal Honcho in 2008, Dipmac in 1984, Tina Marina in 1996 and Climate Control in 2003) are the Irish-based trainers to have tasted major Derby success on the track in two countries.

The attempts of one man to couple success in the coursing field with that on the racetrack have become almost legendary. Based near Tipperary Town, Michael O'Donovan sent out the Waterloo Cup winners Hear And There (1985),

React Fragll (1988), React Robert (1995), Dashing Oak (1996), Judicial Inquiry (1999) and Why You Monty (2004). Unfortunately, his six Waterloo Cup successes in the open terrain at Altcar have been matched exactly by his near-misses in the confines of Powerstown Park. It all began in 1987 with Hard Rain running up to Big Interest, which Johnny McCarthy trained at Banteer, County Cork, for Patsy Byrne.

Moving on to 1992 and O'Donovan's Aulton Berto lost out to Brendan Matthews' Newry Hill and, the following year, O'Donovan's Johns Good was foiled by Fraser Black's Owens Sedge. A hat-trick of finalists was completed by Johns Gang losing out to outsider Fungies First. Into the new century and nothing much had changed, with Matt Hyland losing out to Tom O'Dwyer's Smokey Marshall in 2001 and Judicial Castlelu out-pointed by Danaghers Best

Easter Cup

Shelbourne Park

525 yards: 1928–2007; 550 yards: 2008 onwards

Year	Winner	Time	Year	Winner	Time	Year	Winner	Time
1928	Old Blade	30.64	1960	Springvalley Grand	29.92	1992	Farloe Melody	28.95
1929	Old Blade	30.71	1961	Tiny's Trousseau	29.66	1993	Jacks Well	29.54
1930	Hannah's Pup	30.59	1962	The Grand Canal	29.93	1994	Valais Express	29.13
1931	Lion's Share	30.71	1963	General Courtnowski	29.98	1995	Lacken Prince	29.38
1932	Monologue	30.78	1964	Ballet Dante	30.27	1996	Ballyduag Manx	29.23
1933	Rustic Martin	30.59	1965	The Grand Time	29.50	1997	Park Jewel	29.27
1934	Brilliant Bob	30.29	1966	Clomoney Grand	29.50	1998	Mr Pickwick	29.81
1935	Khun Khan	30.54	1967	Tiny's Tidy Town	29.59	1999	Chart King	28.40
1936	Mooncoin Captain	30.54	1968	Itsamint	29.63	2000	Mr Bozz	28.94
1937	Cardinal Puff	30.50	1969	Move Gas	30.29	2001	Late Late Show	28.60
1938	Pagan Miller	30.27	1970	Monalee Gambler	29.52	2002	Late Late Show	28.74
1939	Abbeylara	30.27	1971	Postal Vote	29.36	2003	Mobhi Gamble	28.47
1940	Shy Sandy	30.34	1972	Catsrock Daisy	29.01	2004	Premier Fantasy	28.08
1941	Prince Norroy	30.32	1973	Newpark Arkle	29.40	2005	Mineola Farloe	28.39
1942	Wayside Clover	30.39	1974	Aquaduct Rosy	29.52	2006	Ahane Lad	28.21
1943	Monarch Of The Glen	30.43	1975	Tantallon's Flyer	29.60	2007	Ardkill Jamie	28.30
1944	Empor Lassie	30.35	1976	Cindy's Spec	29.20	2008	Tyrur Kenny	29.91
1945	Astra	29.86	1977	Weigh In First	29.58	2009	Droopys Noel	29.91
1946	Astra	30.40	1978	Rokeel Light	29.50			
1947	Patsy's Record	30.15	1979	Shady Bunch	29.42			
1948	Castlecoman	29.90	1980	Indian Joe	29.16			
1949	Flash Prince	29.85	1981	Murrays Mixture	29.15			
1950	Sandown Champion	29.85	1982	Speedy Wonder	29.40			
1951	Clogher McGrath	30.03	1983	Wicklow Sands	29.64			
1952	Wee Chap	30.12	1984	Spartacus	29.22			
1953	not run		1985	Oran Express	29.67			
1954	Spanish Battleship	30.17	1986	Baby Doll	29.37			
1955	Spanish Battleship	29.72	1987	Spartafitz	29.36			
1956	Baytown Duel	29.67	1988	Joannes Nine	29.65			
1957	Doon Marshall	30.41	1989	Annagh Bar	29.61			
1958	Sharavogue	29.96	1990	Lassana Champ	29.34			
1959	War Dance	29.76	1991	Farloe Melody	29.53			

in 2003. His Swing Out Sister lost out in the coursing Oaks (1989) and Champion Stakes (1990) before Bexhill Cottage won the 1996 Oaks.

Michael O'Donovan enjoyed greater success when turning his hand to training for the track, and Judicial Pride's Shelbourne Park win (2000) gave the trainer and owner Pat Daly a rare Waterloo Cup–Irish Derby double. Michael O'Donovan's brother, Tim O'Donovan, has enjoyed a commendable strike rate in both codes. He Said So won the Irish Derby of 2005 and Tim O'Donovan was also responsible for Limousine, the coursing Oaks winner of 2002, and Micks Magic, the Irish Cup winner in the 2000–01 coursing season. It obviously takes a degree of good fortune but also an enormous element of dedication and know-how to win a Classic in coursing and racing.

There are those who have won the Waterloo Cup at Altcar; the coursing Champion Stakes, Derby and Oaks at Powerstown Park; the Irish Cup (through its renewals at Clounanna and Patrickswell in County Limerick and Tralee in County Kerry); the English Derby (at White City and Wimbledon); and the Irish Derby and associated Classics on the domestic front (at Shelbourne Park and elsewhere).

The Grand Slam

But the winning of the 'grand slam' has eluded everyone. Matt O'Donnell has come close in the latter half of the history of greyhound racing. For his times, of limited communications and transport restrictions, Mick Horan must be remembered for winning an English Derby (Mick The Miller 1929) and an Irish Derby (Guidless Joe, 1932).

Most but not all of the great greyhounds were Irish. Toms The Best remains the only greyhound to have won an Irish Derby (1997) and an English Derby (1998), and was the product of Cypriot Nick Savva's English-based breeding-owning-training line. Savva's stock is clearly identified by the 'Westmead' prefix, and the Toms The Best era was followed by the English Derby dominance of Westmead Hawk (2005 and 2006) and Westmead Lord (2007).

History still awaits the greyhound who will win the English Derby and Irish Derby in the same season. Westmead Hawk (2005) is just one of those to have gone close. Matt O'Donnell rattled the bar in 1992 with Farloe Melody. Charlie Lister has had more ammunition than most and was nearly on target with his dual English Derby winner Rapid Ranger at Shelbourne Park in 2000 and with Some Picture in 1997. Some Picture had also gone from Lister's Nottingham base and won the Scottish Derby at Shawfield in 1997; and the dream of the same greyhound winning the Scottish–English–Irish treble in the same season may be forever elusive.

Pride and joy ... Trainer Michael O'Donovan goes to collect his winner Judicial Pride (2) after the first Irish Derby of the millenium at Shelbourne Park.

Irish Oaks

Run at Shelbourne Park, except in the asterisked years:
* Harold's Cross, ** Cork, *** Limerick, **** Clonmel
550 yards: 1932; 525 yards: 1933 onwards

Year	Winner	Time	Year	Winner	Time	Year	Winner	Time
1932	Queen of the Suir****	31.80	1964	Knock Her*	29.98	1996	Fossabeg Maid	29.51
1933	Loophole****	30.55	1965	Drunsough Prince	29.76	1997	Borna Best	28.86
1934	Chocolate Kid*	31.18	1966	Hairdresser*	29.40	1998	April Surprise	28.95
1935	The Fenian Bride	30.73	1967	Kevinsfort Queen	29.79	1999	Borna Survivor	28.67
1936	Chicken Sandwich*	30.73	1968	Orwell Parade*	29.96	2000	Marinas Tina	28.56
1937	Godivas Turn	30.61	1969	Itsamint	29.35	2001	Marinas Tina	28.60
1938	Gentle Sally Again*	30.13	1970	Rosmore Robin*	29.60	2002	Lifes Beauty	28.70
1939	Janetta Hunloke**	30.47	1971	Blissful Pride*	29.30	2003	Axle Grease	28.64
1940	not run		1972	Brandon Velvet*	29.45	2004	Legal Moment	28.59
1941	not run		1973	Romping To Work*	29.20	2005	Graylands Pixie	28.78
1942	Fair Mistress***	30.10	1974	Fur Collar*	29.40	2006	Shelbourne Becky	28.58
1943	Mad Printer**	30.05	1975	Main Avenue*	28.98	2007	Ms Firecracker	28.54
1944	My Little Daisy*	30.08	1976	Clashing Daisy*	29.64	2008	Oran Majestic	29.02
1945	Paladin's Charm	30.70	1977	Snow Maiden	29.09	2009	Skywalker Queen	28.24
1946	Cold Christmas*	29.86	1978	Hail Fun	29.40			
1947	Belle o' Manhattan	30.46	1979	Nameless Pixie*	29.34			
1948	Lovely Louisa*	29.90	1980	Strange Legend*	29.24			
1949	Coolkill Darkie	30.36	1981	Claremont Mary*	29.52			
1950	Celtic Gem*	30.00	1982	My Last Hope*	29.32			
1951	Glenco Pearl	30.23	1983	Quick Suzy*	29.38			
1952	Peaceful Lady*	29.95	1984	Burnpark Sally*	28.92			
1953	Peaceful Lady	30.11	1985	Airmount Jewel*	29.06			
1954	Wild Iris*	30.04	1986	Meadowbank Tip*	29.34			
1955	Prairie Peg	29.55	1987	Yale Princess*	29.42			
1956	Baytown Dell*	29.99	1988	Tracy Budd*	29.26			
1957	Gallant Maid	30.02	1989	Picture Card*	29.40			
1958	Ballet Festival*	29.73	1990	Bornacurra Liz*	29.10			
1959	Last Landing	30.09	1991	Gentle Soda*	29.12			
1960	Tristam*	30.03	1992	Old Spinster*	29.42			
1961	Just Sherry	29.95	1993	Libertys Echo	29.48			
1962	Purty Good*	29.78	1994	Shimmering Wings	29.23			
1963	Cherry Express	29.87	1995	Cool Survivor	29.35			

'Byrning' up the track . . . Cool
Performance shows scorching pace to
lead in the Paddy Power Irish Derby at
Shelbourne Park in 2001. Owned by
Patsy Byrne, Cool Performance held on
to beat Pat Kenny's Late Late Show in
a thrilling photo-finish.

19 OWNERSHIP

THE DREAM LIVES ON

Every year, the expectations of Eddie Costello and his wife Grace and his entourage were higher, heightened by his dogs' fast trials and rave reviews in the *Sporting Life*. The trade press carried regular features on what Costello had bought with the English Derby in mind.

The Breeds of Owner

There are many branches to the greyhound family tree. The afghan, borzoi, saluki and whippet are just some of those that can claim a relationship to the finished article. The purebred greyhound itself can be divided into those used for racing on the track and the more robust type seen coursing in the field.

Racing greyhounds are bred and trained to excel over distances ranging from 300 yards to 1,025 yards (two laps of the track) and beyond. Also coming in infinite varieties are the owners. There are those wealthy enough to dabble in the sport and buy a rising star with the prospect of winning a prestigious pot. There are others who are interested in all aspects of the game and, while their initial intention was to simply own a winning greyhound, they become so caught up

Eddie Costello: his vain pursuit of victory in the English Derby at White City, London, made him a greyhound-racing legend.

with the whole business that it takes over their lives. They find themselves hooked and end up as breeders and trainers.

Eddie Costello and the English Derby

Eddie Costello surely qualifies for a category all of his own. A Roscommon man, he went to London in the late 1950s. Like so many others in the greyhound game, he made his fortune in the construction business. A decade later, and already the local-boy-makes-good-to-the-folks-back-home, the winning of the greyhound Derby at White City was a full-blown obsession for Costello.

He wanted a Derby trophy; and, seemingly, at any price. He put everything into his pursuit. He had the top agents scouring Ireland for likely winners, and he had the money to pay for the pups. After that, he entrusted his purchases to the leading trainers. Paddy Keane, Ger McKenna, Eugene McNamara and Francis Murray all tried valiantly on Costello's behalf.

Francis Murray – the son of Michael Murray, an established trainer of earlier years – effectively became Costello's private trainer at his base at Crookedwood, County Westmeath, and prepared the Costello team for the annual sortie to White City in London. Costello himself virtually set up camp in the White City restaurant with his sidekick Fred Warrell. Warrell knew greyhounds, and greyhound people. He had dogs with Ger McKenna for the track and with the coursing 'maestro', Jack Mullan, for the field. Every year, the expectations of Eddie Costello, his wife Grace and his entourage were higher, heightened by his dogs' fast trials and rave reviews in the *Sporting Life*. The trade press carried regular features on what Costello had bought with the English Derby in mind. It replicated a situation on the coursing scene, which, weeks before the coursing Derby, buzzed with excitement over which dog would be running in the name of Mary McGrath from Coalisland, County Tyrone.

The latter stages of the 1980 English Derby came down to two principals. Hurry On Bran was recommended to Costello, who bought him and gave him to his favoured trainer Murray. Costello regularly sourced promising greyhounds in the Limerick area, and would also have been aware of Indian Joe, a dog trained on Shannonside by John Hayes and who had won that year's Easter Cup at Shelbourne Park. Indian Joe was owned by Kevin Frost, from a well-to-do family in Limerick business life. Costello would have assumed that Indian Joe was not for sale. And, anyway, there was a rumour going around that he was carrying an injury in the English Derby. Above all, Costello had Hurry On Bran.

The record books tell us what happened. Belfast bookmaker Alfie McLean made Frost an offer that he did not refuse; Indian Joe won the 1980 English Derby final at White City … and Hurry On Bran was second. Still, Costello had the bug. The following year, he entered no fewer than eleven greyhounds for the English Derby. The Murray string got a mysterious virus, and Hurry On Bran, Calandra Champ and Murray's Mixture and others had to be withdrawn.

There was to be another twist to the 1981 renewal. The one Costello-owned dog to survive past the entry stage was Prince Spy, not from an Irish kennel but trained by Geoffrey DeMulder. Running in the name of Grace Costello, it was 33/1 chance Prince Spy who avoided Joe Kelly's prone Barley Field and John Haynes' hapless Rahan Ship and chased home Parkdown Jet, trained by Ger McKenna, in the English Derby final.

Like Hurry On Bran before him, Calandra Champ came back to contest the Irish Derby. It looked all set up for him; but an hour before the meeting, it rained cats and dogs. The rain did not effect the going because the rain lodged on the track rather than seeping into it. However, Calandra Champ could not cope, while Bold Work, which normally struggled to stay 525 yards, skimmed over the surface water … and won.

At that point, in the early 1980s, Costello was thought to be shelling out a mind-blowing £60,000-plus per annum on greyhounds, simply to try and win a Derby. An infamy grew around Costello's ill-luck. It had turned to paranoia. One owner refused to part with his greyhound at any price. 'I'd have been signing the dog's death warrant. The dog would break a leg at least,' he said, as whispers went around the ever-superstitious greyhound racing community that the owner and or his trainer(s) were jinxed. Whatever the cause and

effect, there was an extraordinary trend that saw greyhounds seemingly cursed when they changed ownership. It happens all the time and some owners do not sell their dogs as they believe it is tantamount to selling their luck.

As the buyer of other people's dogs, Eddie Costello seemed blighted. And it made no difference who trained them. Keane and McKenna had Derby winners for others but even the latter's touch seemed to desert him when it came to Costello's dogs. Under Francis Murray, Calandra Champ did go on to win the National Breeders' Produce Stakes at Clonmel and Murray's Mixture followed Indian Joe into the Easter Cup annals at Shelbourne Park and won the Irish Cesarewitch at Navan, all in 1981.

Eddie Costello and the Irish Derby

Costello did not get where he was on the London-Irish ladder by being thwarted. Even though he had not had any

Happier times … Denis Brosnan (then of the Kerry Group and later chairman at Horse Racing Ireland) (second from left) presents the trophy to Grace Costello after Hurry On Bran won the 1980 Champion Stakes at Shelbourne Park. Also pictured are (extreme right) owner Eddie Costello, trainer Francis Murray and his wife Kathleen Murray.

Bookmaker Alfie McLean's expensive purchase Indian Joe beat Eddie Costello's Hurry On Bran in the English Derby final at White City, London, in 1980.

Rathgallen Tady (pictured with trainer's son John McKenna, trainer Ger McKenna and his wife Josie) won the Irish Derby at Shelbourne Park in 1987, the evening after owner Eddie Costello's wife Grace had died.

joy in the English Derby, there was still Shelbourne Park and the Irish Derby. But when the presentation for the 1987 Irish Derby was made, there was no sign of the now forty-nine-year-old Costello. The photograph shows John McKenna, the trainer's son, holding Rathgallen Tady. This was the third Irish Derby winner for Ger McKenna, but in the presentation photographs he is not looking at the camera, but gazing somewhere off in the distance, lost in his own thoughts. Josie McKenna, the trainer's wife, holds the trophy.

Rathgallen Tady was the most unlikely of Ger McKenna's Derby winners. He was not a favourite at White City, as Parkdown Jet (1981) and Lartigue Note (1989) were. He was not a speedster like Own Pride, which won the 1969 Irish Derby at Harold's Cross in 29.20, won the Irish St Leger at the Market's Field in 30.95 and ran up the 1970 Irish Derby at Shelbourne Park. He was certainly no Bashful Man, which won the 1973 Irish Derby at Shelbourne Park for McKenna in an outrageous 28.82 on turf.

So in 1987, it was not a Classic Irish Derby final line-up, but Matt O'Donnell had a worthy favourite in Ardfert Seán and Christy Daly's Randy would go on and win that year's Irish St Leger. The omens were good, however, for Rathgallen Tady. A naturally wide runner, he was given trap six in the draw, an advantage that he surely needed in the decider. The previous year, the distance of the Irish Derby had been lengthened from 525 yards to 550 yards. That was another plus for a greyhound not endowed with phenomenal early pace, and which needed a particular box and a longer trip. For all the things that appeared to be falling in his favour, he was that rarity: a Ger McKenna-trained outsider in a Derby final. McKenna had a second runner in Balalika. In any other year, with another trap draw, over any other distance … in any other circumstances, Rathgallen Tady would not have won the Irish Derby. And when it came to the presentation party, the centrepiece – the owner – was not there.

Twenty-four hours before this Saturday evening in September, Grace Costello – who had been such an integral part of her husband's business success and who had endured all the highs and lows of his pursuit of greyhound racing's most coveted prize – had died. Years later, Eddie Costello would say: 'The race didn't matter to me. When I watch it on video, I am still not interested because I was not involved. With Grace so ill, I was simply aware that he was in the Derby and that was all. Grace rang on the Saturday of the semi-finals to see if he had qualified but, in the end, she had no sense of time and asked me that week if the dog won the final.'

Rathgallen Tady won in a photo-finish blur that seemed to take the judge an age to decipher. Eddie Costello won a first prize of £27,500 and a first Derby … and had spent over £600,000 in achieving it. Even today, more than two decades on, £600,000 is a substantial sum of money. Long after the Costello era, Francis Murray would win his Derby with Droopys Sandy in Scotland in 1994.

The Story of Ownership

The story of Eddie and Grace Costello would be but a poignant chapter in the story stretching back through the millenniums to ancient Egypt of a burning wish to own the fastest greyhound, the one that is fleeter than the other man's. Such a pride was known to the court of Pharaohs, and to the most aristocratic circles of the Romans and later to the British nobility. Lord Lurgan had the wealth to purchase the first recognised coursing colossus in Master M'Grath; and Albert Williams had the money to buy track titan Mick The Miller, which, in turn, was sold to another man of means Arundel Kempton. Mick The Miller won the English Derby for both Williams and Kempton (in the name of his wife Phyllis) in 1929 and 1930, respectively.

The value placed on the most-prized greyhound reached new heights when Alfie McLean, a bookmaker like Albert Williams, purchased Indian Joe before he won the 1980 English Derby. Money changed hands but the fortune held good, too. 'Luck money' – the vendor giving some of his money back as a token to the purchaser – plays a major part in the folklore of greyhound sport.

Late Late Show

In the modern era, syndication has become popular as it allows those who might not otherwise afford involvement to share the purchase price and the ancillary costs such as

training fees. The story of a dog called Late Late Show sets it apart from the thousands that have been re-told over the greyhound generations. This greyhound was named after the longest-running chat show in the history of global television. Pat Kenny had taken over from Gay Byrne on the RTÉ programme, and happened to be the host when Bord na

Pat's a winner … RTÉ presenter Pat Kenny parades his Late Late Show after one of the dog's many successes.

The almost unbearable pre-race tension culminates in literally seconds of frenzied action. In the immediate aftermath, there is the realisation for the owner of what has happened: the disappointment of defeat or the exhilaration of victory.

Tragic end . . . Josie McKenna, wife of trainer Ger McKenna, receives the trophy after Time Up Please had won the Irish St Leger at Market's Field, Limerick, in 1971. Minutes earlier, the dog's owner Michael Loughnane had collapsed and died on the steps of the stand.

gCon hit on the idea of naming the greyhound and gifting him to the host.

And so Pat Kenny, with an address at the RTÉ Studios in Donnybrook, Dublin, became the proud owner of one of the sport's most decorated racers.

It was a high-risk strategy. The dog, which actually appeared on the Friday-night programme, could have flopped spectacularly. In fact, Late Late Show was put into the care of Paul Hennessy at Gowran, County Kilkenny, and became one of the greatest four-legged ambassadors in the annals of the sport.

A win in the Irish Derby of 2001 narrowly eluded him when he failed to catch Cool Performance. But he was a major attraction at Shelbourne Park, winning the Easter Cup in both 2001 and 2002, as well as a host of other open races. Appropriately, some of his most scintillating displays were reserved for the nights when the television cameras were present.

Time Up Please

There is no doubt that the greyhound, in whatever code, sets the blood coursing and the pulse racing. The almost unbearable pre-race tension culminates in literally seconds of frenzied action. In the immediate aftermath, there is the realisation for the owner of what has happened: the disappointment of defeat or the exhilaration of victory.

In 1971 at the Market's Field, Limerick, Mick Loughnane proudly watched Ger McKenna parade his Time Up Please. The dog won the Irish St Leger in 30.56 – 0.10 seconds inside the clock recorded by Prince Of Bermuda in 1956. It was a time they said would never be beaten. Mick Loughnane's neighbours from Roscrea, County Tipperary, turned to congratulate him. The last thing that the owner had seen was the digits on the track clock. He had collapsed and died. The photograph would be eerily recreated at Shelbourne Park in 1987 with Rathgallen Tady: a presentation with no owner.

Winning Owners

Two years later, in 1973, McKenna would bring Bashful Man to Shelbourne Park and win the Irish Derby in the fastest time ever run in the final (28.82). The greyhound was owned by Deirdre Hynes, and purchased for her by her father Con Hynes, a businessman from Portumna, County Galway. Picturesquely situated on the banks of the River Shannon, Portumna was also the base for trainer Tony Fahy, who had a greyhound in training for Deirdre Hynes. Peruvian Style just fell short of being top class. However, his exploits caught the public imagination when he became a prolific winner. The trainer set his sights on the record of twenty consecutive wins held by the bitch Westpark Mustard. In 1974, Westpark Mustard had passed the nineteen-in-a-row of Mick The Miller, and the new mark was already under threat. Peruvian Style equalled the twenty-in-a-row of Westpark Mustard but ran second in a race at Galway when attempting to set a new standard.

Another owner blessed was Tim O'Connor from Killorglin, County Kerry, who turned his hand to breeding and training to such effect, and who gave us the 'Spanish' brigade – 1949 Irish Derby winner 'Lad', the 1949 and 1950 Irish Laurels winner 'Chestnut' and, above all, 'Battleship', who won the Irish Derby on three occasions (1953, 1954, 1955), as well as the 1955 Irish Laurels and the 1954 and 1955 Easter Cup.

Eddie Costello has not been alone in putting much into the sport and getting a scant return. Others have flirted with greyhound racing and benefited handsomely. More have been there for the long haul. Noel Ryan was a steadfast patron of Paddy Keane when the trainer returned to Ireland in 1969. Ryan went into joint ownership with Paschal Taggart and their Dipmac won the 1984 Irish Derby when in the care of Séamus Graham. Ryan, as an octogenarian, welcomed in Loyal Honcho as an appropriately named Graham-trained winner of the English Derby in 2008. Pat Daly has patronised the Michael O'Donovan kennels and been rewarded with a Waterloo Cup winner (Judicial Inquiry in 1999) and Irish Derby winner (Judicial Pride in 2000).

Arguably, nobody has given more to greyhound sport in its long history than Patsy Byrne. Like Eddie Costello, Byrne's wealth is based on the building business in Britain. His ambition matches that of Costello but, unlike his fellow Irishman, Byrne's altruism has been tempered by an approach that allows him to see greyhound sport as part-hobby and part-business. A richly varied association with greyhound sport has seen Byrne win the English Derby as a trainer (Ballinderry Ash, 1991), an Irish Derby (Cool Performance, 2001), a coursing Derby (Big Interest, 1987) and a cabinet of other coursing trophies.

Even his achievements in the field would pale, however, when compared to those of Mary McGrath. Her stamp and that of her husband Colm McGrath will be inked forever in the history of greyhound sport. Across the two codes, coursing and racing, the Coalisland, County Tyrone, couple can claim to be greyhound sport's most successful team.

An A–Z of Greyhounds

W   Weight

Weights of greyhounds differ greatly, not just between dogs and bitches, but within the males of the breed also. Master M'Grath's weight is thought to have been fifty-four pounds, while Mick The Miller weighed in at sixty-four pounds and Spanish Battleship at just sixty pounds. The dog that many would regard as the greatest park-coursing champion of all time, Master Myles, is thought to have weighed nintey-five pounds.

Tartan Khan, one of the many champions to feature Clonalvy Pride in his breeding, pictured after winning the 1975 English Derby at White City, London, the first to be run over 500 metres. Second from left is Liam Garrahy, who sold the dog to owner Derek Law (seen receiving the trophy), and who is the father of former Bord na gCon regulations manager, John Garrahy.

20 BREEDING
WHEN MUTTON CUTLET WAS TOP DOG

A 'grand' dog ... Bord na gCon chairman
Dr P.J. Maguire (left) pictured with owner/
trainer Paddy Dunphy and his 1962
English Derby winner The Grand Canal.

Mutton Cutlet

A greyhound called Milo sired Milanie, the first winner of the Waterloo Cup at Altcar in 1836. The name of the stud dog does not resound through the pages of greyhound sport's history. Unlike thoroughbred horses, early greyhound sport does not boast sires like the Darley Arabian, Godolphin Arabian and Byerley Turk, which are the breeding pillars of the sport. Thoroughbred equine breeding was already well structured by the end of the eighteenth century in Britain, the Darley Arabian having been brought into the country in 1704.

The first *Greyhound Stud Book* was published in 1882 and T.A. Morris, to whom so much is owed, began the *Irish Greyhound Stud Book* in 1923. He was not only responsible for the publication of the *Irish Stud Book* but for many of the original landmark entries. For T.A. Morris had also imported Mutton Cutlet, which, given Morris' initial animosity to greyhound racing, added a dash of irony in becoming the first dual-purpose sire. Mutton Cutlet was also responsible for one of the all-time great dual-purpose greyhounds in Monologue, which won the 1933 Irish Derby on the track at Shelbourne Park having already lifted the coursing Oaks at Powerstown Park in 1932. And he came up with the 1933 winner of the English Derby (Future Cutlet) when mated to Wary Guide, a daughter of Guiding Hand, sire of the winner of the first official Irish Derby in 1932 (Guidless Joe).

The innumerable credits of Mutton Cutlet included siring Queen of the Suir, which won the Irish Oaks in 1932, which was run that year over 550 yards at Clonmel, and the English Oaks in both 1932 and 1933, then run at London's White City. Queen of the Suir was dam to the Irish-Derby-winning bitch Brave Damsel. Queen of the Suir was nine years of age when the Brave Damsel litter was whelped and the sire, Maiden's Boy, was an eleven-year-old.

Mutton Cutlet was also grand-sire to Davesland, which won the 1934 English Derby; and Mutton Cutlet brought his influence to bear on the distaff side in the 1937 (Wattle Bark) and 1938 (Lone Keel) winners. If there are such things as 'foundation sires' in the history of greyhound racing, then Mutton Cutlet has to be right up there.

Astra

It could be argued that the racing bitches – the dams of the breeding paddocks – do more than the male lines to perpetuate the prowess of the species. That was certainly true of Astra, which won the Irish Puppy Derby in 1944 and followed up by taking the Easter Cup in both 1945 and 1946. She had been alone in completing the Irish Puppy Derby–Easter Cup double until the Pat Buckley-trained Droopys Noel won the 2008 Irish Puppy Derby and doubled up in the Easter Cup in April 2009. Unlike many other hard-raced bitches, Astra passed on her ability even though she only had one litter. That mating (with Paddy The Champion) produced Astra's Son which in turn sired Prairie Vixen, dam of the 1955 Irish Oaks heroine Prairie Peg. Prairie Peg was sent to one of the cornerstones of greyhound breeding in Hi There, and gave us Prairie Flash.

Astra was by Tanist (ex-Mad Darkie) and a repeat mating gave the sport Mad Tanist. Astra's younger full brother sired a whole generation of winners including the 1951 Irish Derby winner Carmody's Tanist.

The mating of Prairie Vixen (to The Grand Champion) resulted in Prairie Peg, and the latter (in a mating with Champion Prince) produced Pigalle Wonder. Pigalle Wonder started his racing days in Kilkenny (as Prairie Champion) but was sold to the owner of the Pigalle Club in London, Al Burnett, and owed much of his ability to a dam-line that featured many of the Paddy Dunphy 'Grand' bloodlines. It was certainly a shrewd buy, as Pigalle Wonder took the 1958 English Derby at White City.

Further benefits were to accrue and A.S. Lucas from Bray, County Wicklow, stepped in to buy Pigalle Wonder at the end of his racing days. As a sire, Pigalle Wonder was responsible for Jack Mullan's 1964 Irish Derby winner Wonder Valley and Tom Lync's Russian Gun, which won the Irish Derby of 1967 and ran up the 1968 renewal.

Lineage

Three decades after the introduction of greyhound racing to these islands, the lineage required for getting track winners was becoming apparent. Tim O'Connor was a breeder hugely favoured by fortune, and his combining of Spanish Chestnut and Ballyseedy Memory (which he had leased from a neighbour) gave him Spanish Battleship, winner of the Irish Derby on three occasions (1953, 1954, 1955). Spanish Chestnut had a Classic-winning history of his own (Irish Laurels 1949 and 1950).

Imperial Dancer had a less illustrious track career, but sired the 1956 Irish Derby winner in Keep Moving and the winner of the 1957 renewal in Hopeful Cutlet. Another to produce back-to-back Irish Derby winners was Knock Hill Chieftain with Chieftain's Guest and Shane's Legacy in 1961 and 1962, respectively. Monalee Champion, with Hi There and The Grand Prince as grand-sires, repeated the feat in 1976 and 1977 with his respective winners Tain Mor and Linda's Champion. Monalee Champion stood with Jack Mullan, and the Newry, County Down, trainer had the record of handling Classic winners on track and field as well as one of the all-time great greyhound-racing sires.

Clonalvy Pride produced Always Proud, the 1966 Irish Derby winner, and he, in turn, gave us the 1969 winner and 1970 runner-up in Own Pride. Clonalvy Pride also came up with the 1967 Irish St Leger winner Yanka Boy, and that canine line was to be particularly kind to Ger McKenna and his owner Mick Loughnane, from Roscrea, County Tipperary. Clonalvy Pride appears three generations back in the breeding on both Cairnville Jet and Gabriel Ruby, sire and dam of McKenna's 1981 English Derby winner Parkdown Jet. Loughnane also owned Time Up Please, and his story is ultimately a sad one in that the owner died as Time Up Please crossed the line after winning his first Irish St Leger in Limerick in 1971. Time Up Please went on to sire Paddy Keane's Irish Derby winner of 1978, Pampered Rover. In the same period, Clonalvy Pride re-emerges as the grand-sire of consecutive winners of the English Derby in Tartan Khan (1975) and Mutts Silver (1976). It is not the first time that he did so as he was also grand-sire of dual English Derby winner Patricias Hope (1972 and 1973). He also pops up in the back-breeding of the 1977 English Derby winner Balliniska Band through Lively Band, Jack Murphy's winner of the Irish Derby and Irish St Leger in 1974.

The first *Greyhound Stud Book* was published in 1882 and T.A. Morris, to whom so much is owed, began the *Irish Greyhound Stud Book* in 1923.

Throughout the history of the sport, the message has been that success on the track can regularly be translated into success as a sire; but it does not always work out that way. The temptation, of course, is to go back to dogs and bitches which have already produced the goods in competition and try to replicate the success.

That's my 'Boy'...Trainer Ger McKenna and Roscrea, County Tipperary, owner Michael Loughnane after the success of Yanka Boy in the Irish St Leger at Market's Field, Limerick. Mick Loughnane later owned the dual Irish St Leger winner Time Up Please (1971–72). Yanka Boy was by the influential Clonalvy Pride and Time Up Please was a son of the great Newdown Heather.

Throughout the history of the sport, the message has been that success on the track can regularly be translated into success as a sire; but it does not always work out that way. The temptation, of course, is to go back to dogs and bitches that have already produced the goods in competition and try to replicate the success. The potential problem is that sires become over-used, with the result that their potency becomes diluted, and that too many bitches can become too closely related.

Prairie Peg and Prairie Flash

The same does not apply to dams, and few did more for the purity and strength of the breed than Prairie Peg. With grand-sires in Mad Tanist and Astra's Son, and parents in The Grand Champion and Prairie Vixen, Prairie Peg was brought to Hi There with the odds seemingly favouring a blessed litter. It was one of those occasions that all the portents worked out, with the Hi There–Prairie Peg mating producing nine pups. One of the number was Prairie Flash, a dog that not only had an exciting racing career but a sensational stud career, stretching over nine years. Even when Prairie Flash was diagnosed with cancer in his hind leg at the age of eleven (in 1969), his career did not end. Owner Tony Nugent saved his prized greyhound through amputation, and Prairie Flash comfortably returned to stud duties, albeit on a limited scale.

He sired a string of greyhounds with the 'Greenane' prefix, owned by either Tony Nugent or his brother Paddy. Blue blood of the canine kind was in the veins of Prairie Flash and he appropriately sired the Duke of Edinburgh's 1968 English Derby winner Camira Flash.

Sand Man

A seismic change in greyhound breeding in Britain and Ireland came about when an Irish-American priest, Father Dan Green, imported Sand Man from the US. Sand Man was a well-bred American racer (Friend Westy–Miss Gorgeous) but proved unfashionable as a sire Stateside. Reversing the old trend by which Bord na gCon had sought to swamp the American market with Irish stock, 1973

whelp Sand Man left his mark throughout Irish greyhound genealogy. This was partly because the time was opportune for a fresh injection into Irish blood lines, with suitable out-crosses becoming increasingly hard to find and the gene pool being pretty limited.

Sand Man stood at Portlaoise with John Fitzpatrick and Joe Dunne. The latter was a baker in the County Laois town and his son Michael Dunne has continued a family tradition in importing sires, mainly from Australia in more recent times. The early criticism of Sand Man was that his male progeny were 'soft' and, indeed, many went to finals but failed to win. He ultimately produced the goods when Dipmac won the 1984 Irish Derby at Shelbourne Park for Séamus Graham, the same year as another son in Whisper Wishes won the last English Derby to be run at White City in London for Charlie Coyle.

Whisper Wishes

As shrewd as T.A. Morris's importing of Mutton Cutlet, A.S. Lucas' purchase of Pigalle Wonder and, indeed, Dan Green's importing of Sand Man, was the purchase by Patsy

Newdown Heather stood at the kennels of racing and coursing trainer Jack Mullan and was one of the most prolific sires of winners in the annals of greyhound sport.

Prairie Flash with three of owner Tony Nugent's children: (L–R) Catherine, Mike and Tony (jnr).

X   Xenophobia

Greyhound racing began in Australia in the same month and the same year as at Shelbourne Park – May 1927. New South Wales is the sport's traditional home in Australia, and the country is renowned for its rigid regulation, particularly in matters relating to betting. A number of Irish greyhounds were exported to stand at stud in Australia, and Irish breeders had a rather xenophobic approach to foreign stock. However, more recent times have seen firstly American and now Australian bloodlines playing an important part in Irish breeding.

Byrne from John Duffy of Whisper Wishes on the night that he won the English Derby. Whisper Wishes (Sand Man–Micklem Drive) was, along with his father, a foundation sire of modern greyhound racing – his bitches being in particular demand because of their future breeding potential.

Other important sires followed, though Phantom Flash – from the Nick Savva 'Westmead' line – died before realising his full potential. He did, however, sire many notable winners including Séamus Graham's 1996 Irish Derby winner Tina Marina. Top Honcho became a pillar of the Michael Dunne range and Staplers Jo became noted as a sire of outstanding bitches, particularly brood bitches.

The Clergy

Apart from the dogs, it is remarkable the part played by the Catholic clergy in the development of, and key moments in, greyhound racing. Father Martin Brophy bred Mick The Miller and sold him on the steps of the White City grandstand on the eve of his first English Derby win in 1929. The great Tanist, the 1940 Irish Derby winner at Shelbourne Park, and sire of the 1947 Harold's Cross hero Daring Flash, was bred by a priest. Fearing disapproval from the hierarchy, the parish priest of Killenaule, County Tipperary, appeared on the card as Mr W. Twyford.

At the end of the 1944–45 coursing season, the Irish Cup at Clounanna was won by Mountain Emperor, which was nominated and owned by a Mr N. Ennis. Three years later, the real Mr N. Ennis was 'unfrocked' when Carlow man Revd William Dowling was elected as president of the Irish Coursing Club.

High-office Breeders and Owners

The ICC nominees to Bord na gCon were often there because of their knowledge of breeding. Consequently, ownership and high office were not always separate, and the list of Irish Coursing Club presidents is peppered with the names of fortunate owners.

Thomas Ahern had two spells in the ICC post (1938–42 and

1951–52) and served on Bord na gCon (1958–63). His Celbridge Chance won the Irish Laurels in Cork in 1959 and the owner nominated him to win the Irish Cup at Clounanna in both 1960 and 1961.

Joining T.A. Morris in the first ICC administration was Philip O'Sullivan and the Limerick City man gave eight years (1916–24) service as president. Bernard Rahill from Leixlip, County Kildare, served, like Thomas Ahern, for two spells as ICC president (1953–56 and 1959). Like Aherne, P.J. Cox from Newbridge, County Kildare, had long and productive tenures with both the ICC and Bord na gCon. Owner of Newbridge track, Cox spent six years at the ICC helm (1960–66), and was the longest-serving member of Bord na gCon (1962–82). Being on controlling bodies for both codes did not ensure harmony, and Cox found himself on Bord na gCon and dithering over whether to license the greyhound track in Ballybunion, County Kerry, when its owner Matthew Sullivan was the ICC president (1966–72).

Another man of considerable energy was William Russell. He lived at Kilross, County Tipperary, but was the backbone of the annual Galbally coursing fixture. An astute political animal, Russell was ICC president (1978–81) and a Bord na gCon member (1973–77).

The names of those who served on the Irish Coursing Club executive and Bord na gCon in or around the same time do not necessarily appear in the breeding credits. However, the ICC representatives staunchly voiced the concerns of the breeders at Bord na gCon level. It would have been felt that Bord na gCon was more concerned with the needs of owners and trainers than those of the grassroots breeder.

As a man with an interest in both camps, Russell would have been undoubtedly happy when the 1976 Waterloo Cup winner Minnesota Miller sired the winner of the Irish Derby at Shelbourne Park in 1980, Suir Miller. The victory of Suir Miller capped a remarkable rise in the ranks for trainer Michael Barrett, the Tipperary man who had also been responsible for the 1977 Irish Derby winner Linda's Champion. Russell was succeeded at the ICC by Arthur (A.J.) Morris, who had served a stint as secretary with his father Thomas (T.A.) Morris (1948–52) before going solo (1952–56).

Breeding and Coursing

A half-century after the advent of greyhound racing in Ireland, coursing and track breeding had effectively gone their separate ways. The coursing influence had still been strong for many years after the artificial lure was first seen. For instance, Irish Cup and coursing Derby winner White Sandhills crops up in the 'tree' of Priceless Border and Endless Gossip, the respective winners of the English Derby in 1948 and 1952.

Jack Mullan was in the happy situation of standing the leading coursing sire (Newdown Heather) and track sire (Monalee Champion) at one and the same time. Newdown Heather was arguably the most dominant coursing sire ever, while Mary McGrath's Best Man exercised an almost total monopoly in park coursing at one point. The greyhound likely to exert the most lasting influence in coursing in the coming years is Hilltown, through the numerous litters he sired. Bred by Garry Anderson, and trained by Brendan Matthews for his son Paul, Hilltown was the offspring of another Matthews inmate in Newry Hill.

The mating of Newry Hill and the bitch Shauns Dilemma was always going to produce something special. Hilltown won the coursing Derby in 1997 and the Champion Stakes of the following season. It became commonplace for Hilltown to sire multiple winners in a season, including winners at the national meeting. A high point included the 2007 dividing of the coursing Oaks by two of his daughters, Chubbys Accord and Qualityandgold.

Minnestota Mama . . . Mary Ryan, Cashel, County Tipperary, with Minnesota Yank and Minnesota Miller which won the Waterloo Cup in successive seasons (1976–77). They were full brothers from different litters. Pictured on right is Carmel Looby with Letesia, dam of both dogs.

LEFT
A stud advertisement dating from the 1940s for Quare Times, a greyhound based at Killenaule, County Tipperary, with trainer Billy Quinn.

At the off . . . Another well-bred sextet
of canine athletes springs into action and
goes in pursuit of a valuable prize on one
of the three nights of racing held weekly at
Shelbourne Park, Dublin.

21 GOING TO THE DOGS

THEN AND NOW

The layout of Dunmore Stadium suited the running style of those transferring from the coursing field, and track greyhounds from coursing stocks excelled here.

Like coursing venues before them, greyhound tracks were founded and tended to prosper in urban areas where they constituted commercially sound propositions for local businessmen, or where there was a sufficient population of greyhounds and a greyhound-rearing community to keep the show going. Belfast and Dublin were ideal venues for tracks as they were cities of size while, at the same time, within easy reach of rurally based greyhound owners. The snag was that the vast spaces needed as greyhound racing venues also attracted land speculators and developers.

Celtic Park and Dunmore Stadium

Easter Monday in 1927 saw the first greyhound race staged in Ireland, and won by Mutual Friend, at Celtic Park. The ground was already the home of Belfast Celtic Football Club; and bookmaker, coursing enthusiast and greyhound racing pioneer Hugh McAlinden was on the board of directors at the soccer club. The track was the home of the Ulster Derby and even staged a couple of early runnings of the Irish St Leger in 1932 and 1943. In an uncertain period, Celtic Park closed in 1978, re-opened in 1980 and closed again, finally, in 1983.

Dunmore Stadium in Belfast opened sixteen months after Celtic Park and outlived it by sixteen years. A circuit of massive dimensions (576 yards), Dunmore Stadium was the home of the Irish National Sprint. The 435-yard race provided a fantastic spectacle. It was won in 1943 by Fair Mistress, which had won the Irish Oaks at Limerick in the

previous season. Mad Tanist (1944), Sandown Champion (1950), Hi There (1954), and Bauhus (1965) all won here before going on to notable stud careers.

Among the sons of Sandown Champion was the 1954 English Derby winner Pauls Fun, while Bauhus sired the White City champion of 1969, Sand Star. Bauhus was followed by the great Hairdresser, which emulated Fair Mistress by winning at Dunmore in 1966 and also taking the Irish Oaks (Harold's Cross).

The layout of Dunmore Stadium suited the running style of those transferring from the coursing field, and track greyhounds from coursing stocks excelled here. Mullaghroe Hiker won the coursing Derby in 1967 and then transferred to the kennel of Jack Mullan for his track schedule. At the stage when he won the Irish National Sprint, he had been bought by Luke Kilcoyne, whose son Pat part-owned the 1984 Waterloo Cup winner Tubbertelly Queen. I'm Slippy, owned by Derryman John Quinn, completed the 1983 Irish National Sprint–English Derby double.

Dunmore Stadium fell under the hammer in 2000; like Celtic Park, its demise was hastened by civic unrest.

Tracks No Longer in Existence

Belfast aside, the core tracks have largely remained intact in the past eighty years. Others no longer in existence or which never got off the ground include:

ARKLOW: Bord na gCon received an application for the operation of a track in the County Wicklow seaside town in 1959. The application was refused and an appeal failed.

BALLINA: A greyhound racing company was set up in 1947 in the County Mayo town, but there is no evidence that official public races ever took place there.

BALLYBUNION: The existence of the track by the seaside in County Kerry, run by a local hotelier, was a short-lived venture. Bord na gCon refused to renew the licence in 1964 and the Ballybunion racing days went to Tralee. The track resurfaced in 1966 but went off the map again in 1975.

The way we were . . . The stand at Dunmore Stadium, 1987

BOYLE: A company in the County Roscommon town applied to the new Bord na gCon for a licence to race in 1959, but there is no further mention of racing ever having taken place there, under licence at least.

CHAPELIZOD: Bord na gCon received an application to race from the owners of the track in the County Dublin village. The application was initially refused but granted on appeal. It was well-regarded by trainers, bookmakers and patrons, but, asked to compete on the same schedule as the other Dublin tracks, it faded out.

CLONES: This track was operated by a company incorporated back in 1935 but the County Monaghan venue had ceased trading by 1964.

KILRUSH: A greyhound racing company was set up in 1947 but there is no evidence that public races ever took place in the County Clare seaside town.

NAVAN: The County Meath venue opened on the Trim Road in 1950 and was the home of the Irish Cesarewitch. The operators were the Boyne Valley Greyhound Racing Company Limited.

SANTRY: The venue on the outskirts of Dublin city was one of many 'flapping' – or unlicensed – tracks that failed to survive the stricter regulated regime enforced by Bord na gCon.

Current Tracks

Other tracks have provided an invaluable service to the greyhound industry although their fortunes (and those of their operating companies) have fluctuated over the years.

CLONMEL, County Tipperary, was originally opened in 1931 at the showgrounds on Davis Road, beside the offices of the Irish Coursing Club. The same Clonmel Greyhound Racing Company also ran the local agricultural society, had an interest in Waterford and had shares in Kilkenny.

Clonmel stages the National Breeders' Produce Stakes (originally the Sapling Stakes), a long-established Classic. Notable winners have included the Fraser Black pair

Droopys Jaguar (1987) and Clashaphuca (1997), and the Dolores Ruth-trained winner of the English Derby, Shanless Slippy (1996). Its other main event is the programme designed around the National Coursing Meeting at nearby Powerstown Park. Clonmel also hosted runnings of the Irish Oaks (1932 and 1933) and the Irish St Leger (1933).

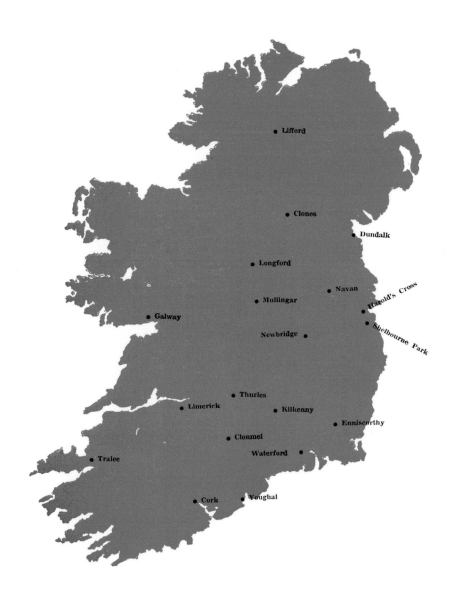

Location of tracks licensed by and under Rules of Racing of Bord na gCon, 1960–63.

Men with their greyhounds
in Derry city, 1955

Purchased by Bord na gCon in 1974, Clonmel went back into private ownership in February 1991, through the Clonmel Leisure Group.

Greyhound racing in CORK has had a number of homes since 1928. There was an initial spell at Ballintemple before the move to Western Road, besides University College, Cork, in 1936. The Leeside venue was purchased by Bord na gCon in 1969.

The circuit near Curraheen on the outskirts of the suburb of Bishopstown is now the home of the Irish Laurels. The Irish Laurels has never moved out of Cork, which also staged an Irish Derby in 1942 and had the hosting of the Irish Oaks in 1939 and 1943.

Racing in DERRY commenced in 1932. The track was closed for a period because of civil unrest, but opened again in 1973. The Brandywell has been also the home of Derry City, a team that has had matches in both the Irish League and the League of Ireland.

Racing at LISBURN, County Antrim, has witnessed a number of changes. The new track is at Drumbo Park, which directly replaced Ballyskeagh, where the management raced on a circuit around the football field used by Distillery in the Irish League.

Across the Louth county boundary at DUNDALK, they started racing in 1930 under the Dundealgan Greyhound Racing Company Limited. Its established home was at the Ramparts, but greyhound racing now forms a unique partnership with horse racing and harness racing at a floodlit all-weather facility opened with grants from both semi-state racing bodies in the Republic of Ireland, Horse Racing Ireland and Bord na gCon. The Irish National Sprint moved here when Dunmore Stadium closed. Dundalk is the venue for one of the really genuine representative races in the 'International', which is made up of three Irish-trained and three British-trained runners.

Matt O'Donnell's Farloe Melody won the 'International' twice (1991 and 1992), and Mary McGrath lifted the feature with Cooladine Super (1981) and Quick Suzy (1983). The 1983 renewal can arguably lay claim to having been the greatest finish to a major event, as five of the sextet flashed over the line together. After a protracted examination of the photo-finish print, Quick Suzy was deemed the winner. She was a short head in front of Mam's Bank and Yankee Express, which dead-heated for second place. Just a neck away in fourth place was Whisper Wishes, with Brideview Sailor only a head further back. The time was a slowish 29.94, again proving that, in greyhound racing, time is not everything.

Mary McGrath's local track was DUNGANNON. The County Tyrone track opened at Oaks Park in 1930 in an area that also had a small but vibrant coursing club.

There was also a strong connection between ENNISCORTHY (opened in 1932) and the club which coursed in the next-door field.

Many Irish greyhound tracks have doubled as soccer venues. GALWAY, where racing began in 1935, is situated on the College Road and is home to the Connacht Branch of the Irish Rugby Football Union. Bord na gCon bought out the Galway company, which had been incorporated back in 1932, in 1974. Galway is one of the much-improved stadiums, and stages the Classic Golden Jacket on the banks of the River Corrib. Galway's other important dates coincide with the summer's horse racing festival at Ballybrit.

It came to be dubbed as the capital's second track but, in fact, HAROLD'S CROSS shared top billing with Shelbourne Park from the start and alternated as the venue for the Irish Derby. Harold's Cross first staged the Irish Derby in 1934 and continued to stage this major event intermittently until 1970.

The Dublin Greyhound and Sports Association set up Harold's Cross in 1928 and it was purchased by Bord na gCon in 1970. Besides the Irish Derby, it has staged the Irish Grand National (which it was allocated by the Irish Coursing Club in 1932) – before it went to Kilkenny, Thurles and Shelbourne Park – as well as a number of renewals in the Irish St Leger (1935, 1937 and 1942). The Irish Oaks was first staged here in 1934 and continued to be run intermittently at Harold's Cross until 1995. The Irish Puppy Derby and Corn Cuchulainn are events still synonymous with Harold's Cross.

A sunlit view of the new track at Galway

The Irish Grand National lapsed for a period but was revived by Bord na gCon in 1959 and allocated to KILKENNY in 1960 and 1961. St James' Park was tied into the ownership of Clonmel and was operated by the Kilkenny Greyhound Racing Company Limited, which was incorporated in 1946. Bord na gCon purchased Clonmel's minority share in the track in 1974.

The County Donegal circuit at LIFFORD provides, along with Derry, a strong base for owners in the north-west. It was licensed from 1960 and is another track to have strong ties with the local (East Donegal) coursing club.

LIMERICK is the home of Bord na gCon and the Irish St Leger, arguably the second-most prestigious Classic after the Derby itself and which had been allocated by the Irish Coursing Club to Celtic Park in 1932. The Shannonside racing circuit opened in 1937 and was based at the Market's Field. The track saw the staging of the Irish Derby in 1939, the Irish Oaks in 1942, and the Irish St Leger in 1940, and has been the home of the last-named since 1944. The company, the Limerick Greyhound Racing Company, had been incorporated as far back as 1933.

The venue was the home for Limerick soccer clubs under various guises and was purchased by Bord na gCon in 1975. With horse racing now taking place in Patrickswell, plans are at an advanced stage to move the greyhound track and Bord na gCon head office to the old Limerick racecourse at Ballinacurra.

Tracks in north Leinster to have served local owners well are LONGFORD, where the Park Road venue opened for business in 1939, and MULLINGAR, with the County Westmeath circuit open for racing since 1932. The latter inherited a number of important events on the closure of Navan, including the Irish Cesarewitch.

Still in the eastern province is NEWBRIDGE, to which greyhound racing originally came in 1948. Dog racing, in the heart of the County Kildare horse-racing region, moved to its location outside the town in 1968. Its main event, the Cox Cup, remembers Patrick J. Cox who served on Bord na gCon from 1962 until 1982 and became its longest-serving member. Also a former president of the Irish Coursing Club, he was synonymous equally with both the greyhound track in the town, where he ran a successful cash-and-carry business, and with Naas racecourse. Both his son Dermot and grandson David have continued the family involvement with greyhound racing, as well as horse racing at Punchestown.

Of course, SHELBOURNE PARK is the colossus not just of the east coast but of the whole greyhound racing scene. The oldest track in the Republic of Ireland, it opened on 14 May 1927. The original company, the National Greyhound Racing Company Limited, was set up in 1926 and purchased by Bord na gCon in 1968. This fine galloping Dublin track is the undisputed home of greyhound racing and is the jewel in the Bord na gCon crown.

Since the first official Irish Derby was held here in 1932, the venue has staged (and continues to stage) most of the important events on the calendar.

The Irish St Leger was held here in 1934, 1936, 1938 and

Turning for home . . . Exciting action at Galway track

Z Zenith

Here is the zenith of greyhound racing trivia, the ultimate teaser for greyhound anoraks. There is only one recorded case of a greyhound competition run on a right-handed track. It was an experiment tried just once at White City in London in the late 1930s. The winner of the decider, if you are ever asked, was Scattering Illusion.

1939. There have been several runnings of the Irish Grand National here. Apart from the Irish Derby, the Irish Oaks, Tote Gold Cup and the Easter Cup are just some of the glittering events hosted by the premier track.

Shelbourne Park was also the home of Shelbourne Football Club both before and during the greyhound-racing era. Shelbourne FC also used Harold's Cross for a period. St Patrick's Athletic used both Harold's Cross and Chapelizod as home venues. The Football Association of Ireland utilised the ground as a neutral venue for cup games. Both Shelbourne Park and Chapelizod staged speedway racing in the 1950s.

THURLES, opened at Town Park in 1950, has always been compared favourably to Shelbourne Park. It was, unusually, set up under a public company – Thurles Greyhound Racing and Sports Association – in 1948. It staged the Irish Grand National from 1962 to 1985 and is the home of the Tipperary Cup.

Munster has a particularly strong clutch of tracks, with TRALEE ideally located in north County Kerry and within easy reach of County Limerick. Tralee was opened in 1929 at Ardfert and relocated to Oakview in 1930. The Kingdom Greyhound Racing Company Limited temporarily lost its licence (the track re-opened in May 1960) and was purchased by Bord na gCon in 1972.

Adding to the track strength in Munster is WATERFORD.

The well-manicured track at Harold's Cross sees three nights racing per week.

Kilcohan Park, where racing commenced in 1947, was another greyhound venue to see soccer action. It was being operated by the Clonmel Greyhound Racing Company Limited and was purchased by Bord na gCon in 1974.

Cork is one of the few counties to have had more than one greyhound track operating in the one era. Counties Antrim (Celtic Park and Dunmore Stadium in Belfast), Dublin (Chapelizod, Harold's Cross and Shelbourne Park), Kerry (Ballybunion and Tralee) and Tipperary (Clonmel and Thurles) are the others. YOUGHAL opened in 1948. It was closed by Bord na gCon for a period (re-opened 19 August 1960) and eventually purchased by the semi-state body in 1971.

Tralee track under lights

Munster has a particularly strong clutch of tracks, with Tralee ideally located in north County Kerry and within easy reach of County Limerick. Tralee was opened in 1929 at Ardfert and relocated to Oakview in 1930.

Dan Walsh at Tralee track. He was a bookie for many years as well as being a trainer and owner, who sold the first £1,000-dog out of Tralee. Tralee legend has it that he also went to Shanghai in 1920 with seventy-five greyhounds.

ACKNOWLEDGEMENTS
BIBLIOGRAPHY
CHRONOLOGY
INDEX

Author Acknowledgements

The author is grateful to the following, who so generously gave of their time and knowledge in the researching of this book: Bob Betts, *Sporting Press* (and former greyhound editor, *Sporting Life*); Matthew Bruton, breeder; Seán Collins, Chief Officer, Bord na gCon (1989–97), President, World Greyhound Racing Federation (1993–95), General Secretary, World Greyhound Racing Federation (1997–2009); Mary Conway, Bord na gCon; J.L. Desmond, Secretary, Irish Coursing Club (1986–2008), Secretary General, World Greyhound Racing Federation (1993–95), President, World Greyhound Racing Federation (2002–04); Terence Dixon, solicitor; Séamus Farrell, bookmaker; Patricia Griffin, Head of Wagering, Bord na gCon; Noel Holland, Cork; Ann Lenihan, Tote Administrator, Dublin tracks; Gerry McCarthy, former Greyhound Correspondent, Irish Press Group; Gus Ryan, Limerick; Paddy Ryan, Shelbourne Park.

Picture Acknowledgements

Every effort has been made to trace copyright holders of images before publication. If notified, the publishers will rectify any errors or omissions at the earliest opportunity. Where there is no information listed for an image, it is because the publishers have been unable to trace the copyright holder or because they believe the image is out of copyright. The publishers and author would especially like to thank Bord na gCon and the Irish Coursing Club for all their help in sourcing images.

Foreword

9   © Éadaoin Ní Mhuircheartaigh

1: The Journey Begins

10–11   The Art Archive / HarperCollins Publishers

12   The Art Archive / Gianni Dagli Orti

13   The Art Archive / Musée du Louvre Paris / Gianni Dagli Orti

14   *Old English Sports and Pastimes: Coursing* (litho) by Aldin, Cecil Charles Windsor (1870–1935) / Private Collection / © The British Sporting Art Trust / The Bridgeman Art Library

15   The Art Archive / Victoria and Albert Museum London / Eileen Tweedy

16–17   The Waterloo Cup Coursing Meeting, 1840 (oil on canvas), Ansdell, Richard (1815–1885) / © Walker Art Gallery, National Museums Liverpool / The Bridgeman Art Library

2: Celtic Roots

21   The Art Archive

22   With thanks to the Greyhound Board of Great Britain

3: Bord na gCon 1958–1968

29   © Imelda Grauer

31   © Steve Nash, www.steve-nash.co.uk

4: The Totalisator

34–5   Kurt Hutton / Picture Post / Getty Images

36   Edward G. Malindine / Topical Press Agency / Getty Images

38   © Pacemaker Press International

5: Flying the Flag

42	© Biscayne Kennel Club, Miami, Florida
44	© Sean F. Cooke
45	David Parry / PA Archive / Press Association Images

6: The Life of Ned Reily

50–1	© Steve Nash, www.steve-nash.co.uk
54 (bottom)	© Joe McGrath
55	© Dolores Ruth, reproduced by her kind permission

7: 'The Dogs' Updated

56–7	© Steve Nash, www.steve-nash.co.uk
59	© Imelda Grauer

8: Victory at Waterloo

64–5	© Private collection, reproduced by permission
66	© Private collection, reproduced by permission
67	© Private collection, reproduced by permission
69	© Private collection, reproduced by permission
71	Suzanne Collins LIPF ARPS; © Suzanne Collins Photography (www.scollinsphoto.com)

9: Coursing in their Veins

72–3	© John D. Kelly
74	© Sean F. Cooke
76	© Ruth Rogers
77 (top)	© Ruth Rogers
77 (bottom)	© Ruth Rogers
78 (top)	© Bridget Byrne, reproduced by her kind permission
78 (bottom)	© W.J. Boland

10: An Affair of the Heart

85	Popperfoto / Getty Images
86	PA / PA Archive / Press Association Images

11: The Greening of the White City

90	Kurt Hutton / Picture Post / Getty Images
95	© Steve Nash, www.steve-nash.co.uk

12: The Maestro Finds the Right Note

96–7	© Steve Nash, www.steve-nash.co.uk
102	© Steve Nash, www.steve-nash.co.uk

13: The Irish Derby 1932–1952

108	© Greyhound Racing Association, London

14: Tom Lynch

112	© Jim Connolly photography

15: Séamus Farrell

125	© Séamus Farrell

16: Classic Connections

128	© Steve Nash, www.steve-nash.co.uk
135	© Steve Nash, www.steve-nash.co.uk

17: Matt O'Donnell

136–7	© Steve Nash, www.steve-nash.co.uk
138	© Ruth Rogers
139	© Ruth Rogers
141	© Imelda Grauer
142	© Imelda Grauer

18: The Easter Cup

144–5	© Steve Nash, www.steve-nash.co.uk
146	© Dolores Cassidy, reproduced by her kind permission
149	© Steve Nash, www.steve-nash.co.uk
152	© Steve Nash, www.steve-nash.co.uk

19: Ownership

154–5	© Steve Nash, www.steve-nash.co.uk
156	© Steve Nash, www.steve-nash.co.uk

20: Breeding

162–3	© Greyhound Racing Association, London
167 (bottom)	© Catherine Kerr, reproduced by her kind permission
169 (left)	© Mollie Standbridge, reproduced by her kind permission

21: Going to the Dogs

170–1	Reproduced by kind permission of Bord na gCon
172	© Pacemaker Press International
173	Reproduced by kind permission of Bord na gCon
174	Bert Hardy / Picture Post / Getty Images
176	Reproduced by kind permission of Bord na gCon
177	Reproduced by kind permission of Bord na gCon
178	Reproduced by kind permission of Bord na gCon
179 (top)	Reproduced by kind permission of Bord na gCon
179 (bottom)	© Don Walsh, reproduced by his kind permission

180–1	© Ruth Rogers
192	Suzanne Collins LIPF ARPS; © Suzanne Collins Photography (www.scollinsphoto.com)

Bibliography

BOOKS

Blanning, Charles and Sir Mark Prescott, *The Waterloo Cup – The First 150 Years* (Heath House Press, 1987)

Comyn, John (ed.), *Trap to Line: 50 Years of Greyhound Racing in Ireland, 1927–1977* (Aherlow Publishers, 1977)

Dack, Barrie, *Greyhound Derby: The First Sixty Years* (Ringpress Books, 1990)

Dangerfield, Stanley and Elsworth Howell (eds.), *The International Encyclopaedia of Dogs* (Pelham Books, 1984)

Edwards Clarke, H. (revised by Charles Blanning), *The Greyhound* (Popular Books, 1980)

Genders, Roy, *The Encyclopaedia of Greyhound Racing* (Pelham Books, 1981)

Genders, Roy and National Greyound Racing Club, *The National Greyhound Racing Club Book of Greyhound Racing* (Penguin Books, 1990)

Hyland, Francis P.M., *Taken for a Ride: Betting Coups and Scandals* (Gill and Macmillan, 2006)

Lennox, Alan, *Guide to Good Stud Dogs* (Greyhound Magazine, 1978)

Martin, John, *Ger McKenna on Greyhounds* (Ringpress Books, 1989)

Montagu-Harrison, H., *The Greyhound Trainer* (Cashel Press, 1962)

MAGAZINES AND NEWSPAPERS

Fortune, Michael (ed.), *Irish Greyhound Derby* (1932 onwards)

——, *Irish Greyhound Review* (1979 onwards)

Sporting Press (previously *Irish Coursing Calendar*) (1924 onwards)

IRISH GOVERNMENT AND BORD NA GCON PUBLICATIONS

Totalisator Act (1929)

Betting Act (1931)

Report of the Advisory Committee on the Greyhound Industry (1952)

Gaming and Lotteries Act (1956)

Greyhound Industry Act (1958)

Joint Committee on Commercial State-sponsored Bodies: Bord na gCon (1990–91)

Bord na gCon Annual Reports (1960 onwards)

The Sporting Greyhound: A Chronology

1576	Rules for hare-coursing drawn up
1776	Coursing club formed at Swaffham, Norfolk
1836	Inaugural running of the Waterloo Cup
1858	National Coursing Club founded
1868	Master M'Grath first Irish-trained winner of Waterloo Cup
1864	Joseph Oller invents the Totalisator / Pari-Mutuel
1882	*National Greyhound Stud Book* published
1909	First greyhound racing track opens in Tuscon, Arizona
1912	Greyhound racing patented by American O.P. Smith
1916	Irish Coursing Club founded
1923	*Irish Greyhound Stud Book* published
1924	The *Sporting Press* published (as the *Coursing Calendar*)
1925	National Coursing Meeting inaugurated in Clonmel
1926	First greyhound race in Britain (at Belle Vue, Manchester)
1927	
April	First greyhound race in Ireland (at Celtic Park, Belfast)
May	First greyhound race in Ireland outside Belfast (Shelbourne Park, Dublin)
October	English Derby inaugurated (at White City, London)
1928	Irish Coursing Club assume control of greyhound racing
1929	
July	(Irish) Totalisator Act
July	Mick The Miller first Irish-trained winner of English Derby
1932	Irish Derby inaugurated (at Shelbourne Park, Dublin)
1952	Report of Advisory Committee on the Greyhound Industry published
1955	Spanish Battleship wins Irish Derby for the third time
1958	Bord na gCon sets up under Greyhound Industry Act
1960	Bord na gCon assumes control of greyhound racing in Republic of Ireland
May	Irish greyhound racing's first Totalisator (at Harold's Cross, Dublin)
1961	Bord na gCon moves to Limerick
1968	Bord na gCon purchases Shelbourne Park
1971	World Greyhound Racing Federation founded
1999	On-course betting tax discontinued
2005	Totalisator betting reaches new yearly record of €51,272,597
2006	Richard (Dick) O'Sullivan becomes the eighth chairman of Bord na gCon
2007	Adrian Neilan becomes the fifth chief executive of Bord na gCon

Abbeylara 111, 114, 143, 147, 151
Adraville Bridge 44, 61–2
Advantage Johnny *144*
Ahane Lad 142, 151
Air Hawk 46
Airmount Champ 143
Airmount Grand 61–2, 90, 149
Airmount Jewel 148, 153
Airmount Rogue 143, 149
Alans Judy 143
Always Kelly *139*, 140
Always Proud 109, 111, 132, 165
Annagh Bar 151
Annual Award 61
Apollo Again 131, 143
April Surprise 148, 153
Aquaduct Rosy 151
Ardfert Mick 44, 111, 141, 150
Ardfert Seán 158
Ardkill Jamie 61–2, 148, *149*, 151
Ardnalee Pal 44
Arrancourt Duke 141
Asdee Stranger 44
Ashleigh Honour 61–2
Ashmore Fairy 44
Ashmore Melody 44, 78
Astra 114, 142, 147, 151, 165
Astra's Son 165, 167
Aulton Berto 150
Autumn Crystal 79
Axle Grease 153

Bab-At-The-Bowster 68
Baby Doll 151
Back Garden 61–2, 131, 133
Balalika 158
Ballet Dante 151
Ballet Festival 153
Ballinaveala Hobo 77
Ballinderry Ash 77, 92, 94, 101, 161
Balliniska Band 103, 165
Ballinrea Express 61
Ballintubber One 44, 141, 143
Ballyard Yank 77
Ballybeg Prim 44, 131, 133, 143
Ballybeg Surprise 143
Ballyduag Manx 151
Ballyduff Bobby 77
Ballyhenry 63
Ballylanigan Tanist 93, 109
Ballymac Ruso *144*
Ballyowen Chief 44, 111, 132
Ballyowen Pride 132
Ballyregan Bob 48
Ballyseedy Memory 116, 165
Bar Blackstone 143
Barefoot Dash 141, 143
Barefoot Marty 143, 149
Barefoot Ridge 61–2, 148
Barley Field 100, 157
Barnacre Boy *63*
Bashful Man 111, 131, 149, 158, 161
Batties Rocket 111, 141, 150
Batties Spirit 140–1, 143
Bauhus 76, 131, 133, 172
Baytown Dell 153
Baytown Duel 151
Beau Lion 143
Believe Him 78

Belle o' Manhattan 153
Belvedere Bran 111
Best Man 79, 169
Bexhill Cottage 152
Bexhill Drive 76
Bexhill Eoin 77
Big Fella Thanks 44
Big Interest 44, 77, 150, 161
Big Kuda 131
Big Oran 61
Billy Playback *56*
Black Rock 77
Blissful Pride 153
Blonde Dino *95*
Boavista 44
Boherash Gaoithe 143
Boherduff Light 61–2, 134, 142
Bold Work 111, 157
Borna Best 153
Bornacurra Liz 153
Borna Survivor 153
Boro Parachute 61
Boston Point 79
Brandon Velvet 153
Brave Damsel 111, 164
Brideview Sailor 175
Bright Lad 71
Brilliant Bob 143, 151
Brook Jockey 143
Brook Prancer 61
Burnpark Sally 153
Butterfly Billy 131
Buzzing Dick 132
Bypass Byway 44, 111

Cabra Cool 90
Cairnville Jet 133, 165
Calandra Champ 157
Calvo 46
Camira Flash 87, 94, 167
Cardinal Puff 151
Careless Border 61
Carmody's Tanist 109, 111, 132, 165
Carra's Son 143
Cashen Legend 61
Castleoman 151
Castle Eve 143
Castleisland Lad 76
Castleland Dream 143
Castlemartyr 44, 77
Castle Pines 44, 77
Catsrock Daisy 44, 111, 132, 147, 151
Catunda Ashmore 78, 142
Catunda Harry 44, 61–2, 134, 142
Cecil's Delight 54
Celbridge Chance 61, 75, 168
Celtic Gem 143
Champion Prince 165
Charity Maid 132
Chart King 44, 90, 94–5, 103, 147, 151
Cheers For Ballyduff 143
Cherry Express 153
Cherrygrove Cross 143
Chicken Sandwich 114, 143, 153
Chieftain's Guest 111, 165
Chittering Clapton 92
Chocolate Kid 153
Chubbys Accord 169
Cill Dubh Darkey 131

Cindy's Spec 151
Claremont Mary 153
Clashaphuca 149, 173
Clashing Daisy 153
Climate Control 44, 111, 148, 150
Clogher McGrath 151
Clomoney Grand 151
Clonalvy Pride *162*, *165*
Clonbonny Bridge 111, 117, 132
Clounmellane Oak 61
Cold Christmas 153
Colonel Perry 111
Come On Bella 61
Concentration 62, 131
Cooladine Super 111, 175
Coolkill Darkie 153
Cool Performance 77, 111, *154*, 160–1
Cool Survivor 148, 153
Cordial Moonlight 116
Courthouse 76
Crafty Champion 78
Crafty Roberto 44, 78
Crafty Tessie 70–1
Cross Country 77
Crossmolina Rambler 109, 111
Cryptogram 46

Dainty Man 7
Daleys Denis 78, 111
Danaghers Best 150
Dandy Man 78
Daring Flash 109, *109*, 111, 168
Dark Baby 61–2
Dark Shadow 143
Dashing Oak 70–1, 150
Davesland 164
Deerfield Bypass 61–2, 131, 142
Deerfield Sunset 75, 143
Dereen Star 141, 143
Dew Reward 44
Dillies Pigalle 76
Dipmac 53, 111, *147*, 148, 150, 161, 167
Dismal 110
Donald 37, 70
Donovan's Ranger 44, 79, *79*
Doon Marshall 151
Doonmore Dreamer 143
Doonshean Banks 8
Double Shadow 61
Down Signal 117
Droopys Jaguar 134, 149, 173
Droopys Kewell 143
Droopys Maldini 44, *56*
Droopys Marco *56*, 90, 134, 149
Droopys Noel 151, 165
Droopys Sandy 90, 159
Droopys Scholes 54, 94, 103
Druids Johno 94
Drumahiskey Venture 111
Drumsough Princess 132
Drunsough Prince 153
Druze 132
Dry Flash 33, 63
Dubedoon 70
Dublin Eily 61
Dunsilly Queen 76

Ella's Ivy 143
Empor Lassie 151

Endless Gossip 93, 169
Entry Badge 82, 93, 106
Eoin Rua 44
Express Ego *149*
Extra Dividend 141, *141*, 142–3
Eyeman 44, 111

Fair Mistress 153, 172
Fair Moving 63
Faithful Hope 62, 91–2, 101, 142, 148
Famous Knight 111
Fancy Stuff 44, 76
Farloe Melody 44, 93–4, 103, 106, *136*, 139, 142, 147, 150–2, 175
Farloe Verdict 93
Felicitas 76
Fenian Bride, The 153
Fire Fly 54, 139, 143
Firgrove Snowman 143
Flaming King 61
Flash Prince 151
Flashy Flair 44
Follow A Star 61–2, 131, 133
Form Of Tender 44
Fossabeg Maid 149, 153
Fred Flintstone 93
Fridge, The 75
Friend Westy 167
Frisby Flashing 143
Frisco Hobo 107, 111, 132
Frozen Fast *75*
Fullerton 114
Fungies First 150
Fur Collar 153
Future Cutlet 164

Gabriel Blue 133
Gabriel Boy 61, 76, 131, 133
Gabriel Ruby 133, 165
Gallant Maid 119, 153
Gay Comfort 44
Gayline 79
General Courtnowski 143, 147, 151
Gentle Sally Again 153
Gentle Soda 149, 153
Gift 46
Gipsy Gem 76
Glenco Pearl 153
Godivas Turn 153
Gortaleen 143
Grand Canal, The 54, 90–1, *91*, 94, 98, 103, 147, 151, *164*
Grand Champion, The 165, 167
Grand Prince, The 165
Grand Time, The 151
Graylands Pixie 153
Guiding Hand 164
Guidless Joe 107, 111, 117, 131, 138, 152, 164

Hack Up Fenian 44, 140, 150
Hail Fun 153
Hairdresser 44, 153, 172
Handball 134
Hannah's Pup 151
Happy Acceptance 46
Hard Rain 150
Headleys Bridge *144*
Hear And There 70–1, 150
Heathermore King 75

Henrietta *58*, 70–1
He Said So *56*, 77, 111, 152
Hilltown 77, 169
Himalayan Climber 70
Hi There 165, 167, 172
Honeymoon 37, 70
Hopeful Cutlet 78, 111, 165
Hunters Guide 76
Hurry On Bran 156–7, *157*, *158*

Imperial Dancer 117, 165
Imperial Jimmy 63
I'm Slippy 44, 172
Indesacjack 143
Indian Joe 25, 44, 53, 76, 93–4, 103, 147, 151, 157, *158*, 159
Inler 109
In The Horrors 44
Itsamint 125, 151, 153
Ivy Hall Flash 44, 61–2, 142

Jacks Well 151
Janetta Hunloke 153
Jerry's Clipper 143
Joannes Nine 149, 151
Johns Gang 150
Johns Good 150
Joyful Tidings 44, 111
Judicial Castlelu 150
Judicial Inquiry 70–1, 150, 161
Judicial Pride 44, 76, 111, 152, *152*, 161
July The Fourth 78
Just Sherry 153

Kals Fairy 75
Kansas Rebel 141
Keen Laddie 22
Keep Moving 111, 118, 132, 165
Keep Whistling 63
Keeragh Sambo 141
Kevinsfort Queen 153
Khun Khan 151
Kilbracken Style 61–2, 142
Kilcasey Streak 61
Kilcaskin Kern 143
Kilvil Skinner 143
Knockash Rover 44, 78
Knockeen Master 61–2
Knock Her 153
Knock Hill Chieftain 165
Knockrour Favourite 61
Knockrour Girl 61, 76
Knockrour Slave 61–2, 76, 131
Knockrour Tiger 76
Kryponite *95*
Kyle Guest 78
Kyle Jack 54, 111

Lacken Prince 151
Larking About 141, 143, 148
Lartigue Note 93–4, *96*, 102, *102*, 103, 131, 133, 149, 158
Lassana Champ 142, 151
Last Landing 153
Last Lap 61
Late Late Show 44, 148, 151, *154*, 159, *159*, 160
Latin Lover 75
Legal Moment 153
Letesia 71, *169*
Libertys Echo 153
Lifes Beauty 153
Like A Shot 111, *128*, 134, *135*, 142
Lilac's Luck *108*, 111

Limousine 77, 152
Linda's Champion 44, 111, 149, 165, 168
Lion's Share 151
Lisglass Lass 61
Listowel Laddie 78
Little Scotch 44, 76
Little Shoe 71
Lively Band 44, 111, *123*, 143, 148, 165
Local Kate 143
Lone Keel 164
Loophole 153
Lovely Chieftain 76, 131, 133, 143
Lovely Louisa 117, 153
Loyal Honcho 91, 94–5, *95*, 103, *147*, 148, 150, 161
Lughill Jo 134, 139, 142–3
Lumber Boss 61–3, 141
Lusty More 44, 76

Machu Picchu *144*
Macoma 87, 146
Maddest Daughter 143
Madd Darkie *see* Tanist (formerly Mad Darkie)
Mad Printer 108, 153
Mad Tanist 109, 165, 167, 172
Maiden's Boy 164
Maid Of Devenish 63
Main Avenue 148, 153
Make History 44, 111
Mam's Bank 175
Manorville Magic 44, 111, 117
Manx Treasure 111, 117
Marchin' Thro' Georgia 109, 111
Marinas Tina 148, 153
Mark Anthony 44, 119, 143
Market Rascal 61
Martry Scotch 79
Master Adams 46
Master M'Grath 20, 37, *64*, *66*, 67, *67*, 68, *69*, 70, 74, 79, 82, 114, 118, 159, 161
Master Myles 44, 70, 78, *78*, 79, 161
Matt Hyland 150
Meadowbank Tip 153
Mets Champion 39
Micklem Drive 168
Micks Magic 44, 77, 152
Mick The Miller *81*, 82–3, *83–4*, 84–5, *85*, 87, 90–4, 98, 103, 107, 109, *115*, 117–19, 131, 146–7, 152, 159, 161, 168
Milanie 164
Millers Toast 78
Milo 164
Mineola Farloe 148, 151
Minnesota Miller 70–1, 93, 106, 140, 150, *168*
Minnesota Yank 70, *169*
Minstrel Rover 107, 111
Miss Gorgeous 167
Mistley 23, 46
Moaning Lad 93
Mobhi Gamble 151
Monalee Champion 165, 169
Monalee Gambler 119, 151
Monalee Pride 111, 132
Monarch Of The Glen 114, 143, 147, 151
Monologue 78, 107, 111, 114, 147, 151, 164
Mooncoin Captain 151
Moonshine Bandit 61
Moon View *63*
Moran's Beef 44, 131–3, 140, 143
Moresby 143
Morning Lass 71
Morning Prince 107, 146
Mountain Emperor 75, 168
Mountleader Peer 44

Mountleader Rolf 143
Mount Nagle Surprise 143
Mourne Marine 75
Mourne Monarch 44, 76
Movealong Santa 143
Move Gas 131, 151
Move On Swanky 44, 75, 78
Mr Bozz 148, 151
Mr Pickwick 61–2, 148, 151
Ms Firecracker 153
Muinessa 16, 111, 117
Mullaghroe Hiker 172
Multibet 44, 77
Munster Hotel 61
Murrays Mixture 151, 157
Murtys Gang 44
Mustang Rooster 78
Mutton Cutlet 164, 167
Mutts Silver 165
Mutual Friend 46, 106, *107*, 172, 175
My Last Hope 153
My Little Daisy 153

Nameless Pixie 44, 131, 133, 153
Nameless Star 61, 131, 133, 143
Narrogar Ann 93
Nearly You Sir 75
Needham Ash 44, 77
Needham Bar 76
Needham Wonder 77
Negro's Crown 143
Never Give Up 93
Newdown Heather *166–7*, 169
Newhill Printer 33, 63
Newmore King 75
Newpark Arkle 151
Newry Hill 44, 77, 150, 169
Nikita Billie 61–2
No Relation 143
Not Flashing 87

Ocean Swell 143
Odell King 61–2
Old Bea 46
Old Blade 114, 141, 147, 151
Old Kentucky Minstrel 70, 75
Old Spinster 153
Oran Express 151
Oran Jack 143
Oran Majestic 153
Orwell Parade 153
Oughter Brigg 131
Owens Sedge 44, 149–50
Own Pride 44, 109, 111, 119, 131, 133, 143, 149, 158, 165

Paddy The Champion 165
Pagan Miller 151
Paladin's Charm 153
Palatinus 83
Pampered Rover 44, 91, 111, 142, 148, 165
Parameter 46
Parkdown Jet 44, 93–4, 98–101, *101*, 102–3, 131, 133, 139–40, 149, 157–8, 165
Park Jewel 151
Patricias Hope 92, *92*, 93–4, 165
Patsy's Record 151
Pauls Fun 93, 172
Peaceful Lady 116–18, 148, 153
Peerless de Wit 74
Penny County 76, 111, *124*
Perry's Apple 111

Peruvian Style 133, 161
Phantom Flash 168
Philotimo 61
Picture Card 153
Pigalle Wonder 124, 165, 167
Pigalle Wonder (formerly Prairie Champion) 124, 165, 167
Play Solo 28, 54, 70–1
Pools Punter 143
Postal Vote 132, *134*, 151
Pouleen Boy 143
Powerstown Proper 61
Powerstown Prospect *91*
Prairie Flash 165, 167, *167*
Prairie Peg 153, 165, 167
Prairie Vixen 165, 167
Premier Fantasy 44, 148, 151
Priceless Border 93, 169
Priceless Rebel 90, 148
Prince Norroy 151
Prince Of Bermuda 60, 118–19, 125, 130–3, 140, 143, 161
Princes Pal 76, 90
Prince Spy 101, 157
Proud Prince 44
Purty Good 153
Pyramid Club 79

Qualityandgold 169
Quare Times *169*
Quarrymount Honi *54*
Quarrymount Riki 44, *54*, 76
Quarrymount Smut 76
Quarter Day 25
Queen of the Suir 108, 153, 164
Quick Suzy 148, 153, 175
Quiet Dandy 44

Rahan Ship 101, *101*, 140, 143, 157
Ramona Hiker *77*
Randy 44, 140, 143, 158
Rapid Ranger 93, 152
Rather Grand 61
Rathgallen Tady 111, 131, 149, 158, *158*, 161
Razldazl Billy 44, 55, 111, 142, 150
Razor Ashmore 77
React Fragll 70–1, 150
React Robert 70–1, 150
Real McCoy 46
Rebel Abbey 116
Rebel Blue 44
Redbarn Panther 143
Red Rasper 131, 143
Resolute Time *72*
Rhu *138*, 140–1, 143
Ringa Hustle 44
Rita's Choice 132
Robeen Printer 61
Rocking Ship 48–9, *49*, 76
Rokeel Light 151
Romping To Work 44, 143, 148, 153
Rosmore Robin 132, 153
Rossa Rose 44, 79
Rough Waters 39, 110, *110*, 111, 123
Round Tower Rose 61
Roving Yank 111
Rugged Mick 61–2, 131, 133
Rusheen Gallant 44
Russian Gun 44, 111, *112*, 119, *119*, 124–5, 130, 165
Rustic Martin 151
Ryland R 85

Safety Circle 44
Sand Man 49, 93, 167
Sandown Champion 151, 172
Sand Star 92, 94, 172
Sandy Sea 44, 77
Sarah's Bunny *124*
Scattering Illusion 178
Scotch Lady 79
Scurlogue Champ 48
Shady Bunch 151
Shaggy Lad 116
Shamrock Point *134*
Shane's Legacy 111, 165
Shanless Slippy 55, 94, 103, 142, 150, 173
Sharavogue 151
Shauns Dilemma 169
Shelbourne Aston *31*, 44, 111, *144*
Shelbourne Becky 153
Shifting Shadow 111
Shimmering Wings 153
Shy Sandy 151
Silent Thought 61–2, 142
Silver Earl 143
Simply Terrific 75
Sir Frederick 111
Sir Lancelot 79
Skipping Tim 61–2
Skip's Choice 132
Skywalker Queen *140*, 141, 153
Slippy Blue 94
Slip The Lark *144*
Small Dash 39
Smokey Alice 76
Smokey Flavour 76
Smokey Marion 76
Smokey Marshall 76, 150
Snipefield Glory 44
Snow Maiden 153

So Careful 78
Sole Aim 111
Some Picture 44, 93, 152
Sonic Flight 61, 142
Spanish Battleship *26*, 60–2, 111, 114, 116, *116*,
       117–18, *118*, 119, 122, 130, 132, 142,
       147–8, 151, 161, 165
Spanish Chestnut 61–2, 116, 161, 165
Spanish Lad 111, 116–17, 161
Sparkys Girl 76
Spartacus 142, 151
Spartafitz 142, 151
Speedy Wonder 151
Spiral Citrate *56*
Spring Time 111
Spring Twilight 75
Springvalley Grand 119, 151
Standard Image 61–2
Staplers Jo 168
Star Point 143
Steve 111
Storm Villa 44, 141, 143
Stormy Champ 76
Strange Baffy 46
Strange Legend 153
Stranger, The 61–2, 143
Sudborne Stiff 46
Suir Miller 111, 149, 168
Supreme Tiger 44, 141, 143
Swanky Star 44
Swanlands Best 131, 143
Swing Out Sister 152

Tain Mor 44, 111, 165
Talis 109
Tame Hero 76
Tanist (formerly Mad Darkie) 109, *109*, 111, 131,
       138–9, 165, 168

Tantallon's Flyer 151
Tanyard Heather 61
Tartan Black 76
Tartan Khan *162*, 165
Templenow Rebel 61
Tender Heartache 76
Tender Heartrob 76
Tender Heather 76
Tender Hero 76
Tender Hillside 76
Tender Honey 76
Terrydrum Tiko 61
Thurles Queen 130
Tigers Eye 61, 63
Time Up Please 131, 133, 143, *160*, 161, *165*
Tina Marina 111, 150, 168
Tiny's Tidy Town 151
Tiny's Trousseau 151
Tipperary Hills 106, 109, 131
Toms The Best 93, 111, 152
Top Honcho 168
Townbrook Bimbo 77
Tracy Budd 153
Tragumna Dasher 61
Trajectory 44
Tranquilla 109
Tristam 153
Tubbercurry Lad 111
Tubbertelly Queen 28, 70–1, 93, 102, 139, 149, *150*, 172
Tullamore 79
Turkish Maid 130
Tyrur Kenny 148, 151
Tyrur Kieran 90, *95*, 148
Tyrur Laurel *95*
Tyrur Rhino 111, *148*
Tyrur Ted 61–2, 148

Uacterlainn Riac 109, 111
Unsinkable Girl *142*

Valais Express 151

War Dance 151
War Girl 130
Wary Guide 164
Wattle Bark 164
Wayside Clover 151
Wee Chap 151
Weigh In First 151
Western Post 109, 111
Westmead Hawk *56*, 93, 152
Westmead Lord 93, 152
Westpark Ash 61
Westpark Mustard 161
Whisper Wishes 49, 92–3, 101, 167–8, 175
Whiteleas Tim 140–1, 150
White Sandhills 75, 77, 169
Who's Me Da? 116
Why You Monty 70–1, 150
Wicklow Sands 151
Wild Iris 153
Wild Woolley 103
Windgap Heresay *72*
Wonder Valley 78, 111, 124, 165

Yacht Club 134
Yale Princess *140*, 141, 153
Yanka Boy 44, *99*, 131, 133, 143, *165*
Yankee Express 175
Yellow Bud 61
Yellow Printer 91–2, 111, 119, *119*, 125
Yolanda Belle 44, 76

Index: General

Italicised page reference indicates an image

A

Adeane, Sir Robert 91
Advisory Committee on the Greyhound Industry 25, 30–1, 46
Ahern, Thomas 28–9, 79, 168
Aintree racecourse 68
All-age Bitch Stake 22
Allen, Chesney 87
Allen, Harry 123
Altcar coursing club 16, 20, 28, 68–71, 75, 106, 150, *150*, 152, 164
Anderson, Garry 169
Anglim, Patrick (Paddy) 138, 140–1
Anglo-Irish International Race Series 46–7
Arkle (horse) 114
Arrian (Roman) 13
Ashbourne track 126

B

Ballina track 31
Ballybeggan Park coursing venue 75
Ballybunion track 41, 45, 168, 172, 179
Barnett, Seán 99–100
Barrett, Michael 149, 168
Barry, Ann 33, 54, 139
Barry, Bernard 71, 122
Barry family 122
Barry, Harry 122
Bassett, John 125
Belfast Celtic Football Club 23, 106, 172
Belle Vue stadium (Manchester) 22, 23, 46, *63*, 122
Berners, Dame Juliana 14
Betting Act (1926) 37
Betting Act (1928) 37
Betting Act (1931) 37
Betting and Lotteries Act (UK) 39
Bexhill Cottage coursing venue 76
Biscayne Kennel Club (Miami, US) *42*
Biscayne track (Miami, US) *48*, 49
Biss, Stan 83
Black, Fraser 90, 94, 134, 141, 149–50, 173
Black (née McKenna), Paula 134, 149
Blanning, Charles 114
Bolger, Jim 78
Bolton track 45
Bord na gCon (Irish Greyhound Board) 30, 37, 40, 44, 47–9, 52–5, 60, 63, 69, 76, 95, 98, 107, 110, 122, 130, 173, 176
    assumes racing responsibilities 29–30, 146
    bookmaker levies 37, 39–40
    broadening of support base 59
    control committee 30
    denies licence to Ballybunion track 172
    dog jacket regulations 69, 175
    drug-testing facility 53
    female members 54
    financing of operations 52–3, 55, 58–60, 175
    foundation of 8, 23, 25, 37, 39
    inaugural board meeting 28
    location of offices 28
    location of tracks, 1960–3 *173*
    maintenance of integrity 44, 46, 58, 61, 98
    management of the totalisator 30, 37, 39–41, 60 *see also* totalisator (tote)
    members 33, *33*, 139, 176
    membership of WGRF 46
    names Late Late Show 159–60
    officers 32, 53–5, 58–9, 71, 75–6, 108, 141, 148, 168

overseas activities 47–9, 133, 167
    prize money 30, 49, 52, 60, 62, 109, 130, 148
    purchases tracks 31, 44–5, 62, 175–9
    recognises Chapelizod track 126
    revises classics list 130
Borris-in-Ossory coursing venue 74
Boylesports 22
Boyne Valley Greyhound Racing Company Ltd 173
Brassil, Noel 32, *33*, 52
Brennan, James 33, *33*
Bristol track 45
Broadbent, Sam 126
Brophy, Fr Martin 82–3, 87, 117, 146–7, 168
Brosnan, Denis *157*
Browne, Jimmy 77
Bruton, John 79
Bruton, Matthew J. 79
Buckley, Pat 90, 165
Burnett, Al 165
Butler, Kitty 20, 54, *54*, 75, 79 *see also* Kitty Butler Stake
Byerley Turk (horse) 164
Byrne, Gay 159
Byrne, Larry *40*
Byrne, Paddy 78, 142
Byrne, Patsy 77–8, *78*, 92–4, 150, *154*, 161, 167–8

C

Cahill, David 48–9
Canterbury track 45
Cantwell family 122
Cardiff track 87, 92
Carey, Max *42*
Carlisle racecourse 39
Carrick-on-Shannon coursing venue 74
Carrick-on-Suir coursing venue 74
Carroll, Jeremiah 78, *78*
Carroll, Patrick 33
Cashman, David 62
Catford track 45
Cavlan, Frank 87
Celtic Bookmakers 59
Celtic Park track (Belfast) 18, 23–4, *24*, 25, 39–40, 45–6, 63, 106, 114, 122, 139, 143, 147, 172, 175–6, 179
Cesarewitch (Irish) 99, 106, 117, 130–3, *134*, 157, 173, 176
Chambers, P.J. 79
Champion Stakes 22, 75–8, 142, 152, *157*, 169
Chandler, Ronnie 75, 78
Chapelizod track 122–3, 126, *126–7*, 173, 178–9
Chaucer, Geoffrey *14*
Chestnut, Joe 70
Christopher, Geraldine *139*
Cleary, Fr Michael 117
Clerkin, Andy *110*
Clifford, Kathleen 141
Clifford, Noel 141
Clones track 31, 41, 45, 173
Clonmel coursing venue 74, *74*, 107
Clonmel Greyhound Racing Company Ltd 173, 179
Clonmel Leisure Group 175
Clonmel track 41, 45, 60, 67, 106, 108, 119, 139, *139*, 140, 142, 173, 175, 179
Clounanna coursing venue 22, 30, 74–5, *77*, 152, 168
Coffey, Peter P. 79
Collins, J.J. (James) *26*, 28
Collins, Niall 28

Collins, Seán *26*, 28, *29*, 32, 46, 52–3, 58
Connery, Seán 122
Cork track 23, 40–1, 44, 59–60, 62, 107–9, 111, 116–18, 131, 133, 139, 142, 148, 175, 179
Corn An Tostal 117
Corn Cuchulainn 106, 130, 175
Costello, Eddie 77, 101, 156, *156*, 157, *157*, 158, *158*, 159, 161
Costello, Grace 101, 156–7, *157*, 158, *158*, 159
Costigan, John 33
County Limerick Coursing Club 20, 22, 44, 75
Cox Cup 176
Cox, David 29, 177
Cox, Dermot 29, 177
Cox, Helen *29*
Cox, Patrick J. 29, *29*, *32*, 33, 54, 79, 168, 176
Coyle, Charlie 93, 167
Cradley Heath track 45
Craigie, Eric 126
Crowley, Jerry 109
Cuddy, Don 48–9
Cuddy, Joe 49
Curley, Cathal 33
Curragh, the 107
Cutler, Bill 126

D

Dalton, Pat *42*, 48–9, *49*, 76, 133
Daly, Christy 140, 158
Daly, Pat 71, 152, 161
Darby O'Gill and the Little People (film) 122
Darley Arabian (horse) 164
Davis, John 93, 142
Delaney, Ronnie 125
Delargy, James P. 33, 53
DeMulder, Geoffrey *124*, 157
Department of Agriculture 25, 30, 40, 52, 54
Derby (city) track 45
Derby (coursing, Irish) 75–9, 140–1, 149–50, 152, 156, 161, 169, 172
Derby (English) 55, 62, 71, 76–7, 80, *80*, 82–4, 86, *86*, 87, 90–1, *91*, 92, *92*, 93–5, *95–6*, 98–100, *100*, 101, *101*, 102–3, 106–7, 109, *115*, 117, *124*, 131, 133, *136*, 139–42, 147–50, 152, 156, *156*, 157–8, *158*, 159, 161, *162*, 164, *164*, 165, 167–9, 172–3
Derby (Irish) 9, 16, 22, 30–1, *31*, 39, *50*, 53–5, *56*, 60, 62, 76–8, 91, 93, 103, 106–8, *108*, 109, *109*, 110, 110, 111, *112*, 114, 116–18, *118–19*, 122–3, *123*, 124, *124*, 125, *128*, 130–4, *134–5*, 138–42, *144*, 147, *147*, 148–9, *149*, 150, 152, *152*, *154*, 157–8, *158*, 159–61, 164–5, 167–8, 175–8 *see also* Puppy Derby (Irish)
Derby (horseracing, Irish) 107
Derby (National) *see* Derby (Irish)
Derby (Scottish) 46, 76, 90, 92, 95, 134, 148–9, 152, 159
Derby (Ulster) 172
Derby (Welsh) 87, 92
Derry City FC 175
Derry track 175
Desmond, Dermot 122
Desmond, Jeremiah L. 20, 46, 58, *58*, 79
Diana (the huntress) *13*
Dickes, William *21*
Dillon, James 25
Distillery FC 175
Divilly, Brian 70–1, 78–9

Divilly, Martin 78
Dixon, Denis 126
Dixon, James Tallis 126
Dixon, Terence 126
Doran, J.J. 109
Douglas, R.M. 70
Dowling, Revd William (pseud. N. Ennis) 79, 168
Downes, Cyril 28
Doyle, Tamarisk 29
Dreaper, Tom 114
Drumgoole, Noel 28
Dublin coursing venue 74
Dublin Greyhound and Sports Association 24, 106, 175
Dublin Greyhound Stadium Ltd 126
Duffy, Desmond *32*, 33
Duffy, John 93, 168
Duleek coursing venue 192
Dundalk and Drogheda Dairies 91
Dundalk coursing venue 74
Dundalk track 8, 40–1, 47, 60, 139, 175
Dundealgan Greyhound Racing Company Ltd 175
Dundee track 45
Dungannon coursing club 175
Dungannon track 175
Dunlavin coursing venue 74
Dunmore Stadium (Belfast) 23, 33, 38, *38*, 39, 63, 106, 133, 139, 172, *172*, 175, 179
Dunne, Joe 167
Dunne, Michael (Mick) 82, 167–8
Dunphy, Patrick (Paddy) 33, 54, 90–1, *91*, 94, 98, 147–8, *164*, 165
Dunraven, Earls of 22, 74

E

East Donegal coursing club 176
Easter Cup 53, 62, 106–7, 114, 117–18, 130–1, 141–2, 146–9, 151, 157, 160–1, 165, 178
Eddery, Pat 107
Edinburgh, Duke of (Prince Philip) *86*, 87, 94, 167
Edinburgh track 45
Edward, Prince 94
Edward VII, King 90
Ellesmere manuscript *14*
Emigrant Newsletter 82
Enniscorthy coursing club 175
Enniscorthy track 40, *40*, 41, 175
Ennis, N. *see* Dowling, Revd William (pseud. N. Ennis)

F

Fahy, Tony 161
Fairyhouse racecourse 36
Farrell, Charlie 122
Farrell, Paul (father of Séamus Farrell (bookmaker)) 122
Farrell, Paul (son of Séamus Farrell (bookmaker)) 122
Farrell, Paul (brother of Séamus Farrell (bookmaker)) 122
Farrell, Philomena 122
Farrell, Raymond 122
Farrell, Séamus (bookmaker) 117, *120*, 122–5, *125*, 126, 142
Farrell (jnr), Séamus *120*, 122
Farrington, Norman *75*
Feeney, Pádraig 33
Fennin, Tim 107
Fermoy, Lord 74
Field, John 54
Field, Michael 32, 54
Fitzgerald, Barry 122

Fitzgerald, Brendan 77–8
Fitzgerald, Pa 77–8
Fitzgerald, Tony 28
Fitzgibbon, Thomas 28–9, 33
Fitzpatrick, Comdt. Joseph 20, *53*, 79, 91, 116
Fitzpatrick, John 167
Fives, Michael 79
Flagler track (US) 49
Flaherty, Timmy 77
Flanagan, Bud 85
Flanagan, Gerard 28
Flanagan, Michael 28
Flanagan, Séamus 25, 28, 30–2, *32–3*, 44, 46, 52–4, 58, 61
Flanagan, Seán 28
Football Association of Ireland 178
Forde, Liam 28, 33
Forest Laws 13
Frost, Jim 25, 28, 53, 76
Frost, Kevin 25, 32, 53, 76, 93, 157

G
Gaelic Athletic Association 20
Galbally coursing venue 168
Galway, James 68
Galway track 41, 45, 106, 139, 161, 175, *176*, *177*
Garrahy, Diarmaid *141*
Garrahy, Eoin *141*
Garrahy, John 141, *141*, *162*
Garrahy, Liam 141, *141*, *162*
Gaskin, Bill 71
Geller, Ike 126
Gilbert, Timothy 33, 108
Glasgow track (Shawfield) 48, 90, 92, 130, 134, 148, 152
Gleeson, Joe *132*
Gleeson, Stephen 33
Gleeson, Steven *139*
Godolphin Arabian (horse) 164
Gold Cup (horseracing) 114
Golden Jacket 106, 130, 175
Golden Miller (horse) 115
Gosforth Park coursing venue (and racecourse) 68
Grady, Séamus 79
Graham, Séamus 9, 53, 55, 91, 94–5, *95*, 147, *147*, 148, 150, 161, 167–8
Grand National (greyhound, Irish) 106, 130–2, 134, 141, 149, 175–6, 178
Greene, Michael 82–3
Green, Fr Dan 167
Greyhound Bar, The (Blanchardstown, Co. Dublin) 117, 123, 125
Greyhound Industry Act (1958) 28, 30–1, 37, 39, 53
Greyhound of the Year Awards 44
Greyhound Racing Association (GRA) 36, 92, 95
Griffin, John 79
Griffin, Patricia *41*
Griffin, Thomas 33
Guinness 600 44

H
Hackney track 45
Hanrahan, Desmond 30–2, 44, *44*, 47–9, 52, 58
Harold's Cross track 39, 41, 44, 60, 106–8, *108–9*, 111, 114, 116–19, 122–4, 126, 131–2, 138–9, 143, 147–8, 153, 158, 168, 172, 175, 178, *178*, 179
Harringay track 23, 45, 93
Harte, Thomas 79
Hatfield Park *10*
Haughey, Charles 91
Haughey, Maureen 91
Haydock Park coursing venue (and racecourse) 68

Hayes Hotel (Thurles) 20
Hayes, John 25, 93–4, 147, 157
Hayes, Tom 76, *76*
Haynes, John 101, *101*, 140, 157
Healy, Philip 33
Heffernan, Kevin 32, 53, 58, 148
Hegarty, John 33
Henehan, Seán 29, 33
Hennessy, Paul 62, 90, 141, 148, *149*, 160
Hewitt, Karl 90, 94–5
Hewitt, Ralph 90, 94–5, 147
Hialeah track (Florida, US) 103
Histon, D.J. 20, 79
Hoare, John 79
Hockfield Light 63
Hogan, P.J. 28–9, 33
Holland, Monita 28, 54, 71
Holland, Pat 28, 46, 54, 70–1
Hollywood track (US) 49
Horan, Adrian 83
Horan, Bill 83
Horan, Mick 55, 76, 83, 94, 107, 117, 131, 146–7, 152
Horse Racing Ireland (HRI) 29, 37, 40, 60, 175
Hotel Minella (Clonmel) 22
Hutchinson, W.F. 70
Hynes, Con 161
Hynes, Deirdre 161

I
International (race, Dundalk) 47, 175
Irish-American International Classic *48*
Irish Coursing Calendar (aka *Irish Coursing and Racing Calendar*) 23
Irish Coursing Club (ICC) 20, 23–5, 29–31, 37, 46, 54, 70–1, 75, 91, 106–10, 116, 122, 138, 173
   assumes control of racing 23, 58, 106
   devises classics list 130–1, 175–6
   foundation of 20, 74
   introduces muzzles 58
   Irish Greyhound Stud Book 20, 23–5, 58, 116, 164
   membership of Bord na gCon 25, 53, 55
   presidents 79, 168, 176
   retains authority in Northern Ireland 25
   secretaries 79
Irish Cup 20, 30, 69, 74–8, 152, 168–9
Irish Greyhound Board *see* Bord na gCon (Irish Greyhound Board)
Irish Greyhound Owners' Association 25
Irish Horseracing Authority 37
Irish Racecourse Bookmakers Assistants' Association 25
Irish Rugby Football Union 175

J
Jackson, Adam 92
Jordan, Lt.-Col. C.L. *26*

K
Kavanagh, Patrick 8
Keane, Olive 91
Keane, Paddy 62, 91, *91*, 95, 142, 148, 156, 161, 165
Keen, Tom 103
Kelliher, Eileen 33, 54–5
Kelly, Helen 148
Kelly, Joe 100, 157
Kelly, Larry 148
Kelly, Lt.-Col. J.P. 79
Kempton, Arundel 84, 159
Kempton Park coursing venue (and racecourse) 68
Kempton, Phyllis *83–4*, 84, *115*, 159
Kenny, Joe 75

Kenny, Pat *154*, 159, *159*, 160
Kerin, Christopher 79
Kerry Group 59
Kiely, Gerry 62, 90, 148–9
Kilcoyne, Carmel 28
Kilcoyne, Luke 28, *33*, 54, 172
Kilcoyne, Pat 28, 71, 172
Kilkenny Greyhound Racing Company Ltd 176
Kilkenny track 41, 45, 118, 175–6
Kilrush track 31, 173
Kingdom Greyhound Racing Company Ltd 178
Kitty Butler Stake 22
Kulchinsky, Aaron 47, *47*

L
Ladbrokes '600' 106, 130
Lalor, Gary 110
Lalor, Henry 110, *110*
Lalor, Jim 110
Lalor, Jimmy 39, 110, *110*, 117, 123
Lalor, John 110
Lalor, Michael 123
Lalor, Patricia (née Cummins) 110
Lantry, James 29, 33
Lartigue, Charles 103
Laurels (English) 131
Laurels (Irish) 61–3, 75–6, 106, 116–18, 130–1, 133–4, 139, 141–2, 148, 161, 165, 168, 175
Law, Derek *162*
Lawlor, Jack 33
Laws of the Leash 14
Leeds track 45
Leyden, Patrick J. 29, *32*, 33
Licensed Greyhound Trainers' Association 25
Lifford track 30, 41, 176
Limerick City Coursing Club 30
Limerick Coursing Club, County *see* County Limerick Coursing Club
Limerick Greyhound Racing Company 176
Limerick Leader 30, 44
Limerick racecourse 53, 176
Limerick track 41, 45, 54, 59–60, 62, 107–9, 111, 119, 131–2, 134, *138*, 139–40, *141*, 142, 147, 152, 158, 160, 161, 165, *166*, 172, 176
Lisburn track 83
Lister, Charlie 93, 152
Liverpool track 23
Longford track 41, 54–5, 176
Looby, Carmel *169*
Loughin, Pat 71
Loughnane, Michael (Mick) *160*, 161, *165*
Lucas, A.S. 165, 167
Lurgan coursing venue 68
Lurgan track 20
Lurgan, Lord 68–9, 74, 79, 159
Lynch, Denis 76, 108
Lynch family (Aughabullogue, Co. Cork) 62
Lynch (née McKenna), Peg 117, 132, 134
Lynch, Terence 33, *33*
Lynch, Tom 110, *112*, 116–17, 119, 123–4, 130, 132–4, 148, 165
Lynch (jnr), Thomas 119, 134
Lyne, James 48
Lynn, William 68

M
Mackey, John *54*, 76
MacSharry, Ray 28
Maguire, Dr Patrick J. *26*, 28, 30, 32, *32*, 44, 59, *164*
Maher, Luke 78, 107
Mallon, Séamus 33
Mallow racecourse 36
Manchester track *see* Belle Vue stadium (Manchester)

Marley, Hugh *112*, 124
Matthews, Brendan 76–7, 108, 150, 169
Matthews, Paul 77, 169
McAlinden family 122
McAlinden, Hugh 23, *23*, 106, 122, 172
McCalmont Cup 118
McCann, Terry 28, 71, *150*
McCarthy, Cathal 102–3
McCarthy, Johnny 150
McEllistim TD, Tom *26*
McGauran, Louis 28
McGirr, Frank 94
McGirr, Pat 76
McGrath, Colm 78–9, 161
McGrath, Mary 78–9, *79*, 148, 156, 161, 169, 175
McKenna, Anthony 33
McKenna, Gay 132–3, *133*, 134, 140–1, 149
McKenna, Ger 28, 55, 62, 70–1, 76, 78, 93–5, *96*, 98–9, *99*, 100, 102, *102*, 103, 119, 126, 130–2, *132*, 133–4, 138, *138*, 139–42, 149, *150*, 156–8, *158*, *160*, 161, *166*
McKenna (jnr), Ger 99, *99*
McKenna, G.J. (Ger) 134, 149
McKenna, Joe 117, 131–2, *132*, 134
McKenna, John 99, *99*, 158, *158*
McKenna, Josie 99, *99*, 158, *158*, 160
McKenna, Malachy 131–2, *132*
McKenna, Owen 62, 78, 99, *128*, 131, 133–4, *134–5*, 139, 142
McKenna, Paula *134*
McLean, Alfie 25, 53, 76, 93, 157, *158*, 159
McNair, Leslie 125
McNamara, Eugene 77, 156
McNamee, Anthony 79
Meehan, Paddy 110
Mentzis, Theo 93
Mereruka (Egyptian) *12*
Middlesbrough track 45
Miller, Mick 82
Milligan, Paddy *119*
Milton Keynes 45
Moclair, Paddy 109
Molloy family 122
Monahan, Pádraig 33
Mooney, Noel 76
Moore, Tom 102–3
Moriarty, John 28, *32*, 33
Morris, Arthur J. 20, 70, 79, 168
Morris, Thomas Aloysius 20, *20*, 22–5, 54, 58, 79, 116, 122, 79, 164–5, 167–8 *see also* T.A. Morris Stake
Morton, Billy 125
Moylan, Jack 107
Muldoon, Frank 124
Mulhall, M.J. 79
Mullan, Brendan 78
Mullan, Jack 76, *77*, 78, 156, 165, *167*, 169, 172
Mulligan, Luke 33
Mullingar track 30, 41, 55, 106, 139, 176
Murphy, Bryan 141
Murphy, Christopher 33, *33*
Murphy, Cornelius 29, *32*, 33
Murphy, Jack *123*, 148, 165
Murphy, Michael 79
Murphy, Michael 78–9
Murray, Francis 90, 156–7, *157*, 159
Murray, Kathleen *157*
Murray, Michael 156

N

Naas racecourse 29, 177
National Breeder and Produce Stakes *see* National
    Breeders' Produce Stakes
National Breeders' Produce Stakes 22, 106, 119,
    130–1, 134, *139*, 140–2, 149, 157, 173 *see
    also* National Sapling Stakes
National Coursing Club (NCC) 20
    Stud Book 20
National Greyhound Awards 44, 133
National Greyhound Racing Club (NGRC) 25, 45,
    91–2, 94
National Greyhound Racing Company Ltd 23–4,
    31, 36, 39, 106, 177
National Sapling Stakes 130, 173 *see also* National
    Breeders' Produce Stakes
National Sprint (Irish) 33, 63, 76, 106, 130–3, 172,
    175
Natural History Museum (Tring, Hertfordshire) 114
Navan track 31, 40–1, 45, 122, 124–5, 157, 173, 176
Neary, Séamus 71
Neilan, Adrian 32
Newbridge track 8, 29, 41, 54, 168, 176
Newmarket racecourse 39
Nolan, Mary *40*
Norfolk, Duke of 14
Norton Canes track 45
Nugent, Catherine *167*
Nugent, Helen 33, 54
Nugent, Mike *167*
Nugent, Paddy *167*
Nugent, Tony *167*, *167*
Nugent (jnr), Tony *167*

O

Oaks (coursing) *72*, 75–9, 107, 147, 152, 164, 169
Oaks (English) 164
Oaks (Irish) 106, 108, 114, 116–19, 125, 130–2,
    140, 141, 148–9, 164–5, 172–3, 175–6, 178
O'Brien, Aidan 98, 109
O'Brien, Paddy *see* O'Neill, Patrick
O'Brien, Patrick 79
O'Brien, Phonsie 78
O'Brien, Vincent 78, 98, 109
O'Callaghan, Christy 62
O'Connell, Francis 33
O'Connor, John 92, *92*, 94
O'Connor, Moss 62
O'Connor TD, Tim *26*, 114, 116, *116*, 161, 165
O'Dea, Jimmy 122
O'Donnell, Matt 55, 62–3, 70–1, 93–4, 106, *136*,
    138, *138*, 139, *139*, 140, *140*, 141–2, 147,
    149, 152, 158, 175
O'Donnell (née Wallis), Pauline 91, *119*
O'Donoghue, Paddy *110*, 126, 146
O'Donovan, Michael 70–1, 75, 150, 152, *152*, 161
O'Donovan, Tim 77, 152
O'Driscoll, Noel 33
O'Dwyer, Tom 76, 150
O'Dwyer, William 33
Old Crescent Rugby Club (Limerick) 28
O'Leary, Cormac 33
Oller, Joseph 37
O'Malley, Patrick 33
Ó Muircheartaigh, Micheál *9*
O'Neill, Donal J. 29, 33
O'Neill, Patrick 32, 52
O'Reilly, Edward (aka Ned Reilly) 33, *33*, 52, *53*,
    54–5
Orford, Lord 16
Oriel Cup 8
O'Rourke, Jack 79
Orr, Hamilton 92, 94

Orton, Sidney 84, 87
O'Sullivan, Paddy 75
O'Sullivan, Philip 79, 168
O'Sullivan, Richard (Dick) 32–3, 59, *59*, 75
O'Toole, Mick 78

P

Paddy Power Derby *see* Derby (Irish)
Paget, Dorothy *115*
Pari-Mutuel (PMU) 37, 41
Patrickswell coursing venue (Co. Limerick) 75, 152
Perry Barr track (Birmingham) 45
Peters, Brian 94
Piccadilly (horse) 107
Pigalle Club (London) 165
Potters Bar kennels 95, 98–9, 102
Power, Ned 62
Powerstown Park coursing venue (and racecourse,
    Clonmel) 20, 22, *72*, 76, 78, *78*, 79, 140,
    142, 147, 149–50, 152, 164, 173
Prendiville, Donal 48
Prescott, Sir Mark 114
Punchestown racecourse 29, 59, 177
Puppy Derby (Irish) 106, 114, *134*, 142, 147, 165,
    175

Q

Quigley, Jimmy 75
Quinlan, Ann 33, 54, *54*, 55, 76
Quinlan, Kevin *54*
Quinn, Billy 106, 109, 131, 138–9, *169*
Quinn, John 172

R

Racing Board 25, 37, 40
Rahill, Bernard 79, 168
Ramsgate track 45
Reading track 45
Reilly, Daniel J. 33, 54, 94
Reilly, Ian 54, 94–5
Reilly, Ned *see* O'Reilly, Edward (aka Ned Reilly)
Revenue Commissioners 25
Reynolds, Albert 52
Reynolds, Leslie 93
Roberts, Robert 33
Roche, Helen 92
Rogers, Ruth 33
Rogers, Terry 126, 131
Ross, Capt. John 28, *32*, 33, 53
Royal Canal flapping track 122
Royal Dublin Society (RDS) 28
Royal Marines Music School 94
RTÉ (Radio Telefís Éireann) 52, *52*, 102, 107, 159
Russell, William 29, 33, 79, 168
Ruth, Dolores 55, *55*, 94–5, 141, *141*, 142, *142*,
    150, 173
Ruth, Frances 55, *55*, 94, 141
Ryan, Dick 70, 75, *75*, 76, 78
Ryan, Jeremiah 146
Ryan, Jim 70
Ryan, John M. 29, 33
Ryan, J.P. 77
Ryan, Mary 70, *169*
Ryan, Noel 91, 95, *95*, *147*, 148, 161
Ryan, Tommy 71
Rye House 45

S

Santry Stadium (athletics) 125
Santry track 122, 173
Savva, Nick 93, 108, 152, 168
Scahill, Des *52*
Scallon, Oliver 33, *33*, 53, 76

Scallon, Rosemary (Dana) 53
Sefton, Earl of 20
Sevenhouses coursing club (Co. Kilkenny) 71
Shannon, Robert 99
Sharkey, Paddy *40*
Sharpe, Albert (actor) 122
Sharpe, Albert (nephew of Albert Sharpe, actor) 122
Sharpe, Albert (son of Albert Sharpe and Philomena
    Farrell) 122
Sharpe, Paul 122
Shawfield track, Glasgow *see* Glasgow track
    (Shawfield)
Sheffield track 100
Shelbourne FC 178
Shelbourne Park 31, *31*, 39, 41, 44, 48, 52–3, 55,
    59–60, 62, 67, 76–8, 82, 91, 93, 106–7,
    109–10, *110*, 114, 116–19, *120*, 123–6, *128*,
    131–3, 138–9, 141–2, *142*, *144*, 146–7, *147*,
    148, *149*, 152, *152*, 154, 157, *157*, 158, *158*,
    160–1, 164, 167–8, *170*, 175, 177–9
Shepherd's Bush (White City) track *see* White City
    Stadium (Shepherd's Bush)
Slide On (horse) 107
Slough track 45
Smith, O.P. 103
Southport coursing venue 75
Spennymoor track 45
Spillers (dog-food company) 93
Sporting Life 100, 156
Sporting Press 23, 25
Spratt, Joan 54
Stack, Liz 76
Stack, Tommy 76, 92
Stanley, Brian 92
St Leger (English) 13
St Leger (Irish) 54, 62, 74–6, 106, 114, 119, *123*,
    130–4, *138*, 139–41, *141*, 142–3, 147–9,
    158, 160, 161, 165, 172–3, 175–7
St Patrick's Athletic AFC 126, 178
Stud Book, Greyhound (1882) 164
Sullivan, Matthew 79, 168
Sunderland track 47
Swaffham coursing club (Norfolk) 16, 20, 68, 74
Swaffham track 45
Swaffield, Alice 141

T

Taggart, Paschal 8, 32, 54, 59, *59*, 60, 141, *147*, 148,
    161
Taggart, Shane 141
T.A. Morris Stake 22
Thornton, Tom 75
Thurles Greyhound Racing and Sports Association
    178
Thurles track 41, 118, 141, 175, 178–9
Tickner, David 93, 142
Tiernan, Seán 192
Tipperary Cup 118, 178
Tompkins, Barbara 92
totalisator (tote) 30, *34*, 36–7, 39–41
    foundation of 24, *26*, 30, 36, 39
    history of 37
    income 39–41
    supervision of 28
    Totalisator Act (1929) 37
    'Tote-A-Manuel' 36
Tote Gold Cup 178
Trabolgan coursing venue 74
Tralee coursing venue 152
Tralee track *26*, 30, 41, 45, 48, 54–5, 60, 106, 172,
    178–9, *179*
Tramore racecourse 36
Travers, Matt 76, 90, *124*

Tubridy, Gerry 76
Tuite, Jim 106–7, *107*
Turf Club 37, 110
Turner, Nick 63
Tuscon track (Arizona, US) 103
Twyford, W. (priest, Killenaule, Co. Tipperary) 109,
    168
Tynan, Aidan 32
Tynan, P.J. *139*

U

Unraced Classic 106, 130

V

Victoria, Queen 69

W

Wall, Teresa 33
Walsh, Dan 7, *179*
Walshe, Deirdre (née Desmond) *58*
Walshe, James (Jimmy) *58*, 70–1
Walshe, John 70
Walsh, Thomas 25
Walsh, William A. 33
Walthamstow track 45, *45*, 75
Ward, David 33
Warrell, Fred *79*, 156
Waterford track 41, 45, 54–5, 60, 178–9
Waterloo Cup 16, *16*, 17, 20, 23, 28, 37, 46, 54,
    68–71, 75, *75*, 76, 79, 82, 93, 102, 106, 114,
    122, 139–40, 149–50, *150*, 152, 161, 164,
    168, *169*, 172
Weatherbys 20
Wembley track 23, 25, 45, 53
West Ham track 85
White City Stadium (Shepherd's Bush) 23, 25, *34*,
    45, 47, 53–4, 62, 71, 76, *80*, 83, 85, *86*, 87,
    88, 90, *90*, 91, *91*, 92, *92*, 93–4, 98–100,
    100–1, 102, 106–7, *115*, 133, 140–1, 147,
    152, 156, *156*, 157–8, *158*, *162*, 164–5,
    167–8, 172, 178
Who, The (rock group) 87
Wild Boy (film) 85, *85*
Williams, Albert (A.H.) 83–4, 159
Wimbledon track 13, 53–5, 71, 85, 87, 92–4, *95–6*,
    102, 103, 106, 133, *136*, 141–2, 147–8
Wisbech track 45
World Greyhound Racing Federation (WGRF) 46, 54

Y

Yates, Ivan 59
York racecourse 37
Youghal track 30, 41, 44, *179*

One man and his dog . . . Seán Tiernan at the Duleek coursing meeting, February 1995

First published in 2009 by
Blackstaff Press
4c Heron Wharf
Sydenham Business Park
Belfast BT3 9LE
with the assistance of Bord na gCon/Irish Greyhound Board

© Text, John Martin, 2009
© Foreword, Micheál Ó Muircheartaigh, 2009
© Photographs, see pages 182–3. The picture acknowledgements on pages 182–3 constitute an extension of this copyright page.

Design by Lisa Dynan

Printed in Italy by Sedit

A CIP catalogue for this book is available from the British Library

ISBN 978-0-85640-845-8

www.blackstaffpress.com
www.igb.ie